MOST REQUESTED
RECIPES

Taste of Home

TASTE OF HOME BOOKS • RDA ENTHUSIAST BRANDS, LLC • MILWAUKEE, WI

99

198

OUR MOST-SHARED RECIPES EVER

Every year, home cooks like you submit thousands of recipes to our *Taste of Home* community. We rounded up the dishes our readers just can't keep to themselves—most-loved, most delicious, most worthy of Instagram and pinning—inside ***Taste of Home Most Requested Recipes 2020.***

Now in its eighth edition, this ultimate collection showcases 363 delectable homemade creations. You'll find everything from appetizers and entrees to sides, soups, breads, desserts and more. Count on these unforgettable mainstays to deliver flavor your family will love...every time!

Each dish was reviewed and approved by our experts in the *Taste of Home* Test Kitchen, and step-by-step instructions and vibrant full-color photos make it easy to cook with confidence.

Packed with dozens of clever kitchen tips and first-person reader reviews, you'll know why a dish is ranked as one of the best. As an added bonus, this year we've included a roundup of recipes reinvented in five unique ways—the possibilities are truly endless!

And when life gets busy, refer to these handy at-a-glance icons to make the most of your time in the kitchen.

🕐 Quick-to-fix recipes that are table-ready in 30 minutes or less.

5️⃣ Dishes that require no more than five items (not counting water, oil, salt, pepper and optional ingredients). What could be easier?

🏆 Winners and runners-up in one of our *Taste of Home* recipe contests.

❄️ Recipes that can be made ahead and frozen.

Dig in to our readers' most-beloved, raved-over, "I simply LOVED this!" dishes. Whether whipping up cozy comfort food, creating attention-getting potluck pleasers or planning a spread for a special occasion, you're guaranteed to find a new favorite in ***Most Requested Recipes 2020!***

© 2020 RDA Enthusiast Brands, LLC.
1610 N. 2nd St., Suite 102, Milwaukee, WI 53212-3906
All rights reserved. Taste of Home is a registered trademark of RDA Enthusiast Brands, LLC.
Visit us at tasteofhome.com for other Taste of Home books and products.

International Standard Book Number:
D 978-1-61765-961-4
U 978-1-61765-962-1
International Standard Serial Number: 2166-0522
Component Number:
D 119200040H
U 119200042H

Executive Editor: Mark Hagen
Senior Art Director: Raeann Thompson
Editor: Amy Glander

Assistant Art Director: Courtney Lovetere
Designer: Jazmin Delgado
Copy Editor: Amy Rabideau Silvers

Cover Photography:
Photographer: Dan Roberts
Set Stylist: Stacey Genaw
Food Stylist: Josh Rink

Pictured on front cover and title page: Three-Layer Chocolate Ganache Cake, p. 172

Pictured on back cover:
Taco Pinwheels, p. 20
Pressure-Cooker Mushroom Pot Roast, p. 86
Apricot Cranberry Bread, p. 149

Printed in USA
1 3 5 7 9 10 8 6 4 2

122

25

7

45

218

TABLE OF CONTENTS

To find a recipe: tasteofhome.com
To submit a recipe: tasteofhome.com/submit
To find out about other *Taste of Home* products:
  shoptasteofhome.com

f LIKE US facebook.com/tasteofhome

y TWEET US twitter.com/tasteofhome

○ FOLLOW US @tasteofhome

○ PIN US pinterest.com/taste_of_home

Appetizers, Snacks & Beverages

This round-up of favorite appetizers makes it easy to find the perfect hot, cold or easy-as-can-be party pleaser.

BUFFALO WING POPPERS

The taste of Buffalo wings and pepper poppers pair up in these hot bites. They will disappear fast—so make a double batch and have copies of the recipe handy.
—Barbara Nowakowski, Mesa, AZ

- -

Prep: 20 min. • **Bake:** 20 min.
Makes: 40 appetizers

- 20 jalapeno peppers
- 1 pkg. (8 oz.) cream cheese, softened
- 1½ cups shredded part-skim mozzarella cheese
- 1 cup diced cooked chicken
- ½ cup blue cheese salad dressing
- ½ cup Buffalo wing sauce

1. Cut peppers in half lengthwise, leaving stems intact; discard seeds. In a small bowl, combine the remaining ingredients. Pipe or stuff into pepper halves.

2. Place in a greased 15x10x1-in. baking pan. Bake, uncovered, at 325° for 20 minutes for spicy flavor, 30 minutes for medium and 40 minutes for mild.

NOTE: Wear disposable gloves when cutting hot peppers; the oils can burn skin. Avoid touching your face.

1 PIECE: 57 cal., 5g fat (2g sat. fat), 12mg chol., 159mg sod., 1g carb. (1g sugars, 0 fiber), 2g pro.

READER REVIEW

"Loved this recipe. Easy to make and they taste delicious. It reminds me of a buffalo chicken dip I make quite frequently. Never thought of piping into jalapenos. Yum!"

DADUK, TASTEOFHOME.COM

PARMESAN-BACON BUBBLE BREAD

I had some leftover bread dough I needed to put to good use, so I turned to a recipe I often use for bubble bread and substituted savory ingredients for the sweet.
—*Lori McLain, Denton, TX*

Prep: 20 min. + rising • **Bake:** 20 min.
Makes: 16 servings

- 1 loaf frozen bread dough, thawed (16 oz.)
- ¼ cup butter, melted
- ¾ cup shredded Parmesan cheese
- 6 bacon strips, cooked and finely crumbled, divided
- ⅓ cup finely chopped green onions, divided
- 2 Tbsp. grated Parmesan cheese
- 2 Tbsp. salt-free herb seasoning blend
- 1½ tsp. sugar
  Optional: Alfredo sauce or marinara sauce

1. Turn dough onto a lightly floured surface; divide and shape into 16 rolls. Place butter in a shallow bowl. In a large bowl, combine the shredded Parmesan, half the bacon, half the green onions, grated Parmesan, seasoning blend and sugar. Dip dough pieces in melted butter, then toss with cheese mixture to coat. Stack pieces in a greased 9-in. cast-iron skillet.
2. Cover with a kitchen towel; let rise in a warm place until almost doubled, about 45 minutes. Preheat oven to 350°. Bake until golden brown, 20-25 minutes. Top bread with the remaining bacon and green onions. Serve warm and, if desired, with Alfredo or marinara sauce for dipping.
1 PIECE: 140 cal., 6g fat (3g sat. fat), 14mg chol., 311mg sod., 14g carb. (2g sugars, 1g fiber), 6g pro.

HOMEMADE GUACAMOLE

Ever wonder how to make guacamole? Just whip together this recipe for easy guacamole made with your favorite ingredients.
—*Joan Hallford, North Richland Hills, TX*

Takes: 10 min. • **Makes:** 2 cups

- 3 medium ripe avocados, peeled and cubed
- 1 garlic clove, minced
- ¼ to ½ tsp. salt
- 2 medium tomatoes, seeded and chopped, optional
- 1 small onion, finely chopped
- ¼ cup mayonnaise, optional
- 1 to 2 Tbsp. lime juice
- 1 Tbsp. minced fresh cilantro

Mash avocados with garlic and salt. Stir in remaining ingredients.
¼ CUP: 90 cal., 8g fat (1g sat. fat), 0 chol., 78mg sod., 6g carb. (1g sugars, 4g fiber), 1g pro. **DIABETIC EXCHANGES:** 1½ fat.

TEST KITCHEN TIP
For extra flavor, top your guacamole with black beans and corn. This fun combination is popular in Mexican restaurants. The bright colors and contrasting textures make them a tasty addition to creamy guac. For even more flavor, grill the corn first.

MOCHA PUNCH

I first tried this smooth, creamy punch at a friend's holiday open house. It was so special and distinctive I didn't leave until I had the recipe. Having a frosty glass of this chocolate punch is almost like sipping a chocolate shake.
—Yvonne Hatfield, Norman, OK

Prep: 15 min. + chilling
Makes: 25 servings

- 6 cups water
- ½ cup sugar
- ½ cup instant chocolate drink mix
- ¼ cup instant coffee granules
- ½ gallon vanilla ice cream
- ½ gallon chocolate ice cream
- 1 cup heavy whipping cream, whipped

1. In a large saucepan, bring water to a boil. Remove from heat. Add the sugar, drink mix and coffee; stir until dissolved. Refrigerate, covered, 4 hours or overnight.

2. About 30 minutes before serving, pour mixture into a large punch bowl. Add scoops of ice cream; stir until partially melted. Top servings with whipped cream.

¾ CUP: 254 cal., 13g fat (8g sat. fat), 46mg chol., 87mg sod., 34g carb. (30g sugars, 1g fiber), 4g pro.

TOUCHDOWN BRAT SLIDERS

It's game time when these minis make an appearance. Two things my husband loves—beer and brats—get stepped up a notch with crunchy flavored chips.
—Kirsten Shabaz, Lakeville, MN

Takes: 50 min. • **Makes:** 16 sliders

- 5 thick-sliced bacon strips, chopped
- 1 lb. uncooked bratwurst links, casings removed
- 1 large onion, finely chopped
- 2 garlic cloves, minced
- 1 pkg. (8 oz.) cream cheese, cubed
- 1 cup dark beer or nonalcoholic beer
- 1 Tbsp. Dijon mustard
- ¼ tsp. pepper
- 16 dinner rolls, split and toasted
- 2 cups cheddar and sour cream potato chips, crushed

1. In a large cast-iron or other heavy skillet, cook bacon over medium heat until crisp. Remove to paper towels with a slotted spoon; drain, reserving drippings. Cook bratwurst and onion in drippings over medium heat, breaking into crumbles until meat is no longer pink. Add the garlic; cook 1 minute longer. Drain well.

2. Stir in the cream cheese, beer, mustard and pepper. Bring to a boil. Reduce heat; simmer, uncovered, until thickened, 15-20 minutes, stirring occasionally. Stir in the bacon. Spoon ¼ cup onto each roll; sprinkle with crushed chips. Replace tops.

1 SLIDER: 354 cal., 24g fat (10g sat. fat), 62mg chol., 617mg sod., 23g carb. (2g sugars, 2g fiber), 10g pro.

GARLIC TOMATO BRUSCHETTA

I drew inspiration from my grandma's recipe for this garden-fresh bruschetta. The tomato goodness says welcome to the party, or serve it as a complement to your favorite Italian entree.
—Jean Franzoni, Rutland, VT

- -

Prep: 30 min. + chilling • **Makes:** 12 servings

¼ cup olive oil
3 Tbsp. chopped fresh basil
3 to 4 garlic cloves, minced
½ tsp. salt
¼ tsp. pepper
4 medium tomatoes, diced
2 Tbsp. grated Parmesan cheese
1 loaf (1 lb.) unsliced French bread

1. In a large bowl, combine oil, basil, garlic, salt and pepper. Add the tomatoes and toss gently. Sprinkle with cheese. Refrigerate at least 1 hour.

2. Bring to room temperature before serving. Cut bread into 24 slices; toast under broiler until lightly browned. Top with the tomato mixture. Serve immediately.

2 PIECES : 156 cal., 6g fat (1g sat. fat), 1mg chol., 347mg sod., 22g carb. (0 sugars, 1g fiber), 4g pro.

ZIPPY GARLIC TOMATO BRUSCHETTA: To tomato mixture, add 2 Tbsp. minced seeded jalapeno pepper and 2 tsp. balsamic vinegar.

VERONICA
CALLAGHAN
Glastonbury, CT

ASIAGO BEEF TART

I love simple recipes that are fancy enough for guests. To get a velvety texture in this tart, I use creme fraiche, but sour cream works, too.
—*Veronica Callaghan, Glastonbury, CT*

- -

Prep: 25 min. • **Bake:** 15 min.
Makes: 16 servings

   1   sheet refrigerated pie crust
   ¾   lb. lean ground beef (90% lean)
   1   shallot, finely chopped
   2   large eggs
   ¾   cup sour cream
   ½   tsp. salt
   ¼   tsp. pepper
   ¾   cup shredded part-skim
        mozzarella cheese
   ⅔   cup shredded Asiago cheese
   ⅓   cup oil-packed sun-dried
        tomatoes, coarsely chopped
   ¼   cup coarsely chopped fresh basil
   1   tsp. minced fresh rosemary or
        ¼ tsp. dried rosemary, crushed
TOPPINGS
   2   Tbsp. pine nuts, toasted
        Thinly sliced fresh basil, optional

1. Preheat oven to 400°. On a work surface, unroll pie crust; roll to a 12-in. circle. Press onto bottom and up sides of an ungreased 11-in. tart pan with removable bottom. Refrigerate while preparing filling.
2. In a large skillet, cook beef and shallot over medium heat 5-7 minutes or until beef is no longer pink, breaking up beef into crumbles. Remove from heat.
3. In a small bowl, whisk eggs, sour cream, salt and pepper until blended. Stir in the cheeses, sun-dried tomatoes, chopped basil and rosemary. Stir into beef mixture; pour into tart shell.
4. Bake on a lower oven rack 15-20 minutes or until crust is golden brown and filling is set. Just before serving, add toppings as desired.
NOTE: To toast pine nuts, cook in a skillet over low heat until lightly browned, stirring occasionally.
1 PIECE: 172 cal., 11g fat (5g sat. fat), 54mg chol., 202mg sod., 9g carb. (1g sugars, 0 fiber), 9g pro.

GRILLED WING ZINGERS

My husband fine-tuned this recipe—and the results were spectacular! These spicy-hot grilled wings help make the party. You can easily adjust the heat level by altering the amount of chili powder and cayenne. The wings take a little time, but they're worth it.
—Angela Roster, Greenbackville, VA

Prep: 35 min. • **Grill:** 35 min.
Makes: about 6½ dozen

    8   lbs. chicken wings
    1   cup packed brown sugar
    1   cup Louisiana-style hot sauce
    ¼   cup butter, cubed
    1   Tbsp. cider vinegar
    ⅓   cup sugar
    ½   cup Italian seasoning
    ¼   cup dried rosemary, crushed
    ¼   cup paprika
    ¼   cup chili powder
    ¼   cup pepper
    2   Tbsp. cayenne pepper
    1   cup blue cheese salad dressing
    ½   cup ranch salad dressing
        Celery sticks

1. Cut chicken wings into 3 sections and discard wing tip sections. Set wings aside.
2. In a small saucepan, bring brown sugar, hot sauce, butter and vinegar to a boil. Reduce the heat; simmer, uncovered, until butter is melted and sauce is heated through, 6-8 minutes. Cool.
3. In a large shallow dish, combine sugar and seasonings. Add chicken wings in batches and turn to coat evenly.
4. Grill, covered, over indirect medium heat until juices run clear, 35-45 minutes, turning and basting occasionally with sauce.
5. In a small bowl, combine blue cheese and ranch salad dressing; serve with chicken wings and celery sticks.
NOTE: Uncooked chicken wing sections (wingettes) may be substituted for whole chicken wings.
1 PIECE: 96 cal., 6g fat (2g sat. fat), 18mg chol., 170mg sod., 5g carb. (4g sugars, 1g fiber), 5g pro.

THREE-CHEESE PEPPERONCINI SPREAD

Our big family loves to celebrate with food. Here's my take on a cheesy Greek spread known as Kopanisti. We serve it with pita crisps or crackers.
—Michael Hall, Goodland, IN

Prep: 10 minutes + chilling
Makes: 16 servings

    1   pkg. (8 oz.) cream cheese,
        cubed and softened
    1   cup crumbled feta cheese
    ½   cup crumbled blue cheese
    ½   cup coarsely chopped pepperoncini
    1   Tbsp. juice from pepperoncini
    3   Tbsp. olive oil
    ½   tsp. minced garlic clove
    ½   tsp. pepper
    ½   tsp. crushed red pepper
        flakes, optional
        Assorted crackers

1. Place first the 8 ingredients in a food processor; if desired, add pepper flakes. Pulse just until combined (do not process until smooth).
2. Remove to a bowl; refrigerate, covered, at least 1 hour. Serve with crackers.
2 TBSP.: 105 cal., 10g fat (5g sat. fat), 23mg chol., 172mg sod., 1g carb. (0 sugars, 0 fiber), 3g pro.

AIR-FRYER PICKLES

Like deep-fried pickles? You'll love this version even more. Dill pickle slices are coated with panko bread crumbs and spices, then air-fried until crispy. Dip them in ranch dressing for an appetizer you won't soon forget.
—*Nick Iverson, Denver, CO*

Prep: 20 min. + standing • **Cook:** 15 min./batch
Makes: 32 slices

- 32 dill pickle slices
- ½ cup all-purpose flour
- ½ tsp. salt
- 3 large eggs, lightly beaten
- 2 Tbsp. dill pickle juice
- ½ tsp. cayenne pepper
- ½ tsp. garlic powder
- 2 cups panko bread crumbs
- 2 Tbsp. snipped fresh dill
  Cooking spray
  Ranch salad dressing, optional

1. Preheat air fryer to 400°. Let pickle slices stand on a paper towel until liquid is almost absorbed, about 15 minutes.

2. Meanwhile, in a shallow bowl, combine flour and salt. In another shallow bowl, whisk the eggs, pickle juice, cayenne and garlic powder. Combine panko and dill in a third shallow bowl.

3. Dip pickles in flour mixture to coat both sides; shake off excess. Dip in egg mixture, then in crumb mixture, patting to help coating adhere. Spritz pickles and fryer basket with cooking spray. In batches, place pickles in a single layer in basket and cook until golden brown and crispy, 7-10 minutes. Turn pickles; spritz with additional cooking spray. Continue cooking until golden brown and crispy, 7-10 minutes. Serve immediately. If desired, serve with ranch dressing.

1 PICKLE SLICE: 26 cal., 1g fat (0 sat. fat), 13mg chol., 115mg sod., 4g carb. (0 sugars, 0 fiber), 1g pro.

TEST KITCHEN TIP
In our testing, we have found cook times vary dramatically between brands of air fryers. As a result, we have given wider than normal ranges on suggested cook times. Begin checking at the first time listed and adjust as needed.

🎗 SENSATIONAL SLUSH

Colorful and refreshing, this sweet-tart slush has become a family favorite. I freeze the mix in 2- and 4-cup containers so I can serve it in small portions for individuals or the whole family.
—*Connie Friesen, Altona, MB*

Prep: 25 min. + freezing • **Makes:** 20 servings

- ½ cup sugar
- 1 pkg. (3 oz.) strawberry gelatin
- 2 cups boiling water
- 1 cup unsweetened pineapple juice
- 2 cups sliced fresh strawberries
- 1 can (12 oz.) frozen lemonade concentrate, thawed
- 1 can (12 oz.) frozen limeade concentrate, thawed
- 2 cups cold water
- 2 liters lemon-lime soda, chilled

1. In a large bowl, dissolve sugar and gelatin in boiling water. In a blender, combine the pineapple juice and strawberries; cover and process until blended. Add to gelatin mixture. Stir in concentrates and cold water. Cover and freeze for 8 hours or overnight.

2. Remove from freezer 45 minutes before serving. For each serving, combine ½ cup slush mixture with ½ cup lemon-lime soda; stir well.

1 CUP: 151 cal., 0 fat (0 sat. fat), 0 chol., 22mg sod., 39g carb. (35g sugars, 1g fiber), 1g pro.

NICK IVERSON
Denver, CO

BACON CHEESE SPREAD

Each year, I share Christmas cheer by setting up a buffet at my family's hardware store. This cheese spread is always a favorite.
—Sharon Bickett, Chester, SC

Takes: 15 min. • **Makes:** 4 cups

- 1 pkg. (12 oz.) bacon strips, chopped
- ½ cup chopped pecans
- 4 cups shredded sharp cheddar cheese
- 2 cups mayonnaise
- 1 small onion, chopped
- 2 Tbsp. finely chopped sweet red pepper
- ⅛ tsp. cayenne pepper
  Assorted crackers

Cook bacon until crisp; drain. Meanwhile, in a large bowl, combine the next 6 ingredients. Stir in bacon. Serve with crackers.

2 TBSP.: 184 cal., 18g fat (5g sat. fat), 23mg chol., 216mg sod., 1g carb. (0 sugars, 0 fiber), 4g pro.

CHERRY TOMATO BITES

Cherry tomatoes may be small, but these are full of great flavor. They add color to any table.
—David Bostedt, Zephyrhills, FL

Takes: 30 min. • **Makes:** about 4 dozen

- 2 pints cherry tomatoes
- 1 pkg. (8 oz.) cream cheese, softened
- 6 bacon strips, cooked and crumbled
- ¼ cup finely chopped green onions
- ¼ cup minced fresh parsley
- ¼ tsp. Worcestershire sauce

Cut a thin slice off the top of each tomato. Scoop out and discard pulp. Invert the tomatoes on a paper towel to drain juices. Meanwhile, combine remaining ingredients in a small bowl. Spoon or pipe into tomatoes. Refrigerate until serving.

3 TOMATO BITES: 72 cal., 6g fat (4g sat. fat), 18mg chol., 85mg sod., 2g carb. (1g sugars, 0 fiber), 2g pro.

BAKED ONION DIP

Some people like this cheesy onion dip so much that they can't tear themselves away from the appetizer table to eat their dinner.
—Mona Zignego, Hartford, WI

Prep: 5 min. • **Bake:** 40 min.
Makes: 16 servings (2 cups)

- 1 cup mayonnaise
- 1 cup chopped sweet onion
- 1 Tbsp. grated Parmesan cheese
- ¼ tsp. garlic salt
- 1 cup shredded Swiss cheese
  Minced fresh parsley, optional
  Assorted crackers

1. In a large bowl, combine the mayonnaise, onion, Parmesan cheese and garlic salt; stir in Swiss cheese. Spoon into a 1-qt. baking dish.
2. Bake, uncovered, at 325° until golden brown, about 40 minutes. If desired, sprinkle with parsley. Serve with crackers.

2 TBSP.: 131 cal., 13g fat (3g sat. fat), 11mg chol., 127mg sod., 1g carb. (1g sugars, 0 fiber), 2g pro.

SPARKLING GINGER LEMONADE

Chill out with this delightful cooler, perfect for springtime bridal showers or hot summer days on the deck. It's a quick fix you'll stir up time after time.
—Jodi Blubaugh, Eagle Mountain, UT

Prep: 20 min. + cooling • **Makes:** 5 servings

- 2 cups water
- 1 cup honey
- 2 Tbsp. minced fresh gingerroot
- 2 cups club soda, chilled
- 1 cup lemon juice

1. In a small saucepan, bring the water, honey and ginger to a boil. Remove from heat; cover and steep for 10 minutes. Strain, discarding ginger. Cool.
2. Transfer to a pitcher; stir in soda and lemon juice. Serve immediately over ice.

1 CUP: 220 cal., 0 fat (0 sat. fat), 0 chol., 23mg sod., 61g carb. (57g sugars, 0 fiber), 0 pro.

OLIVE-STUFFED CELERY

My grandmother taught me and my mom how to make this appetizer. We serve it at Christmas and Thanksgiving. The stuffing is so yummy that even if you don't normally care for the ingredients on their own, you'll love this mash-up.
—Stacy Powell, Santa Fe, TX

Takes: 25 min. • **Makes:** 2 dozen

- 1 dill pickle spear plus 1 tsp. juice
- 3 sweet pickles plus 1 tsp. juice
- 6 pitted ripe olives plus 1 tsp. juice
- 6 pimiento-stuffed olives plus 1 tsp. juice
- 1 pkg. (8 oz.) cream cheese, softened
- ⅓ cup Miracle Whip
- ¼ tsp. salt
- ¼ cup finely chopped pecans, toasted
- 6 celery ribs, cut into 2-in. pieces

1. Finely chop the pickles and olives; set aside. In a small bowl, beat cream cheese, Miracle Whip, juices and salt until blended. Stir in the pickles, olives and pecans.
2. Pipe or stuff filling into celery sticks. Store in the refrigerator.
1 PIECE: 61 cal., 5g fat (2g sat. fat), 12mg chol., 228mg sod., 2g carb. (1g sugars, 0 fiber), 1g pro.

JALAPENO POPPER DIP

Here's a fantastic way to deliver all that blazing jalapeno popper taste and without the work. Whenever I bring it to a party, I'm always asked for the recipe. Serve with corn chips, tortilla chips or butter crackers.
—Jennifer Wilke, Collinsville, IL

Prep: 15 min. • **Bake:** 20 min.
Makes: 16 servings

- 2 pkg. (8 oz. each) cream cheese, softened
- 1 cup mayonnaise
- ½ cup shredded cheddar cheese
- 1 can (4 oz.) chopped green chiles
- 1 can (4 oz.) diced jalapeno peppers
- ½ cup shredded Parmesan cheese, divided
- ½ cup seasoned bread crumbs
- 1 Tbsp. olive oil
  Sliced green onions, optional
  Corn chips, tortilla chips or assorted crackers

1. In a large bowl, beat the cream cheese, mayonnaise, cheddar, chiles, peppers and ¼ cup Parmesan until blended. Spoon into an ungreased 1½-qt. baking dish.
2. In a small bowl, combine the bread crumbs, oil and remaining Parmesan. Sprinkle over cheese mixture. Bake, uncovered, at 350° for 20-25 min. or until golden brown. Sprinkle with green onions, if desired. Serve with chips or crackers.
¼ CUP: 245 cal., 24g fat (9g sat. fat), 42mg chol., 322mg sod., 4g carb. (0 sugars, 0 fiber), 4g pro.

BLACK FOREST HAM PINWHEELS

When I served these at my annual Christmas party, people liked the smokiness of the ham and the sweet surprise of the cherries. I enjoy making them for different occasions because they can be done ahead, then all I have to do is slice and arrange them on a tray.
—*Kate Dampier, Quail Valley, CA*

Prep: 20 min. + chilling
Makes: about 3½ dozen

- 1 **pkg. (8 oz.) cream cheese, softened**
- 4 **tsp. minced fresh dill**
- 1 **Tbsp. lemon juice**
- 2 **tsp. Dijon mustard**
  Dash salt and pepper
- ½ **cup dried cherries, chopped**
- ¼ **cup chopped green onions**
- 5 **flour tortillas (10 in.),**
  room temperature
- ½ **lb. sliced deli Black Forest ham**
- ½ **lb. sliced Swiss cheese**

1. In a small bowl, beat cream cheese, dill, lemon juice, mustard, salt and pepper until blended. Stir in cherries and onions. Spread over each tortilla; layer with ham and cheese.
2. Roll up tightly; securely wrap in waxed paper and refrigerate at least 2 hours. Cut into ½-in. slices.
1 PINWHEEL: 78 cal., 4g fat (2g sat. fat), 13mg chol., 151mg sod., 6g carb. (2 sugars, 0g fiber), 4g pro.
APPETIZER PINWHEELS: Omit dill, lemon juice, mustard, salt, pepper, cherries onion, ham and cheese. Beat cream cheese with 1 cup sour cream, 1 can (4¼ oz.) drained chopped ripe olives, 1 can (4 oz.) well-drained chopped green chiles, 1 cup shredded cheddar cheese, ½ cup chopped green onions, dash garlic powder and dash salt until blended. Spread over tortillas and proceed as recipe directs.
REUBEN PINWHEELS: Omit the dill, lemon juice, mustard, salt, pepper, cherries, green onion, ham and cheese. Beat cream cheese with 3 Tbsp. spicy brown mustard and ¼ tsp. prepared horseradish. Spread 1 heaping tablespoonful cream cheese mixture over each tortilla; layer each with 8 thin slices deli corned beef, 3 thin slices Swiss cheese and 1 heaping tablespoon additional cream cheese mixture. Top each with ½ cup well-drained sauerkraut. Proceed as recipe directs.

FESTIVE APPLE DIP

I came up with this peanut butter treat when my dad gave me a big bag of apples. The dip has been one of my favorites ever since. In addition to apples, try it with graham crackers, vanilla wafers, banana chunks or animal crackers.
—*Theresa Tometich, Coralville, IA*

Takes: 20 min. • **Makes:** 8 servings

- 1 **pkg. (8 oz.) cream cheese, softened**
- ½ **cup creamy peanut butter**
- ⅓ **cup packed brown sugar**
- 1 **tsp. vanilla extract**
- ½ **cup miniature marshmallows**
- 1 **jar (11¾ oz.) hot fudge**
  ice cream topping
- 2 **Tbsp. chopped mixed nuts or peanuts**
- 3 **each medium red and green**
  apples, cut into thin wedges
- 2 **Tbsp. lemon juice**

1. For dip, beat first 4 ingredients until smooth; stir in marshmallows. Spoon half the mixture into a 3-cup bowl; top with half the fudge topping. Repeat layers. Sprinkle with nuts.
2. To serve, toss apples with lemon juice. Serve with dip.
¼ CUP DIP WITH ¾ APPLE: 403 cal., 22g fat (9g sat. fat), 29mg chol., 218mg sod., 49g carb. (38g sugars, 3g fiber), 8g pro.

TANGY BARBECUE WINGS

I took these slow-cooked wings to work, and they vanished before I even got a bite! The tangy sauce is lip-smacking good.
—*Sherry Pitzer, Troy, MO*

- -

Prep: 1 hour • **Cook:** 3 hours
Makes: 2 dozen wings (2 sections each)

5	lbs. chicken wings
2½	cups ketchup
⅔	cup white vinegar
⅔	cup honey
½	cup molasses
2	to 3 Tbsp. hot pepper sauce
1	tsp. salt
1	tsp. Worcestershire sauce
½	tsp. onion powder
½	tsp. chili powder
½	to 1 tsp. liquid smoke, optional

1. Preheat oven to 375°. Using a sharp knife, cut through the 2 wing joints; discard wing tips. Arrange the remaining wing pieces in 2 greased 15x10x1-in. baking pans. Bake for 30 minutes; drain. Turn wings; bake until juices run clear, 20-25 minutes longer.
2. Meanwhile, in a large saucepan, combine remaining ingredients; bring to a boil. Reduce heat; simmer, uncovered, 30 minutes, stirring occasionally.
3. Drain wings. Place one-third of the chicken in a 5-qt. slow cooker; top with one-third of the sauce. Repeat layers twice. Cook, covered, on low 3-4 hours. Stir before serving.
NOTE: Uncooked chicken wing sections (wingettes) may be substituted for whole chicken wings.

1 WING (2 SECTIONS): 178 cal., 7g fat (2g sat. fat), 30mg chol., 458mg sod., 19g carb. (19g sugars, 0 fiber), 10g pro.

READER REVIEW

"My family absolutely loves spicy food and these wings are a definite hit with them. It's a recipe we'll be making many more times and it's a keeper, for sure."

TKARINAS, TASTEOFHOME.COM

GRILLED PEACH & PINEAPPLE SANGRIA

Grilled peaches and pineapple slathered in cinnamon butter make this refreshing sangria stand out from the rest. I add grilled lemon and lime slices to each glass for a citrusy boost.
—*Heather King, Frostburg, MD*

- -

Prep: 25 min. + chilling • **Makes:** 8 servings

1	**bottle (750 ml) sauvignon blanc or other white wine**
2	**cups lemonade**
½	**cup orange liqueur**
1	**Tbsp. butter, melted**
1	**Tbsp. sugar**
1	**tsp. ground cinnamon**
3	**medium peeled peaches, pitted and halved**
¼	**fresh pineapple, peeled and cut into 4 slices**

1. Make sangria by combining wine, lemonade and liqueur. Refrigerate. Meanwhile, in a small bowl, combine the melted butter, sugar and cinnamon. Mix well.

2. Brush the butter mixture over cut side of peaches and all over pineapple slices. Grill fruit, covered, on a greased rack over medium direct heat 4-5 minutes. Turn peaches and pineapple. Grill 4-5 minutes more. Remove from grill.

3. Cut each peach half into 5 or 6 slices and each pineapple slice into 5 or 6 pieces. Add three-fourths of fruit to sangria, reserving remainder. Refrigerate at least 2 hours.

4. Before serving, thread several pieces of reserved fruit onto appetizer skewers. Pour sangria over ice; serve with fruit skewers.

¾ CUP: 206 cal., 2g fat (1g sat. fat), 4mg chol., 20mg sod., 25g carb. (21g sugars, 1g fiber), 1g pro.

PUMPKIN PIE DIP

I came up with this rich creamy dip when I had a small amount of canned pumpkin left in the fridge after my holiday baking. It is also great served with sliced pears and apples, or as a spread on zucchini bread or any other sweet nut bread.

—Laurie LaClair, North Richland Hills, TX

Takes: 10 min. • **Makes:** 4 cups

- 1 pkg. (8 oz.) cream cheese, softened
- 2 cups confectioners' sugar
- 1 cup canned pumpkin
- ½ cup sour cream
- 1 tsp. ground cinnamon
- 1 tsp. pumpkin pie spice
- ½ tsp. ground ginger
  Gingersnap cookies

Beat cream cheese and confectioners' sugar until smooth. Beat in pumpkin, sour cream and spices until blended. Transfer to a bowl; serve with gingersnaps. Refrigerate leftovers.

2 TBSP. DIP: 65 cal., 3g fat (2g sat. fat), 8mg chol., 24mg sod., 9g carb. (8g sugars, 0 fiber), 1g pro.

READER REVIEW

"This dip is fantastic. Everywhere I take it, friends and family want the recipe. My dad eats it like pudding without the cookies he likes it so much! It's very quick and easy, too!"

CHARME, TASTEOFHOME.COM

PARTY SHRIMP

The marinade for this dish makes the shrimp so flavorful, you won't even need a dipping sauce. Even those who claim they don't like shellfish dig this appetizer.

—Kendra Doss, Colorado Springs, CO

Prep: 15 min. + marinating • **Broil:** 10 min.
Makes: about 2½ dozen

- 1 Tbsp. olive oil
- 1½ tsp. brown sugar
- 1½ tsp. lemon juice
- 1 garlic clove, thinly sliced
- ½ tsp. paprika
- ½ tsp. Italian seasoning
- ½ tsp. dried basil
- ¼ tsp. pepper
- 1 lb. uncooked shrimp (26-30 per lb.), peeled and deveined

1. In a bowl or shallow dish, combine the first 8 ingredients. Add shrimp; toss to coat. Refrigerate 2 hours.

2. Drain shrimp, discarding marinade. Place shrimp on an ungreased baking sheet. Broil 4 in. from heat until shrimp turn pink, 3-4 minutes on each side.

1 SHRIMP: 14 cal., 0 fat (0 sat. fat), 18mg chol., 18mg sod., 0 carb. (0 sugars, 0 fiber), 2g pro.

BEEFY TACO DIP

Here's a taco dip that combines several of my friends' recipes. I experimented until I came up with my favorite. It's always a hit, no matter where I take it!
—*Faye Parker, Bedford, NS*

Prep: 30 min. + chilling • **Makes:** 20 servings

- 1 pkg. (8 oz.) cream cheese, softened
- 1 cup sour cream
- ¾ cup mayonnaise
- 1 lb. ground beef
- 1 envelope taco seasoning
- 1 can (8 oz.) tomato sauce
- 2 cups shredded cheddar or Mexican cheese blend
- 4 cups shredded lettuce
- 2 medium tomatoes, diced
- 1 small onion, diced
- 1 medium green pepper, diced
  Tortilla chips

1. In a small bowl, beat cream cheese, sour cream and mayonnaise until smooth. Spread on a 12- to 14-in. pizza pan or serving dish. Refrigerate for 1 hour.
2. In a saucepan over medium heat, brown ground beef; drain. Add taco seasoning and tomato sauce; cook and stir for 5 minutes. Cool completely. Spread over cream cheese layer. Chill.
3. Just before serving, sprinkle with cheese, lettuce, tomatoes, onion and green pepper. Serve with chips.
1 SERVING: 216 cal., 18g fat (8g sat. fat), 47mg chol., 383mg sod., 5g carb. (2g sugars, 1g fiber), 8g pro.

BLACKBERRY BEER COCKTAIL

This refreshing hard lemonade has a mild alcohol flavor. The beer adds just enough fizz to dance on your tongue as you sip.
—*Ginger Sullivan, Cutler Bay, FL*

Takes: 10 min. • **Makes:** 10 servings

- 4 bottles (12 oz. each) beer, chilled
- 1 can (12 oz.) frozen raspberry lemonade concentrate, thawed
- ¾ cup fresh or frozen blackberries, thawed
- ½ cup vodka
  Ice cubes
  Lemon slices

In a large pitcher combine the beer, lemonade concentrate, blackberries and vodka. Serve over ice and garnish with lemon slices.
¾ CUP: 151 cal., 0 fat (0 sat. fat), 0 chol., 6mg sod., 21g carb. (19g sugars, 1g fiber), 1g pro.

FRUIT & CHEESE KABOBS

Make these fresh and fruity snacks for the ballpark or beach. The cinnamon-spiced yogurt dip adds that special touch everyone loves.
—*Taste of Home Test Kitchen*

Takes: 20 min.
Makes: 12 kabobs (1½ cups dip)

- 1 cup vanilla yogurt
- ½ cup sour cream
- 2 Tbsp. honey
- ½ tsp. ground cinnamon
- 2 cups fresh strawberries, halved
- 1½ cups green grapes
- 8 oz. cubed cheddar or Monterey Jack cheese, or a combination of cheeses

For dip, mix first 4 ingredients. On 12 wooden skewers, alternately thread strawberries, grapes and cheese cubes. Serve immediately or refrigerate.
1 KABOB WITH 2 TBSP. DIP: 147 cal., 9g fat (5g sat. fat), 22mg chol., 143mg sod., 12g carb. (11g sugars, 1g fiber), 6g pro.

BAKED SPINACH DIP LOAF

Any round loaf works as a serving bowl for this cream-cheesy dip, with spinach, cheddar, water chestnuts and, yes, bacon. Scoop the dip with extra bread and veggies—then eat the bowl!
—*Frieda Meding, Trochu, AB*

- -

Prep: 25 min. • **Bake:** 1 hour 25 min.
Makes: 16 servings

- 6   bacon strips, cooked and crumbled, divided
- 2   pkg. (8 oz. each) cream cheese, softened
- 1   cup mayonnaise
- 1   pkg. (10 oz.) frozen chopped spinach, thawed and squeezed dry
- 1   can (8 oz.) sliced water chestnuts, drained and chopped
- 1¼ cups shredded cheddar cheese, divided
- 2   green onions, chopped, divided
- 1   garlic clove, minced
- 2   tsp. dill weed
- ½   tsp. seasoned salt
- ⅛   tsp. pepper
- 1   unsliced round loaf (1 lb.) sourdough bread
    Cucumber slices

1. Preheat oven to 375°. Reserve 1 Tbsp. crumbled bacon for topping. Beat cream cheese and mayonnaise until smooth. Stir in spinach, water chestnuts, 1 cup cheese, half the green onions, minced garlic, seasonings and remaining bacon.
2. Cut a 1½-in. slice off top of bread. Hollow out the bottom, leaving a ½-in.-thick shell. Cut all removed bread into cubes for serving. Fill shell with dip. Wrap in heavy-duty foil, tenting foil over dip. Bake on a baking sheet 1¼ hours.
3. Open foil carefully, allowing the steam to escape. Sprinkle dip with remaining cheese and green onion and the reserved bacon. Bake until cheese is melted, 10-15 minutes. Serve warm with cucumber and cubed bread.
¼ CUP DIP: 254 cal., 24g fat (9g sat. fat), 41mg chol., 334mg sod., 5g carb. (2g sugars, 1g fiber), 6g pro.

TACO PINWHEELS

These come together quickly when you start with cold leftover taco meat. Enjoy them as an app with salsa or for lunch with a side salad.
—*Cindy Reams, Philipsburg, PA*

- -

Prep: 15 min. + chilling
Makes: 3 dozen pinwheels

- 4   oz. cream cheese, softened
- ¾   cup seasoned taco meat (recipe on page 100)
- ¼   cup finely shredded cheddar cheese
- ¼   cup salsa
- 2   Tbsp. mayonnaise
- 2   Tbsp. chopped ripe olives
- 2   Tbsp. finely chopped onion
- 5   flour tortillas (8 in.), room temperature
- ½   cup shredded lettuce
    Additional salsa

1. In a small bowl, beat the cream cheese until smooth. Stir in the taco meat, cheese, salsa, mayonnaise, olives and onion. Spread over tortillas. Sprinkle with lettuce; roll up tightly. Wrap in waxed paper and refrigerate for at least 1 hour.
2. Unwrap and cut into 1-in. pieces. Serve with additional salsa.
1 PINWHEEL: 51 cal., 3g fat (1g sat. fat), 6mg chol., 84mg sod., 4g carb. (0 sugars, 0 fiber), 2g pro.

TEST KITCHEN TIP
These pinwheels can also be made with leftover chicken taco meat. If you don't have salsa on hand, add chopped red or green bell peppers to the cream cheese mixture for extra flavor and color.

CHERRY CHEESE LOGS

Our guests flock to this gem of an appetizer—cherry-studded cream cheese logs served with graham or water crackers and pears.
—*Elizabeth Godecke, Chicago, IL*

- -

Prep: 15 min. + chilling
Makes: 2 logs (1¾ cups each)

  3 **pkg. (8 oz. each) cream
      cheese, softened**
  2 **Tbsp. sugar**
  1 **Tbsp. orange juice**
  ¼ **tsp. ground ginger**
  1 **jar (10 oz.) maraschino cherries,
      well drained and chopped**
  1 **cup chopped pecans, toasted
      Graham crackers**

1. In a large bowl, beat cream cheese, sugar, orange juice and ginger until smooth. Fold in cherries. Refrigerate, covered, at least 1 hour.
2. Place pecans in a shallow bowl. Shape the cheese mixture into two 7-in.-long logs; roll in pecans to coat evenly. Wrap logs; refrigerate at least 1 hour. Serve with crackers.
NOTE: To toast nuts, bake in a shallow pan in a 350° oven for 5-10 minutes or cook in a skillet over low heat until lightly browned, stirring occasionally.
2 TBSP.: 131 cal., 12g fat (6g sat. fat), 27mg chol., 72mg sod., 6g carb. (5g sugars, 0 fiber), 2g pro.

1

**1 FAVORITE
5 WAYS
*Cheese Logs***

4 NEW TWISTS ON AN OLD-FASHIONED APP

Use cream cheese as the base for each of these creative options. You can make the logs the day before, so they are a perfect buffet option. Each recipe makes two logs and will serve about 10 guests.

BUFFALO
(Recipe 2)

In a large bowl, beat 8 oz. cream cheese with 1 cup shredded sharp cheddar cheese, ½ cup crumbled blue cheese, ¼ cup each minced celery and minced carrot, and 1 Tbsp. hot sauce. Cover and refrigerate at least 2 hours. Roll cheese mixture into 2 logs, about 5 in. long. Roll logs in 1 cup crushed pretzels. Cover and refrigerate until serving.

NACHO
(Recipe 3)

In a large bowl, beat 8 oz. cream cheese with 1 cup shredded sharp cheddar cheese, 1 envelope taco seasoning, 2 Tbsp. minced fresh cilantro and 2 Tbsp. minced jalapeno. Cover and refrigerate at least 2 hours. Roll cheese mixture into 2 logs, about 5 in. long. Roll logs in 1 cup crushed tortilla chips. Cover and refrigerate until serving.

PESTO
(Recipe 4)

In a large bowl, beat 12 oz. cream cheese, 1 cup shredded Parmesan cheese, ¼ cup prepared pesto and 2 minced garlic cloves. Cover and refrigerate at least 2 hours. Roll cheese mixture into 2 logs, about 5 in. long. Roll logs in 1 cup toasted pine nuts. Cover and refrigerate until serving.

REUBEN
(Recipe 5)

In a large bowl, beat 8 oz. cream cheese with 1 cup shredded Swiss cheese, ½ cup chopped pastrami, ⅓ cup well-drained sauerkraut, 2 Tbsp. Thousand Island dressing and 1 tsp. caraway seeds. Cover and refrigerate at least 2 hours. Roll cheese mixture into 2 logs, about 5 in. long. Roll logs in 1 cup chopped toasted pecans. Cover and refrigerate until serving.

Breakfast & Brunch

Wake up to comfort with this tasty mix of classic and inventive a.m. faves. From quick-to-fix dishes for hectic mornings to lazy Sunday brunch ideas, you'll find all the best in breakfast food here!

PRESSURE-COOKER POT ROAST HASH

Who says traditional pot roast has to be reserved for Sunday supper? The magic of my pressure cooker allows me to turn the classic dish into a breakfast-style hash we can enjoy any day of the week!
—Gina Jackson, Ogdensburg, NY

Prep: 20 min. • **Cook:** 45 min. + releasing
Makes: 10 servings

- 1 cup warm water (110° to 115°)
- 1 Tbsp. beef base
- ½ lb. sliced fresh mushrooms
- 1 large onion, coarsely chopped
- 3 garlic cloves, minced
- 1 boneless beef chuck roast (3 lbs.)
- ½ tsp. pepper
- 1 Tbsp. Worcestershire sauce
- 1 pkg. (28 oz.) frozen O'Brien potatoes

EGGS
- 2 Tbsp. butter, divided
- 10 large eggs, divided use
- ½ tsp. salt, divided
- ½ tsp. pepper, divided
  Minced chives

1. In a 6-qt. electric pressure cooker, whisk water and beef base; add mushrooms, onion and garlic. Sprinkle beef chuck roast with pepper; transfer to pressure cooker. Drizzle with Worcestershire sauce. Lock lid; close pressure-release valve. Adjust to pressure-cook on high for 45 minutes. Allow pressure to naturally release for 10 minutes, then quick-release any remaining pressure.

2. Remove roast; when cool enough to handle, shred meat with 2 forks. In a large skillet, cook potatoes according to package directions; stir in the shredded beef. Using a slotted spoon, transfer vegetables from pressure cooker to skillet; heat through. Discard cooking juices.

3. For the eggs, heat 1 Tbsp. butter over medium-high heat in another large skillet. Break 5 eggs, 1 at a time, into pan. Sprinkle with half the salt and pepper. Reduce heat to low. Cook until eggs reach desired doneness, turning after whites are set if desired. Repeat with remaining butter, eggs, salt and pepper. Serve eggs over hash; sprinkle with chives.

1 SERVING: 429 cal., 24g fat (8g sat. fat), 281mg chol., 15mg sod., 15g carb. (2g sugars, 2g fiber), 35g pro.

AVOCADO SCRAMBLED EGGS

Bacon and avocado blend nicely in these quick-to-fix scrambled eggs. They're perfect for breakfast, but I'll also whip them up after a church meeting or football game—or any time friends drop by for coffee and a bite to eat.
—*Sundra Hauck, Bogalusa, LA*

Takes: 10 min. • **Makes:** 6 servings

8 large eggs
½ cup whole milk
½ tsp. salt
¼ tsp. pepper
1 medium ripe avocado, peeled and cubed
2 Tbsp. butter
6 bacon strips, cooked and crumbled

In a bowl, beat eggs. Add milk, salt and pepper; stir in avocado. In a skillet over medium heat, melt butter. Add egg mixture; cook and stir gently until the eggs are completely set. Sprinkle with bacon.
1 SERVING: 233 cal., 19g fat (7g sat. fat), 302mg chol., 434mg sod., 4g carb. (2g sugars, 1g fiber), 12g pro.

BLT BRUNCH PIE

My boys can't wait to pick the first ripe tomatoes in our garden to be used in this terrific pie. It has a tempting filling and tomatoes layered in a melt-in-your-mouth crust. And the crust is so easy to make—you just pat the dough into the pan!
—*Shara Walvoort, Oostburg, WI*

Prep: 20 min. + chilling • **Bake:** 40 min.
Makes: 6 servings

1¼ cups all-purpose flour
2 tsp. baking powder
½ tsp. salt
½ tsp. dried basil
½ cup shortening
½ cup sour cream
FILLING
¾ cup mayonnaise
1 cup shredded cheddar cheese
1 can (4½ oz.) mushroom stems and pieces, drained
8 bacon strips, cooked and crumbled
1 Tbsp. chopped green pepper
1 Tbsp. chopped onion
3 medium tomatoes, peeled and sliced

1. In a large bowl, combine first 4 ingredients. Cut in shortening until crumbly. Stir in sour cream. Cover and refrigerate for 30 minutes.
2. Press dough into a 9-in. pie plate; flute the edges if desired. Bake at 375° for 10 minutes. Cool completely.
3. In a large bowl, combine the mayonnaise, cheddar cheese, mushrooms, bacon, green pepper and onion. Layer half of the tomatoes in crust; top with half of the mayonnaise mixture. Repeat layers.
4. Bake at 350° until a knife inserted in the center comes out clean, 30-35 minutes. Refrigerate leftovers.
1 PIECE: 464 cal., 39g fat (11g sat. fat), 38mg chol., 618mg sod., 19g carb. (3g sugars, 1g fiber), 8g pro.

SWEET POTATO-CRANBERRY DOUGHNUTS

I grew up near Idaho, where they're famous for spudnuts, a doughnut made from mashed potatoes. These use sweet potatoes and tart cranberries. They make a great treat in the fall, but don't let that stop you from enjoying them any time of year!
—Joni Hilton, Rocklin, CA

Prep: 25 min. + rising • **Cook:** 5 min./batch
Makes: 2 dozen

- ¼ cup sugar
- 1½ tsp. active dry yeast
- 1 tsp. ground cinnamon
- ½ tsp. salt
- 4 to 4½ cups all-purpose flour
- 1 cup 2% milk
- ¼ cup shortening
- 2 Tbsp. water
- 2 large eggs, room temperature
- ½ cup mashed sweet potatoes
- ½ cup finely chopped dried cranberries
  Oil for deep-fat frying
- 1 cup confectioners' sugar
- 2 to 3 Tbsp. apple cider or juice

1. In a large bowl, combine the sugar, yeast, cinnamon, salt and 1½ cups flour. In a small saucepan, heat the milk, shortening and water to 120°-130°; add to dry ingredients. Beat on medium speed for 2 minutes. Add the eggs, mashed potatoes and cranberries; beat 2 minutes longer. Stir in enough remaining flour to form a firm dough.

2. Do not knead. Place in a greased bowl, turning once to grease the top. Cover and let dough rise in a warm place until doubled, about 1 hour.

3. Punch dough down. Turn onto a lightly floured surface; roll out to ½-in. thickness. Cut with a floured 2½-in. doughnut cutter; reroll scraps. Place 1 in. apart on greased baking sheets. Cover and let rise until doubled, about 30 minutes.

4. In an electric skillet or deep fryer, heat oil to 375°. Fry doughnuts, a few at a time, until golden brown on both sides. Drain on paper towels. Combine confectioners' sugar and apple cider; dip warm doughnuts in glaze.

1 GLAZED DOUGHNUT: 191 cal., 8g fat (1g sat. fat), 18mg chol., 63mg sod., 27g carb. (10g sugars, 1g fiber), 3g pro.

BREAKFAST LOAF

I make this impressive hearty sandwich when we have company for the weekend. Add sliced mushrooms and olives if you'd like.
—Amy McCuan, Oakley, CA

Prep: 15 min. • **Bake:** 25 min. + standing
Makes: 6 servings

- 6 large eggs
- ¼ tsp. salt
- ⅛ tsp. pepper
- 1 Tbsp. butter
- 1 round loaf (1 lb.) French bread
- 6 oz. sliced deli ham, divided
- ¾ cup shredded Monterey Jack cheese, divided
- ¾ cup shredded cheddar cheese, divided
- ½ medium sweet red pepper, thinly sliced
- 1 medium tomato, thinly sliced

1. Preheat oven to 350°. Whisk together eggs, salt and pepper. In a large skillet, heat butter over medium heat. Pour in egg mixture; cook and stir until eggs are thickened and no liquid egg remains. Remove from heat.

2. Cut one-fourth off top of bread loaf. Hollow out both parts, leaving a ½-in. shell (save the removed bread for another use).

3. Place a fourth of the ham in bread bottom; top with half of each of the cheeses. Layer with red pepper, scrambled eggs, tomato and the remaining cheeses and ham. Press layers gently; replace bread top. Wrap tightly in foil.

4. Bake until heated through, 25-30 minutes. Let stand 10 minutes before cutting.

1 SLICE: 439 cal., 18g fat (9g sat. fat), 230mg chol., 1083mg sod., 42g carb. (5g sugars, 2g fiber), 26g pro.

UPSIDE-DOWN APPLE BACON PANCAKE

I frequently cook Sunday brunch, and I'm always experimenting with new recipes. Apples picked from our tree were the inspiration behind this sweet and savory pancake, which my husband quickly declared a keeper.
—*Sue Gronholz, Beaver Dam, WI*

Prep: 30 min. • **Bake:** 20 min.
Makes: 4 servings

- 4 bacon strips, chopped
- 1 large apple, peeled and sliced
- 2 Tbsp. brown sugar
- ½ tsp. ground cinnamon
- 1 cup all-purpose flour
- 2 Tbsp. sugar
- 1½ tsp. baking powder
- 1 large egg, room temperature
- ¾ cup 2% milk
- 1 Tbsp. butter, melted
- ½ tsp. vanilla extract
  Optional toppings: Confectioners' sugar and maple syrup

1. Preheat oven to 375°.

2. In an 8-in. cast-iron or ovenproof skillet, cook bacon over medium heat until crisp. Using a slotted spoon, remove bacon to paper towels to drain, reserving drippings.

3. Add apples to drippings; cook and stir over medium-high heat until crisp-tender, 2-3 minutes. Remove from heat. Sprinkle with bacon, brown sugar and cinnamon.

4. In a large bowl, combine the flour, sugar and baking powder. In a small bowl, combine egg, milk, butter and vanilla; stir mixture into dry the ingredients just until moistened. Pour over apples.

5. Bake until lightly browned, 20-25 minutes. Invert onto a serving plate. If desired, dust with confectioners' sugar and serve with maple syrup.

1 PIECE: 371 cal., 16g fat (7g sat. fat), 76mg chol., 430mg sod., 46g carb. (20g sugars, 2g fiber), 10g pro.

SUE GRONHOLZ
Beaver Dam, WI

BLACK BEAN & WHITE CHEDDAR FRITTATA

This is one of my favorite comfort foods for breakfast or even a quick dinner. I make it with lime salsa. But if you're looking for something with more kick, use hot salsa or add some chipotle pepper.

—Aysha Schurman, Ammon, ID

- -

Prep: 20 min. • **Cook:** 15 min.
Makes: 6 servings

- 6 large eggs
- 3 large egg whites
- ¼ cup salsa
- 1 Tbsp. minced fresh parsley
- ¼ tsp. salt
- ¼ tsp. pepper
- 1 Tbsp. olive oil
- ⅓ cup finely chopped green pepper
- ⅓ cup finely chopped sweet red pepper
- 3 green onions, finely chopped
- 2 garlic cloves, minced
- 1 cup canned black beans, rinsed and drained
- ½ cup shredded white cheddar cheese
  Optional toppings: Minced fresh cilantro, sliced ripe olives and additional salsa

1. Preheat broiler. In a large bowl, whisk the first 6 ingredients until blended.

2. In a 10-in. ovenproof skillet, heat oil over medium-high heat. Add peppers and green onions; cook and stir 3-4 minutes or until peppers are tender. Add garlic; cook 1 minute longer. Stir in beans. Reduce heat to medium; stir in egg mixture. Cook, uncovered, until nearly set, 4-6 minutes. Sprinkle with white cheddar cheese.

3. Broil 3-4 in. from heat 3-4 minutes or until light golden brown and eggs are completely set. Let stand 5 minutes. Cut into wedges. If desired, serve with toppings.

1 WEDGE: 183 cal., 10g fat (4g sat. fat), 196mg chol., 378mg sod., 9g carb. (2g sugars, 2g fiber), 13g pro. **DIABETIC EXCHANGES:** 2 medium-fat meat, ½ starch, ½ fat.

SAUSAGE BACON BITES

These tasty morsels are perfect with almost any egg dish or as finger foods that party guests can pop into their mouths.

—*Pat Waymire, Yellow Springs, OH*

- -

Prep: 20 min. + chilling • **Bake:** 35 min.
Makes: about 3½ dozen

- ¾ lb. sliced bacon
- 2 pkg. (8 oz. each) frozen fully cooked breakfast sausage links, thawed
- ½ cup plus 2 Tbsp. packed brown sugar, divided

1. Preheat oven to 350°. Cut bacon strips widthwise in half; cut sausage links in half. Wrap a piece of bacon around each piece of sausage. Place ½ cup brown sugar in a shallow bowl; roll sausages in sugar. Secure each with a toothpick. Place in a foil-lined 15x10x1-in. baking pan. Cover and refrigerate 4 hours or overnight.

2. Sprinkle with 1 Tbsp. brown sugar. Bake until bacon is crisp, 35-40 minutes, turning once. Sprinkle with remaining brown sugar.

1 PIECE: 51 cal., 4g fat (1g sat. fat), 6mg chol., 100mg sod., 4g carb. (4g sugars, 0 fiber), 2g pro.

BASIL VEGETABLE STRATA

I've been cooking this healthy strata for years, and my family can't get enough! The fresh basil is a flavor boost.

—*Jean Ecos, Hartland, WI*

- -

Prep: 40 min. + chilling
Bake: 1 hour + standing
Makes: 8 servings

- 3 tsp. canola oil, divided
- ¾ lb. sliced fresh mushrooms
- 1 cup finely chopped sweet onion
- 1 large sweet red pepper, cut into strips
- 1 large sweet yellow pepper, thin strips
- 1 medium leek (white portion only), chopped
- ½ tsp. salt
- ½ tsp. pepper
- 10 slices whole wheat bread, cut into 1-in. pieces
- 1½ cups shredded part-skim mozzarella cheese
- ¼ cup grated Parmesan cheese
- 8 large eggs
- 4 large egg whites
- 2½ cups fat-free milk
- ¼ cup chopped fresh basil

1. In a large skillet, heat 1 tsp. oil over medium-high heat. Add mushrooms; cook and stir until tender, 8-10 minutes. Remove from the pan.

2. In same pan, heat 1 tsp. oil over medium heat. Add onion; cook and stir until golden brown, 6-8 minutes. Remove from pan and add to the mushrooms.

3. Add remaining oil to the pan. Add peppers, leek, salt and pepper; cook and stir until leek is tender, about 6-8 minutes. Stir in sauteed the mushrooms and onion.

4. In a 13x9-in. baking dish coated with cooking spray, layer half of each of the following: bread cubes, vegetable mixture, mozzarella cheese and Parmesan cheese. Repeat layers. In a large bowl, whisk the eggs, egg whites and milk until blended; pour over layers. Sprinkle with fresh basil. Refrigerate, covered, overnight.

5. Preheat oven to 350°. Remove strata from refrigerator while oven heats.

6. Bake, covered, for 50 minutes. Bake, uncovered, until lightly browned and a knife inserted in the center comes out clean, 10-15 minutes longer. Let stand 10 minutes before serving.

1 PIECE: 322 cal., 13g fat (5g sat. fat), 201mg chol., 620mg sod., 28g carb. (9g sugars, 4g fiber), 24g pro. **DIABETIC EXCHANGES:** 2 medium-fat meat, 1½ starch, 1 vegetable, ½ fat.

BIRTHDAY CAKE WAFFLES

These fun waffles—soft on the inside, crisp on the outside—taste just like cake batter! They are quick to whip up anytime, but would make birthday mornings feel even more special.
—*Andrea Fetting, Franklin, WI*

- -

Prep: 20 min. • **Cook:** 25 min.
Makes: 6 waffles

- 1 cup all-purpose flour
- 1 cup (about 5 oz.) confetti cake mix or flavor of choice
- 2 Tbsp. cornstarch
- 3 tsp. baking powder
- ¼ tsp. salt
- 2 Tbsp. rainbow sprinkles, optional
- 2 large eggs, room temperature
- 1¾ cups 2% milk
- ¾ to 1 cup plain Greek yogurt
- ½ tsp. vanilla extract
- ½ tsp. almond extract

CREAM CHEESE FROSTING
- 4 oz. softened cream cheese or reduced-fat cream cheese
- ¼ cup butter, softened
- 1½ to 2 cups confectioners' sugar
- ½ tsp. vanilla extract
- 1 to 3 Tbsp. 2% milk

1. Preheat oven to 300°. Combine the first 5 ingredients and, if desired, the rainbow sprinkles. In another bowl, whisk eggs, milk, yogurt and extracts. Add yogurt mixture to flour mixture; mix until smooth.

2. Preheat waffle maker coated with cooking spray. Pour batter and bake waffles according to the manufacturer's directions until golden brown. Transfer cooked waffles to oven until ready to serve.

3. For frosting, beat cream cheese and butter on high until light and fluffy, 2-3 minutes. Gradually beat in confectioners' sugar, ½ cup at a time, until smooth. Beat in vanilla. Add enough milk to reach desired consistency. Spread over warm waffles. For a cakelike look, cut waffles into fourths and stack them; decorate with birthday candles.

1 WAFFLE: 528 cal., 22g fat (13g sat. fat), 115mg chol., 695mg sod., 72g carb. (45g sugars, 1g fiber), 10g pro.

BREAKFAST BANANA SPLITS

I can't stop bragging about this recipe. It's elegant enough for a formal brunch, yet simple enough for any day of the week. It's nutritious, too. Play around with different fruits and cereals—the variations are endless!
—*Renee Lloyd, Pearl, MS*

- -

Takes: 10 min. • **Makes:** 2 servings

- 1 medium banana
- ⅓ cup each fresh blueberries, halved seedless grapes, sliced peeled kiwifruit and halved fresh strawberries
- 1 cup vanilla yogurt
- ½ cup granola with fruit and nuts
- 2 maraschino cherries with stems

Cut banana crosswise in half. For each serving, split each half lengthwise and place in a serving dish. Top with remaining ingredients.

1 SERVING: 337 cal., 6g fat (1g sat. fat), 6mg chol., 96mg sod., 66g carb. (42g sugars, 8g fiber), 12g pro.

RAINBOW QUICHE

With a bounty of veggies and a creamy egg-cheese filling, this tasty quiche gets two thumbs-up!
—Lilith Fury, Adena, OH

- -

Prep: 30 min. • **Bake:** 40 min. + standing
Makes: 8 servings

- 1 sheet refrigerated pie crust
- 2 Tbsp. butter
- 1 small onion, finely chopped
- 1 cup sliced fresh mushrooms
- 1 cup small fresh broccoli florets
- ½ cup finely chopped sweet orange pepper
- ½ cup finely chopped sweet red pepper
- 3 large eggs, lightly beaten
- 1⅓ cups half-and-half cream
- ¾ tsp. salt
- ½ tsp. pepper
- 1 cup shredded Mexican cheese blend, divided
- 1 cup fresh baby spinach

1. Preheat oven to 425°. Unroll pie crust onto a lightly floured surface, roll to a 12-in. circle. Transfer to a 9-in. deep-dish pie plate; trim and flute edge. Refrigerate while preparing the filling.

2. In a large skillet, heat butter over medium-high heat; saute onion, mushrooms, broccoli and peppers until mushrooms are lightly browned, 6-8 minutes. Cool slightly.

3. Whisk together eggs, cream and salt and pepper. Sprinkle ½ cup cheese over crust; top with spinach and vegetable mixture. Sprinkle with remaining cheese. Pour in egg mixture.

4. Bake on a lower oven rack 15 minutes. Reduce oven setting to 350°; bake until a knife inserted in the center comes out clean, 25-30 minutes. (Cover edge loosely with foil if necessary to prevent overbrowning.) Let stand 10 minutes before cutting.

NOTE: You may also use this recipe to fill 2 frozen deep-dish pie shells. Bake the quiches for 40-45 minutes. Each yields 6 servings.

1 PIECE: 295 cal., 20g fat (10g sat. fat), 115mg chol., 482mg sod., 18g carb. (4g sugars, 1g fiber), 9g pro.

ITALIAN SAUSAGE QUICHE: Omit broccoli and butter. Substitute Italian cheese blend for the Mexican cheese blend. In a large skillet, saute 1 pound bulk Italian sausage, onion, mushrooms and peppers until tender; drain. Add ½ tsp. dried basil, ½ tsp. dried parsley and ⅛ tsp. crushed red pepper to the egg mixture.

SWEET & SPICY BACON

Chili powder, cayenne and curry add an unexpected flavor twist to the taste-tempting bacon. With a touch of cinnamon and maple syrup, the well-seasoned strips complement almost any breakfast entree.
—Taste of Home *Test Kitchen*

- -

Takes: 25 min. • **Makes:** 4 servings

- 1 tsp. chili powder
- ⅛ tsp. cayenne pepper
- ⅛ tsp. curry powder
- ⅛ tsp. ground cinnamon
- 8 bacon strips
- 3 Tbsp. maple syrup

Combine the seasonings; sprinkle over both sides of bacon. Place on a rack in an ungreased 15x10x1-in. baking pan. Bake at 450° for 10 minutes. Drizzle with 1 Tbsp. syrup. Turn bacon and drizzle with remaining syrup. Bake for 6-10 minutes longer or until browned. Remove to paper towels. Serve warm.

2 PIECES: 115 cal., 6g fat (2g sat. fat), 11mg chol., 210mg sod., 11g carb. (10g sugars, 0 fiber), 4g pro.

> **TEST KITCHEN TIP**
> Since you're cooking bacon for breakfast, you may decide to cook the entire package all at once. Chop the extra bacon and use it later to top a soup, salad or baked potato.

FRUITY ORANGE DREAM

A fellow teacher gave me this recipe when I was living in West Virginia. It's a standout for a brunch or party, especially if it's made the night before and the flavors have plenty of time to blend. Plus, children love it—it tastes like a Creamsicle in a bowl!
—Georgeanna Wellings, Dacula, GA

Prep: 15 min. + chilling • **Makes:** 8 servings

- 1½ cups cold 2% milk
- 1 pkg. (3.4 oz.) instant vanilla pudding mix
- ¾ cup sour cream
- ⅓ cup thawed orange juice concentrate
- 2 cans (11 oz. each) mandarin oranges, drained
- 1 can (20 oz.) unsweetened pineapple tidbits, drained
- 1 can (15 oz.) sliced peaches in extra-light syrup, drained
- 2 large red apples, chopped

In a large bowl, whisk milk and dry pudding mix 2 minutes. Stir in sour cream and orange juice concentrate. Gently stir in fruit. Refrigerate, covered, at least 1 hour before serving.
¾ CUP: 194 cal., 5g fat (3g sat. fat), 7mg chol., 91mg sod., 38g carb. (33g sugars, 2g fiber), 3g pro.

> **TEST KITCHEN TIP**
> Feel free to toss other fruits in this salad, such as a banana, fresh berries or maraschino cherries.

AIR-FRYER TOAD-IN-THE-HOLE

Toad-in-the-Hole is a British comfort food dish consisting of sausages baked in Yorkshire pudding. I prepare mine in the air fryer, breakfast-style, even though it's commonly served at suppertime.
—Leigh Rys, Herndon, VA

Prep: 10 min. • **Cook:** 25 min.
Makes: 4 servings

- 8 frozen turkey breakfast sausage links
- 2 large eggs
- 1 cup 2% milk
- ½ cup all-purpose flour
- 1 tsp. onion powder
- 1 tsp. stone-ground mustard
- ⅛ tsp. salt
- ⅛ tsp. pepper
- Optional: 1 bacon strip, cooked and crumbled, and minced parsley

1. Preheat the air fryer to 400°. Cut sausages in half widthwise. Arrange in a greased 6-in. round baking pan. Cook in air fryer until lightly browned, 6-8 minutes, turning once.
2. Meanwhile, in a large bowl, whisk eggs, milk, flour, onion powder, mustard, salt, and pepper. If desired, stir in bacon; pour over sausages. Cook until puffed and golden brown, 10-15. Serve immediately and, if desired, garnish with parsley.
1 SERVING: 257 cal., 15g fat (5g sat. fat), 143mg chol., 494mg sod., 16g carb. (3g sugars, 1g fiber), 16g pro.

3. In a large skillet with high sides, bring vinegar and 2-3 in. water to a boil. Reduce heat to maintain a gentle simmer. Break 1 cold egg at a time into a small bowl; holding bowl close to surface of water, slip eggs into water.

4. Cook, uncovered, 3-5 minutes or until whites are completely set and yolks begin to thicken but are not hard. Using a slotted spoon, remove eggs; place over mushrooms in baking pan. Sprinkle the goat cheese and remaining mozzarella cheese over eggs and mushrooms. Refrigerate, covered, overnight.

5. Remove pan from refrigerator 30 minutes before baking. Preheat oven to 400°. Sprinkle onions over top. Bake, uncovered, until golden brown and heated through, 10-15 minutes. Top with basil just before serving.

1 PIECE: 345 cal., 17g fat (5g sat. fat), 227mg chol., 798mg sod., 29g carb. (6g sugars, 2g fiber), 17g pro.

AVOCADO FRUIT SALAD

This salad is simply delish. I'm glad a friend gave me the recipe. My family loves it, and so do I.
—*Mildred Sherrer, Fort Worth, TX*

Takes: 20 min. • **Makes:** 6 servings

- ½ cup plain yogurt
- 2 Tbsp. honey
- 1 tsp. grated lemon zest
- 1 tsp. plus 2 Tbsp. lemon juice, divided
- 3 medium ripe avocados, peeled and cubed
- 1 medium apple, chopped
- 1 cup halved seedless grapes
- 1 can (11 oz.) mandarin oranges, drained
- 1 medium firm banana, cut into ¼-in. slices

1. For dressing, mix yogurt, honey, lemon zest and 1 tsp. lemon juice. Toss avocados with remaining lemon juice.

2. In a large bowl, combine the remaining ingredients; gently stir in avocados. Serve with dressing.

¾ CUP: 231 cal., 11g fat (2g sat. fat), 3mg chol., 22mg sod., 35g carb. (25g sugars, 6g fiber), 3g pro.

OVERNIGHT BAKED EGGS BRUSCHETTA

I want to spend as much time as I can with my guests when they stay for the holidays, so I rely on make-ahead recipes to help make that happen. Because most overnight brunch casseroles are so similar, I came up with a breakfast bruschetta for a fun change of pace.
—*Judi Berman-Yamada, Portland, OR*

Prep: 45 min. + chilling • **Bake:** 10 min.
Makes: 9 servings

- 1 tube (13.8 oz.) refrigerated pizza crust
- 1 Tbsp. cornmeal
- 3 Tbsp. olive oil, divided
- 1½ cups shredded part-skim mozzarella cheese, divided
- ¾ lb. sliced baby portobello mushrooms
- ¾ tsp. garlic powder
- ¾ tsp. dried rosemary, crushed
- ½ tsp. pepper
- ¼ tsp. salt
- 2 cups pizza sauce
- 1 Tbsp. white vinegar
- 9 large eggs
- 2 oz. fresh goat cheese, crumbled
- ½ cup French-fried onions
  Fresh basil leaves

1. Preheat oven to 400°. Unroll the pizza dough and press onto bottom of a greased 15x10x1-in baking pan that's been sprinkled with cornmeal. Brush dough with 1 Tbsp. oil; sprinkle with ¾ cup mozzarella cheese. Bake 8 minutes.

2. Meanwhile, in a large skillet, heat remaining oil over medium-high heat. Add mushrooms; cook and stir until tender. Stir in garlic powder, rosemary and seasonings. Stir pizza sauce into mushrooms; spread mushroom mixture over baked crust.

COLLEEN DELAWDER
Herndon, VA

SLOW-COOKER HONEY NUT GRANOLA

I lightened up my friend's granola recipe and changed the add-ins to suit our tastes. It's now a family favorite. Get creative and mix up the nuts, seeds or dried fruits.

—*Tari Ambler, Shorewood, IL*

- -

Prep: 20 min. • **Cook:** 1½ hours + cooling
Makes: 8 cups

4½	cups old-fashioned oats
½	cup sunflower kernels
⅓	cup toasted wheat germ
¼	cup unsweetened shredded coconut
¼	cup sliced almonds
¼	cup chopped pecans
¼	cup chopped walnuts
¼	cup ground flaxseed
½	cup honey
⅓	cup water
3	Tbsp. canola oil
1	tsp. ground cinnamon
1	tsp. vanilla extract
½	tsp. ground nutmeg

Dash salt
¾ cup dried cranberries
¾ cup raisins
Yogurt, optional

1. In a 3- or 4-qt. slow cooker, combine the first 8 ingredients. In a small bowl, whisk the honey, water, oil, cinnamon, vanilla, nutmeg and salt until blended; stir into oat mixture. Cook, covered, on high until crisp, 1½-2 hours, stirring well every 20 minutes.

2. Stir in cranberries and raisins. Spread evenly onto waxed paper or baking sheets; cool completely. Store in airtight containers. If desired, serve with yogurt.

NOTE: Look for unsweetened coconut in the baking or health food section.

½ CUP: 267 cal., 12g fat (2g sat. fat), 0 chol., 43mg sod., 39g carb. (19g sugars, 5g fiber), 6g pro.

TEST KITCHEN TIP
Be sure to stir the granola mixture thoroughly every 20 minutes for even cooking.

SOUTHERN HASH BROWNS & HAM SHEET-PAN BAKE

Why not take the convenience of sheet-pan cooking and apply it to breakfast? I love how easily this meal comes together.
—*Colleen Delawder, Herndon, VA*

Prep: 15 min. • **Bake:** 35 min.
Makes: 4 servings

1   pkg. (20 oz.) refrigerated shredded hash brown potatoes
3   Tbsp. olive oil
½   tsp. salt
½   tsp. pepper
¼   cup apple jelly
¼   cup apricot preserves
1   Tbsp. horseradish sauce
1   tsp. Dijon mustard
¼   tsp. garlic powder
¼   tsp. onion powder
2   cups cubed fully cooked ham
4   large eggs
2   green onions, finely chopped

1. Preheat oven to 400°. Place potatoes in a greased 15x10x1-in. baking pan. Drizzle with oil; sprinkle with salt and pepper. Toss to coat. Bake 25-30 minutes or until the edges are golden brown.
2. In a small bowl, combine jelly, preserves, horseradish sauce, Dijon, garlic powder and onion powder. Pour over potatoes; add ham. Toss to coat.
3. With the back of a spoon, make 4 wells in potato mixture. Break an egg into each well. Bake until egg whites are completely set and the yolks begin to thicken but are not hard, 10-12 minutes. Sprinkle with green onions and additional pepper.
1 SERVING: 483 cal., 19g fat (4g sat. fat), 228mg chol., 1340mg sod., 55g carb. (23g sugars, 3g fiber), 24g pro.

AMISH WAFFLES

These waffles are so crispy and delicious, you wouldn't think they could get any better—but then you add the fruity topping and...wow!
—*Neil and Jeanne Liechty, Pensacola, FL*

Takes: 30 min. • **Makes:** 8 servings

- 1 cup all-purpose flour
- 1 cup sifted cake flour
- 1½ cups whole milk
- 2½ tsp. baking powder
- 2 large eggs, room temperature, well beaten
- 5 Tbsp. butter, melted
- 1 tsp. vanilla

TOPPING

- 1⅔ cups water
- ⅔ cup sugar
- 2 Tbsp. cornstarch
- 2 Tbsp. light corn syrup
- 8 oz. frozen blueberries
- 8 oz. frozen raspberries
  Vanilla ice cream, optional

1. Preheat waffle maker. Mix first 7 ingredients in order just until smooth. Bake the waffles according to manufacturer's directions until golden brown.

2. Meanwhile, for topping, combine water, sugar, cornstarch, corn syrup in a small saucepan over medium heat until thickened. Remove from heat; cool. Stir in berries. Serve warm over waffles; if desired, add ice cream.

1 SERVING: 382 cal., 10g fat (6g sat. fat), 79mg chol., 268mg sod., 65g carb. (35g sugars, 2g fiber), 8g pro.

FRUIT-TOPPED BLINTZES

My mother is a wonderful cook who always likes to prepare (and improve on!) dishes she's sampled at restaurants. That's what I did with these blintzes, and my family loves my fruity version even more than the original.
—*Patricia Larsen, Thayne, WY*

Prep: 25 min. • **Cook:** 15 min.
Makes: 8 servings

BLINTZES

- 9 large eggs, room temperature
- 1 cup all-purpose flour
- ¼ cup cornstarch
- ⅛ tsp. salt
- 3 cups 2% milk

FILLING

- 2 pkg. (8 oz. each) cream cheese, softened
- ½ cup confectioners' sugar
  Pureed raspberries or strawberries
  Whipped cream, optional
  Fresh raspberries or strawberries, optional

1. In a large bowl, beat eggs. Add the flour, cornstarch and salt; stir until smooth. Stir in the milk.

2. Heat a lightly greased 8-in. nonstick skillet; pour ⅓ cup batter into the center of skillet. Lift and tilt pan to evenly coat bottom. Cook until the top appears dry; turn and cook 15-20 seconds longer. Keep the blintzes in a warm oven, covered with foil. Repeat with remaining batter.

3. For filling, in a small bowl, beat cream cheese and confectioner's sugar until smooth. Place about 2 Tbsp. in the center of each blintz; overlap sides and ends on top of filling. Place folded side down. Serve with pureed berries; garnish with whipped cream and fresh berries if desired.

2 BLINTZES: 340 cal., 19g fat (10g sat. fat), 283mg chol., 237mg sod., 29g carb. (13g sugars, 0 fiber), 14g pro.

APPLE-SAGE SAUSAGE PATTIES

Apple and sausage naturally go together. Add sage, and you've got a standout patty. They're freezer-friendly, so I make them ahead and grab when needed.

—*Scarlett Elrod, Newnan, GA*

- -

Prep: 35 min. + chilling • **Cook:** 10 min./batch
Makes: 16 patties

1	large apple
1	large egg, lightly beaten
½	cup chopped fresh parsley
3	to 4 Tbsp. minced fresh sage
2	garlic cloves, minced
1¼	tsp. salt
½	tsp. pepper
½	tsp. crushed red pepper flakes
1¼	lbs. lean ground turkey
6	tsp. olive oil, divided

1. Peel and coarsely shred apple; place apple in a colander over a plate. Let stand for 15 minutes. Squeeze apple and blot dry with paper towels.

2. In a large bowl, combine egg, parsley, sage, garlic, seasonings and apple. Add turkey; mix lightly but thoroughly. Shape into sixteen 2-in. patties. Place patties on waxed paper-lined baking sheets. Refrigerate, covered, 8 hours or overnight.

3. In a large nonstick skillet, heat 2 tsp. oil over medium heat. In batches, cook patties until golden brown and a thermometer reads 165°, 3-4 minutes on each side, adding more oil as needed.

FREEZE OPTION: Place uncooked patties on waxed paper-lined baking sheets; wrap and freeze until firm. Remove from pans and transfer to a freezer container; return to freezer. To use, cook frozen patties as directed, increasing time to 4-5 minutes on each side.

1 PATTY: 79 cal., 5g fat (1g sat. fat), 36mg chol., 211mg sod., 2g carb. (1g sugars, 0 fiber), 8g pro.

BROCCOLI QUICHE CUPS

Make this crustless quiche in muffin cups or in a regular-size pie tin. Either way, there's plenty of bacon-y, cheesy goodness to go around.

—*Angela Lively, Conroe, TX*

- -

Takes: 25 min. • **Makes:** 1 dozen

1	cup chopped fresh broccoli
1	cup shredded pepper jack cheese
6	large eggs, lightly beaten
¾	cup heavy whipping cream
½	cup bacon bits
1	shallot, minced
¼	tsp. salt
¼	tsp. pepper

1. Preheat oven to 350°. Divide broccoli and cheese among 12 greased muffin cups.

2. Whisk together remaining ingredients; pour into cups. Bake until set, 15-20 minutes.

2 QUICHE CUPS: 291 cal., 24g fat (12g sat. fat), 243mg chol., 523mg sod., 4g carb. (2g sugars, 0 fiber), 16g pro.

> **TEST KITCHEN TIP**
> Counting calories? Swap half-and-half for whipping cream and save more than 60 calories and 6 grams of saturated fat per serving.

MIGAS BREAKFAST TACOS

Migas—a scrambled egg dish incorporating traditional southwestern ingredients and flavors—make the best filling for my breakfast tacos. The secret ingredient: fried corn tortillas. They are truly something special!
—*Stephen Exel, Des Moines, IA*

- -

Takes: 30 min. • **Makes:** 3 servings

- ¼ cup finely chopped onion
- 1 jalapeno pepper, seeded and chopped
- 1 Tbsp. canola oil
- 2 corn tortillas (6 in.), cut into thin strips
- 4 large eggs
- ¼ tsp. salt
- ⅛ tsp. pepper
- ½ cup crumbled queso fresco or shredded Monterey Jack cheese
- ¼ cup chopped seeded tomato
- 6 flour tortillas (6 in.), warmed
  Optional toppings: Refried beans, sliced avocado, sour cream and minced fresh cilantro

1. In a large skillet, saute onion and jalapeno in oil until tender. Add tortilla strips; cook 3 minutes longer. In a small bowl, whisk the eggs, salt and pepper. Add to skillet; cook and stir until almost set. Stir in cheese and tomato.
2. Serve mixture in flour tortillas with toppings of your choice.
NOTE: Wear disposable gloves when cutting hot peppers; the oils can burn skin. Avoid touching your face.
2 EACH: 424 cal., 21g fat (5g sat. fat), 295mg chol., 821mg sod., 39g carb. (2g sugars, 1g fiber), 21g pro.

> **TEST KITCHEN TIP**
> You can also wrap these tacos in white or yellow corn tortillas instead of flour. Or, put a generous amount of filling into a extra-large soft flour tortilla for a big burrito. Pour some of your favorite jarred salsa on top for a little extra kick.

PRESSURE-COOKER STEEL-CUT OATS & BERRIES

I woke up one Sunday morning and realized I had forgotten to make overnight oats in my slow cooker the night before. I improvised by putting the ingredients in my pressure cooker, and the results were just as good. Serve with your favorite fresh berries.
—*Mary Anne Thygesen, Portland, OR*

- -

Prep: 15 min. • **Cook:** 10 min. + releasing
Makes: 3 servings

- 3¼ cups water, divided
- ¾ cup steel-cut oats
- ¾ cup sweetened shredded coconut
- 6 Tbsp. dried cranberries
- ⅜ tsp. each ground cinnamon, cardamom, allspice and nutmeg
- ⅜ tsp. salt
- 1½ tsp. butter
  Optional toppings: Yogurt, maple syrup and fresh berries

1. Place ¾ cup water, ¼ cup oats, ¼ cup coconut, 2 Tbsp. cranberries, ⅛ tsp. each cinnamon, cardamom, allspice and nutmeg, and ⅛ tsp. salt in each of three 1-pint canning jars. Top each with ½ tsp. butter.
2. Place trivet insert and remaining 1 cup water in a 6-qt. electric pressure cooker. Set jars on trivet. Lock lid; close the pressure-release valve. Adjust to pressure-cook on high for 10 minutes. Let pressure release naturally. Remove jars. Let stand 3 minutes before serving. If desired, serve oats with toppings of your choice.
1 SERVING: 349 cal., 13g fat (9g sat. fat), 5mg chol., 372mg sod., 55g carb. (26g sugars, 7g fiber), 6g pro.

AUNT EDITH'S BAKED PANCAKE

My dear aunt made a mighty breakfast that revolved around what we called "the big pancake." I loved watching her pour the batter into her huge iron skillet, then bake the confection to perfection in the oven.
—*Marion Kirst, Troy, MI*

Prep: 15 min. • **Bake:** 20 min.
Makes: 4 servings

- 3 large eggs, room temperature
- ½ tsp. salt
- ½ cup all-purpose flour
- ½ cup 2% milk
- 2 Tbsp. butter, softened

Confectioners' sugar
Lemon wedges

In a bowl, beat eggs until very light. Add salt, flour and milk; beat well. Thoroughly rub the bottom and sides of a 10-in. cast-iron or other heavy skillet with butter. Pour batter into skillet. Bake at 450° for 15 minutes. Reduce heat to 350° and bake until set, 5 minutes longer. If desired, remove pancake from skillet and place on a large hot platter. Dust with confectioners' sugar and garnish with lemon. Serve immediately.

1 PIECE: 180 cal., 10g fat (5g sat. fat), 158mg chol., 407mg sod., 14g carb. (2g sugars, 0 fiber), 7g pro.

PROSCIUTTO EGG PANINI

Change up the usual bacon and egg sandwich by piling on prosciutto instead. It's a breakfast worth waking up for!
—*Erin Mylroie, Santa Clara, UT*

Takes: 30 min. • **Makes:** 8 servings

- 3 large eggs
- 2 large egg whites
- 6 Tbsp. fat-free milk
- 1 green onion, thinly sliced
- 1 Tbsp. Dijon mustard
- 1 Tbsp. maple syrup
- 8 slices sourdough bread
- 8 thin slices prosciutto or deli ham
- ½ cup shredded sharp cheddar cheese
- 8 tsp. butter

1. In a small bowl, whisk the eggs, egg whites, milk and onion. Coat a large skillet with cooking spray and place over medium heat. Add egg mixture; cook and stir over medium heat until completely set.
2. Combine mustard and syrup; spread over 4 bread slices. Layer with scrambled eggs, prosciutto and cheese; top with remaining bread. Butter outsides of sandwiches.
3. Cook on a panini maker or indoor grill for 3-4 minutes or until the bread is browned and cheese is melted. Cut each panini in half to serve.

½ SANDWICH: 228 cal., 10g fat (5g sat. fat), 111mg chol., 640mg sod., 21g carb. (3g sugars, 1g fiber), 13g pro. **DIABETIC EXCHANGES:** 1½ starch, 1½ fat, 1 lean meat.

TO MAKE AHEAD: Refrigerate the unbaked casserole, covered, several hours or overnight. Preheat oven to 350°. Remove casserole from refrigerator while oven heats. Bake as directed, increasing time by 5 minutes.

1 CUP: 506 cal., 34g fat (14g sat. fat), 243mg chol., 1419mg sod., 27g carb. (5g sugars, 2g fiber), 22g pro.

ASPARAGUS & RED PEPPER FRITTATA

Here's a delicious way to start the morning. This frittata is enriched with asparagus, hash brown potatoes, peppers, herbs and a wonderful blend of cheeses. Serve with a side of seasonal fruit.
—*Toni Donahue, Westerville, OH*

- -

Prep: 20 min. • **Cook:** 25 min.
Makes: 6 servings

  12 fresh asparagus spears, trimmed
  ½ tsp. plus 3 Tbsp. olive oil, divided
  10 large eggs
  3 large egg whites
  ¾ cup 2% milk
  ½ cup shredded Parmesan cheese
  ¾ tsp. salt
  ½ tsp. pepper
  1 pkg. (20 oz.) refrigerated shredded hash brown potatoes
  ½ large sweet red pepper, julienned
  3 fresh basil leaves, thinly sliced
  ½ cup shredded pepper Jack cheese

1. Place asparagus on an ungreased baking sheet; drizzle with ½ tsp. oil. Bake at 400° for 10-12 minutes or until tender, stirring once.
2. In a large bowl, whisk the eggs, egg whites, milk, Parmesan cheese, salt and pepper; set aside. Heat 2 Tbsp. oil in a 12-in. ovenproof skillet over medium heat. Add potatoes and press down lightly. Cook, uncovered, until bottom is golden brown, 6-7 minutes. Drizzle with remaining oil; turn over.
3. Pour egg mixture over potatoes. Cover and cook for 9-11 minutes or until nearly set. Arrange asparagus and red pepper over top. Sprinkle with basil and pepper Jack cheese.
4. Broil 3-4 in. from the heat until eggs are completely set, 2-3 minutes. Let stand for 5 minutes. Cut into wedges.

1 WEDGE: 371 cal., 21g fat (7g sat. fat), 370mg chol., 692mg sod., 24g carb. (3g sugars, 2g fiber), 22g pro.

BREAKFAST BURRITO CASSEROLE

A friend gave me this burrito casserole recipe and I modified it to fit our family. It's perfect for a brunch—just prep it the night before and bake the next morning.
—*Krista Yoder, Abbeville, SC*

- -

Prep: 25 min. • **Bake:** 30 min.
Makes: 8 servings

  8 large eggs
  ⅓ cup 2% milk
  ½ tsp. salt
  ½ tsp. pepper
  1 lb. bulk pork sausage
  1 cup sour cream
  1 can (10¾ oz.) condensed cream of chicken soup, undiluted
  4 flour tortillas (10 in.), cut into 1-in. pieces
  1⅓ cups salsa, divided
  ⅔ cup shredded cheddar cheese
  ⅔ cup shredded part-skim mozzarella cheese
    Optional: Enchilada sauce and thinly sliced green onions

1. Preheat oven to 350°. Whisk together eggs, milk, salt and pepper. In a large skillet coated with cooking spray, cook and stir egg mixture over medium heat until thickened and no liquid egg remains; remove.
2. In same skillet, cook and crumble sausage over medium heat 5-7 minutes or until no longer pink; drain. Stir together sour cream and soup. Spread half the sour cream mixture in an ungreased 13x9-in. baking dish. Layer with half the tortilla pieces, half the salsa, scrambled eggs, sausage and remaining tortillas and sour cream mixture. Top with the remaining salsa; sprinkle with cheeses.
3. Bake, uncovered, until heated through, 30-35 minutes. If desired, serve with enchilada sauce and sliced green onions.

Soups & Sandwiches

Say hello to homemade with these warm soups and hearty sandwiches. Served on their own or as a pair, you don't need to look any further for the very best in comfort food. Ooh yeah!

BROCCOLI BEER CHEESE SOUP

My homemade twist on broccoli cheese soup is amazing with or without the beer. I make extra and pop individual servings into the freezer to enjoy later.
—*Lori Lee, Brooksville, FL*

- -

Prep: 20 min. • **Cook:** 30 min.
Makes: 10 servings (2½ qt.)

- 3 Tbsp. butter
- 5 celery ribs, finely chopped
- 3 medium carrots, finely chopped
- 1 small onion, finely chopped
- 4 cups fresh broccoli florets, chopped
- ¼ cup chopped sweet red pepper
- 4 cans (14½ oz. each) chicken broth
- ½ tsp. pepper
- ½ cup all-purpose flour
- ½ cup water
- 3 cups shredded cheddar cheese
- 1 pkg. (8 oz.) cream cheese, cubed
- 1 bottle (12 oz.) beer or nonalcoholic beer
  Optional toppings: Additional shredded cheddar cheese, cooked and crumbled bacon strips, sour cream, chopped green onions and salad croutons

1. In a Dutch oven, melt butter over medium-high heat. Add the celery, carrots and onion; saute until crisp-tender. Add broccoli and red pepper; stir in broth and pepper. Combine flour and water until smooth; gradually stir into pan. Bring to a boil. Reduce heat; simmer, uncovered, until thickened and vegetables are tender, 25-30 minutes.

2. Stir in cheeses and beer until cheeses are melted (do not boil). Top with additional shredded cheese, bacon, green onions, sour cream and croutons as desired.

FREEZE OPTION: Before adding toppings, cool soup; transfer to freezer containers. Freeze up to 3 months. To use, partially thaw in refrigerator overnight; heat through in a large saucepan over medium-low heat, stirring occasionally (do not boil). Add cheese and other toppings as desired.

1 CUP: 316 cal., 23g fat (13g sat. fat), 69mg chol., 1068mg sod., 13g carb. (5g sugars, 2g fiber), 12g pro.

FRESH VEGGIE POCKETS

One summer I worked at a health food store that sold sandwiches. We were close to a college campus, so I made lots of these fresh filled pitas for the students. With veggies and nutty sunflower kernels, they're a fast-to-fix meal when you're on the go.
—Linda Reeves, Cloverdale, IN

Takes: 15 min. • **Makes:** 4 servings

- 1 carton (8 oz.) spreadable cream cheese
- ¼ cup sunflower kernels
- 1 tsp. seasoned salt or salt-free seasoning blend
- 4 whole wheat pita breads (6 in.), halved
- 1 medium tomato, thinly sliced
- 1 medium cucumber, thinly sliced
- 1 cup sliced fresh mushrooms
- 1 ripe avocado, peeled and sliced

In a large bowl, combine the cream cheese, sunflower kernels and seasoned salt; spread about 2 Tbsp. on the inside of each pita half. Layer with the tomato, cucumber, mushrooms and avocado.

2 FILLED PITA HALVES: 434 cal., 23g fat (9g sat. fat), 37mg chol., 571mg sod., 48g carb. (6g sugars, 8g fiber), 14g pro.

MAPLE SAUSAGE SLIDERS WITH SLAW

Small in size but big in flavor, these dynamite coleslaw-topped sliders are sure to score with hungry fans. They're a welcome change from usual game-day fare.
—Lisa Huff, Wilton, CT

Prep: 25 min. • **Cook:** 10 min./batch
Makes: 1½ dozen

- 2 cups coleslaw mix
- 1 cup shredded peeled apple
- 1 cup crumbled blue cheese
- ¼ cup finely chopped red onion
- 3 Tbsp. olive oil
- 2 Tbsp. cider vinegar
- 1½ tsp. maple syrup
- ½ tsp. Dijon mustard
- ⅛ tsp. salt
- ⅛ tsp. pepper

SLIDER

- 1 cup finely chopped walnuts, toasted
- ½ cup finely chopped red onion
- 2 Tbsp. minced fresh thyme or 2 tsp. dried thyme
- ½ tsp. salt
- ¼ tsp. pepper
- 2 lbs. bulk maple pork sausage
- 18 dinner rolls, split and lightly toasted

1. In a large bowl, combine the coleslaw mix, apple, blue cheese and red onion. In a small bowl, whisk the oil, vinegar, maple syrup, mustard, salt and pepper. Pour over coleslaw mixture; toss to coat. Chill until serving.
2. In a large bowl, combine the walnuts, onion, thyme, salt and pepper. Crumble sausage over mixture and mix well. Shape into 18 patties.
3. In a large skillet, cook patties in batches over medium heat for 3-4 minutes on each side or until a thermometer reads 160°.
4. Top each bottom roll with a burger and 2 Tbsp. coleslaw mixture. Replace roll tops.

1 SLIDER WITH 2 TBSP. SLAW: 331 cal., 22g fat (6g sat. fat), 50mg chol., 678mg sod., 23g carb. (4g sugars, 2g fiber), 12g pro.

CARIBBEAN POTATO SOUP

A blend of veggies—including okra, kale and black-eyed peas—goes into this bright and hearty soup. No kale on hand? Just toss in spinach instead.
—*Crystal Jo Bruns, Iliff, CO*

Takes: 30 min. • **Makes:** 6 servings

- 2 medium onions, chopped
- 2 tsp. canola oil
- 3 garlic cloves, minced
- 2 tsp. minced fresh gingerroot
- 2 tsp. ground coriander
- 1 tsp. ground turmeric
- ½ tsp. dried thyme
- ¼ tsp. ground allspice
- 5 cups vegetable broth
- 2 cups cubed peeled sweet potato
- 3 cups chopped fresh kale
- 1 cup frozen sliced okra
- 1 cup coconut milk
- 1 cup canned diced tomatoes, drained
- 1 cup canned black-eyed peas, rinsed and drained
- 2 Tbsp. lime juice

1. In a Dutch oven, saute onions in oil until tender. Add the garlic, ginger and spices; cook 1 minute longer.
2. Stir in broth and potato. Bring to a boil. Reduce heat; cover and simmer for 5 minutes. Stir in kale and okra. Return to a boil; cover and simmer 10 minutes longer or until potato is tender. Add the milk, tomatoes, peas and lime juice; heat through.

1½ CUPS: 213 cal., 10g fat (7g sat. fat), 0 chol., 954mg sod., 28g carb. (9g sugars, 6g fiber), 5g pro.

CRYSTAL JO BRUNS
Iliff, CO

BUTTERNUT SQUASH CHILI

Add butternut squash to chili for a tasty, filling, energy-packed dish your whole family will love. My crew gives it their stamp of approval!
—*Jeanne Larson, Rancho Santa Margarita, CA*

Prep: 20 min. • **Cook:** 30 min.
Makes: 8 servings (2 qt.)

- 1 lb. ground beef or turkey
- ¾ cup chopped red onion
- 5 garlic cloves, minced
- 3 Tbsp. tomato paste
- 1 Tbsp. chili powder
- 1 tsp. ground cumin
- ½ to 1 tsp. salt
- 1¾ to 2 cups water
- 1 can (15 oz.) black beans, rinsed and drained
- 1 can (15 oz.) pinto beans, rinsed and drained
- 1 can (14½ oz.) diced tomatoes
- 1 can (14½ to 15 oz.) tomato sauce
- 3 cups cubed peeled butternut squash, (½-in. cubes)
- 2 Tbsp. cider vinegar
  Optional: Chopped avocado, plain Greek yogurt and shredded mozzarella cheese

1. In a Dutch oven over medium heat, cook beef and red onion, crumbling meat, until the beef is no longer pink and the onion is tender, 6-8 minutes.
2. Add next 5 ingredients; cook 1 minute longer. Stir in water, both types of beans, diced tomatoes and tomato sauce. Bring to a boil; reduce heat. Stir in squash; simmer, covered, until squash is tender, 20-25 minutes. Stir in vinegar.
3. If desired, serve with chopped avocado, yogurt and shredded mozzarella cheese.

1 CUP: 261 cal., 8g fat (3g sat. fat), 35mg chol., 704mg sod., 32g carb. (6g sugars, 8g fiber), 18g pro. **DIABETIC EXCHANGES:** 2 starch, 2 lean meat.

DID YOU KNOW?
Butternut squash is a bell-shaped squash with a pale tan shell. The shell can be peeled before cooking. The orange flesh has a sweet, nutty flavor similar to pumpkin.

GARBANZO BEAN BURGERS

These meatless burgers are totally awesome. I'd rather have one of these than any old cheeseburger at a restaurant. They rock!
—*Berea Rider, East Point, KY*

- -

Prep: 25 min. • **Cook:** 10 min.
Makes: 4 servings

- 1   can (15 oz.) garbanzo beans or chickpeas, rinsed and drained
- 3   Tbsp. water
- 1   tsp. lemon juice
- 1   cup dry bread crumbs
- 1   large egg
- 1   tsp. Italian seasoning
- ½   tsp. garlic powder
- ½   tsp. onion powder
    Dash crushed red pepper flakes
- 2   Tbsp. canola oil

- 4   whole wheat or whole grain hamburger buns, split and toasted
- 4   slices reduced-fat American cheese
    Optional toppings: Dill pickle slices, fat-free mayonnaise, ketchup, sliced red onion, lettuce and sliced tomato

1. Place the beans, water and lemon juice in a food processor; cover and process until blended. Transfer to a large bowl. Add the bread crumbs, egg and seasonings and mix well. Shape into 4 patties.

2. In a large cast-iron or other heavy skillet, cook patties in oil in batches until lightly browned, 3-4 minutes on each side. Serve on buns with cheese. If desired, top with pickle slices, mayonnaise and ketchup.

1 BURGER: 447 cal., 16g fat (3g sat. fat), 50mg chol., 807mg sod., 60g carb. (10g sugars, 9g fiber), 17g pro.

CREAM OF TURKEY & WILD RICE SOUP

A dear friend brought me some of this soup when I was ill—and it instantly hit the spot. I asked her for the recipe and I've made it since, especially when I have leftover turkey to use up. Now I to take it to friends when they're not feeling well. It's just the filling meal to warm you up on a cold, wintry day.
—*Doris Cox, New Freedom, PA*

- -

Prep: 15 min. • **Cook:** 20 min.
Makes: 6 servings

- 1   medium onion, chopped
- 1   can (4 oz.) sliced mushrooms, drained
- 2   Tbsp. butter
- 3   cups water
- 2   cups chicken broth
- 1   pkg. (6 oz.) long grain and wild rice mix
- 2   cups diced cooked turkey
- 1   cup heavy whipping cream
-     Minced fresh parsley

In a large saucepan, saute onion and mushrooms in butter until onion is tender. Add water, broth and rice mix with seasoning; bring to a boil. Reduce heat; simmer for 20-25 minutes or until rice is tender. Stir in turkey and cream and heat through. Sprinkle with parsley.
1 CUP: 364 cal., 21g fat (12g sat. fat), 100mg chol., 857mg sod., 25g carb. (3g sugars, 1g fiber), 19g pro.

READER REVIEW

"My family loved this, and we will be making it again in the future! It's perfect for using up all that leftover turkey from the holidays."
PUNKYSQUIRREL, TASTEOFHOME.COM

BACON-POTATO CORN CHOWDER

I was raised on a farm, and a warm soup with homey ingredients, like this one, was always a treat after a chilly day working outside. My hearty chowder nourishes the family.
—*Katie Lillo, Big Lake, MN*

- -

Takes: 30 min. • **Makes:** 6 servings

- ½ **lb. bacon strips, chopped**
- ¼ **cup chopped onion**
- 1½ **lbs. Yukon Gold potatoes (about 5 medium), peeled and cubed**
- 1 **can (14¾ oz.) cream-style corn**
- 1 **can (12 oz.) evaporated milk**
- ¼ **tsp. salt**
- ¼ **tsp. pepper**

1. In a large skillet, cook bacon over medium heat until crisp, stirring occasionally. Remove with a slotted spoon; drain on paper towels. Discard drippings, reserving 1½ tsp. in pan. Add onion to drippings; cook and stir over medium-high heat until tender.

2. Meanwhile, place cubed potatoes in a large saucepan; add water to cover. Bring to a boil over high heat. Reduce heat to medium; cook, uncovered, for 10-15 minutes or until tender. Drain, reserving 1 cup potato water.

3. Add corn, milk, salt, pepper and reserved potato water to saucepan; heat through. Stir in bacon and onion.

1 CUP: 271 cal., 11g fat (5g sat. fat), 30mg chol., 555mg sod., 34g carb. (9g sugars, 2g fiber), 10g pro.

SPICY BUFFALO CHICKEN WRAPS

This recipe has a real kick and is one of my husband's favorites. Ready in a flash, it's easily doubled and the closest thing to restaurant Buffalo wings I've ever tasted in a light version.
—*Jennifer Beck, Meridian, ID*

- -

Takes: 25 min. • **Makes:** 2 servings

- ½ **lb. boneless skinless chicken breast, cubed**
- ½ **tsp. canola oil**
- 2 **Tbsp. Louisiana-style hot sauce**
- 1 **cup shredded lettuce**
- 2 **flour tortillas (6 in.), warmed**
- 2 **tsp. reduced-fat ranch salad dressing**
- 2 **Tbsp. crumbled blue cheese**

1. In a large nonstick skillet, cook chicken in oil over medium heat for 6 minutes; drain. Stir in hot sauce. Bring to a boil. Reduce heat; simmer, uncovered, until sauce is thickened and chicken is no longer pink, 3-5 minutes.

2. Place lettuce on tortillas; drizzle with ranch dressing. Top with chicken mixture and blue cheese; roll up.

1 WRAP: 273 cal., 11g fat (3g sat. fat), 70mg chol., 453mg sod., 15g carb. (1g sugars, 1g fiber), 28g pro. **DIABETIC EXCHANGES:** 3 lean meat, 1½ fat, 1 starch.

QUICK CREAM OF MUSHROOM SOUP

My daughter-in-law, a gourmet cook, served this soup as the first course for a holiday dinner. She received the recipe from her mom and graciously shared it with me. Now I'm happy to share it with my own friends and family.
—*Anne Kulick, Phillipsburg, NJ*

Takes: 30 min. • **Makes:** 6 servings

  2   **Tbsp. butter**
  ½   **lb. sliced fresh mushrooms**
  ¼   **cup chopped onion**
  6   **Tbsp. all-purpose flour**
  ½   **tsp. salt**
  ⅛   **tsp. pepper**
  2   **cans (14½ oz. each) chicken broth**
  1   **cup half-and-half cream**

1. In a large saucepan, heat the butter over medium-high heat; saute mushrooms and onion until tender.
2. Mix flour, salt, pepper and 1 can broth until smooth; stir into the mushroom mixture. Stir in remaining broth. Bring to a boil; cook and stir until thickened, about 2 minutes. Reduce heat; stir in cream. Simmer, uncovered, until flavors are blended, about 15 minutes, stirring occasionally.

1 CUP: 136 cal., 8g fat (5g sat. fat), 33mg chol., 842mg sod., 10g carb. (3g sugars, 1g fiber), 4g pro.

CHERRY CHICKEN CROISSANTS

I had a similar chicken salad at a restaurant and created my own version. It may seem like an odd combination, but the ingredients work well together. My children love it, and it only takes a few minutes to cut everything up—so easy!
—*Katrina Gladdish, Grawn, MI*

Takes: 10 min. • **Makes:** 6 servings

  2   **cups diced cooked chicken**
  3   **celery ribs, chopped**
  ½   **cup dried cherries**
  ½   **cup chopped walnuts**
  ½   **cup halved green grapes**
  8   **bacon strips, cooked and crumbled**
  ½   **cup mayonnaise**
  6   **croissants, split**

In a large bowl, combine first 7 ingredients. Serve on croissants.

1 SANDWICH: 616 cal., 39g fat (12g sat. fat), 92mg chol., 613mg sod., 41g carb. (18g sugars, 3g fiber), 24g pro.

OVEN-BAKED BURGERS

A crispy coating mix is the secret ingredient that dresses up these burgers that bake in the oven. I use a sweet and spicy steak sauce for the best flavor.
—*Mike Goldman, Arden Hills, MN*

Takes: 30 min. • **Makes:** 4 servings

  ¼   **cup steak sauce**
  2   **Tbsp. plus ⅓ cup seasoned coating mix, divided**
  1   **lb. ground beef**
  4   **hamburger buns, split**
  4   **lettuce leaves**

1. In a bowl, combine the steak sauce and 2 Tbsp. coating mix. Crumble beef over mixture and mix well. Shape into four 3½-in. patties. Dip both sides of patties in remaining coating. Place on an ungreased baking sheet.
2. Bake at 350° until a thermometer reads 160°, about 20 minutes, turning once. Serve on buns with lettuce.

1 SERVING: 403 cal., 17g fat (6g sat. fat), 70mg chol., 889mg sod., 35g carb. (6g sugars, 1g fiber), 26g pro.

BLACK BEAN-PUMPKIN SOUP

Packed with protein from beans and vitamins from pumpkin, this soup is the definition of healthy. The dollop of light sour cream adds a satisfying touch that feels indulgent.
—Jennifer Fisher, Austin, TX

Prep: 30 min. • **Cook:** 30 min
Makes: 8 servings (2 qt.)

- 2 cans (15 oz. each) black beans, rinsed and drained
- 1 can (14½ oz.) diced tomatoes, drained
- 2 medium onions, finely chopped
- 1 tsp. olive oil
- 3 garlic cloves, minced
- 1 tsp. ground cumin
- 3 cups vegetable broth
- 1 can (15 oz.) pumpkin
- 2 Tbsp. cider vinegar
- ½ tsp. pepper
- 2 Tbsp. bourbon, optional
- ½ cup reduced-fat sour cream
- ½ cup thinly sliced green onions
- ½ cup roasted salted pumpkin seeds

1. Place black beans and tomatoes in a food processor; cover and process until blended. Set aside.
2. In a Dutch oven, saute onions in oil until tender. Add garlic and cumin; saute 1 minute longer. Stir in vegetable broth, pumpkin, vinegar, pepper and bean mixture. Bring to a boil. Reduce heat; cover and simmer for 20 minutes.
3. Stir in bourbon if desired. Garnish each serving with sour cream, green onions and pumpkin seeds.
1 CUP: 238 cal., 8g fat (2g sat. fat), 5mg chol., 716mg sod., 30g carb. (9g sugars, 9g fiber), 13g pro. **DIABETIC EXCHANGES:** 1½ starch, 1½ fat, 1 lean meat, 1 vegetable.

READER REVIEW
"Just made this soup. Definitely one of my favorites! I used fresh roasted pumpkin and blended it together with the black beans and tomatoes."
MARIAGILLZ8R, TASTEOFHOME.COM

MIGHTY HERO SANDWICH

My friend Valerie once served us this sky-high multilayered hero sandwich, also known as a Dagwood. It's easy, colorful and the marinated veggies give it all kinds of oomph.
—Kelley Boyce, Tulsa, OK

Takes: 30 min. • **Makes:** 8 servings

- ¼ cup balsamic vinegar
- 1 Tbsp. minced fresh parsley
- 1 Tbsp. olive oil
- 2 garlic cloves, minced
- ¼ tsp. dried oregano
- ¼ tsp. pepper
- 1 large tomato, halved and sliced
- 1 cup sliced fresh mushrooms
- 2 thin slices red onion, separated into rings
- 1 round loaf (1 lb.) sourdough bread
- 1 small zucchini, shredded
- ½ lb. sliced deli turkey
- 6 slices part-skim mozzarella cheese

1. In a large bowl, whisk the first 6 ingredients until blended. Add the tomato, mushrooms and onion; toss gently to coat. Let stand for 15 minutes.
2. Meanwhile, cut loaf horizontally in half. Hollow out both parts, leaving a ½-in.-thick shell (save removed bread for another use).
3. Drain marinated vegetables, reserving marinade. Brush marinade over inside of bread halves. Top bottom half with zucchini. Layer with half the marinated vegetables, ¼ pound turkey and 3 slices cheese; repeat layers. Replace top of loaf. Cut into wedges.
1 PIECE: 233 cal., 7g fat (3g sat. fat), 24mg chol., 636mg sod., 26g carb. (6g sugars, 1g fiber), 16g pro. **DIABETIC EXCHANGES:** 2 starch, 2 lean meat, ½ fat.

JENNIFER FISHER
Austin, TX

BEEFY MUSHROOM SOUP

This is a tasty way to use leftover roast or steak and get a delicious supper on the table in about a half-hour. The warm, rich taste of this mushroom soup is sure to please.
—*Ginger Ellsworth, Caldwell, ID*

Takes: 30 min. • **Makes:** 3 cups

- 1 medium onion, chopped
- ½ cup sliced fresh mushrooms
- 2 Tbsp. butter
- 2 Tbsp. all-purpose flour
- 2 cups reduced-sodium beef broth
- ⅔ cup cubed cooked roast beef
- ½ tsp. garlic powder
- ¼ tsp. paprika
- ¼ tsp. pepper
- ⅛ tsp. salt
  Dash hot pepper sauce
  Shredded part-skim mozzarella cheese, optional

1. In a large saucepan, saute onion and mushrooms in butter until onion is tender; remove with a slotted spoon and set aside. In a small bowl, whisk flour and broth until smooth; gradually add to the pan. Bring to a boil; cook and stir until thickened, 1-2 minutes.
2. Add the roast beef, garlic powder, paprika, pepper, salt, pepper sauce and onion mixture; cook and stir until heated through. Garnish with cheese if desired.
1 CUP: 180 cal., 9g fat (5g sat. fat), 52mg chol., 470mg sod., 9g carb. (3g sugars, 1g fiber), 14g pro. **DIABETIC EXCHANGES:** 2 lean meat, 2 fat, 1 vegetable.

CHAMPION ROAST BEEF SANDWICHES

When I have time, I prepare a roast with this much-requested recipe in mind. But when I need a quick meal in a hurry, I use deli roast beef with equally delectable results.
—*Ann Eastman, Santa Monica, CA*

Takes: 15 min. • **Makes:** 4 servings

- ½ cup sour cream
- 1 Tbsp. onion soup mix
- 1 Tbsp. prepared horseradish, drained
- ⅛ tsp. pepper
- 8 slices rye or pumpernickel bread
- ½ lb. sliced roast beef
  Lettuce leaves

In a small bowl, combine first 4 ingredients. Spread 1 Tbsp. on each slice of bread. Top 4 slices of bread with roast beef and lettuce; cover with remaining bread.
1 SANDWICH: 318 cal., 11g fat (6g sat. fat), 60mg chol., 1401mg sod., 34g carb. (4g sugars, 4g fiber), 18g pro.

CHEESE CHICKEN SOUP

What's better than veggies and cheese? This comforting soup comes together in a jiffy with the use of everyday convenience items. Yum!
—*LaVonne Lundgren, Sioux City, IA*

Takes: 30 min. • **Makes:** 8 servings

- 4 cups cubed cooked chicken breast
- 3½ cups water
- 2 cans (10¾ oz. each) condensed cream of chicken soup, undiluted
- 1 pkg. (16 oz.) frozen mixed vegetables, thawed
- 1 can (14½ oz.) diced potatoes, drained
- 1 pkg. (16 oz.) Velveeta, cubed

In a Dutch oven, combine first 5 ingredients. Bring to a boil. Reduce heat; cover and simmer until vegetables are tender, 8-10 minutes. Stir in Velveeta just until melted (do not boil).
1⅓ CUPS: 429 cal., 22g fat (11g sat. fat), 116mg chol., 1464mg sod., 23g carb. (6g sugars, 4g fiber), 33g pro.

ASIAN LONG NOODLE SOUP

This flavorful soup is perfect when you want something warm and filling in a flash. If you can't find lo mein noodles, angel hair pasta is a good substitute.
—*Carol Emerson, Aransas Pass, TX*

Takes: 30 min. • **Makes:** 6 servings (2 qt.)

- 6   oz. uncooked Asian lo mein noodles
- 1   pork tenderloin (¾ lb.), cut into thin strips
- 2   Tbsp. soy sauce, divided
- ⅛   tsp. pepper
- 2   Tbsp. canola oil, divided
- 1½ tsp. minced fresh gingerroot
- 1   garlic clove, minced
- 1   carton (32 oz.) chicken broth
- 1   celery rib, thinly sliced
- 1   cup fresh snow peas, halved diagonally
- 1   cup coleslaw mix
- 2   green onions, sliced diagonally
      Fresh cilantro leaves, optional

1. Cook noodles according to package directions. Drain and rinse with cold water; drain well.

2. Meanwhile, toss pork with 1 Tbsp. soy sauce and pepper. In a 6-qt. stockpot, heat 1 Tbsp. oil over medium-high heat; saute the pork until lightly browned, 2-3 minutes. Remove from pot.

3. In same pot, heat the remaining oil over medium-high heat; saute ginger and garlic until fragrant, 20-30 seconds. Stir in broth and remaining soy sauce; bring to a boil. Add celery and snow peas; return to a boil. Simmer; uncovered, until crisp-tender, 2-3 minutes. Stir in pork and coleslaw mix; cook just until cabbage begins to wilt. Add noodles; remove from heat. Top with green onions and, if desired, cilantro.

1⅓ CUPS: 227 cal., 7g fat (1g sat. fat), 35mg chol., 1078mg sod., 23g carb. (2g sugars, 1g fiber), 16g pro.

CHICKEN CAESAR WRAPS

This classic cold sandwich with tender chicken, Parmesan cheese and Caesar croutons uses just the right amount of dressing. It's a quick and tasty lunch or dinner.
—*Nancy Pratt, Longview, TX*

Takes: 15 min. • **Makes:** 6 servings

- ¾   cup reduced-fat creamy Caesar salad dressing
- ¼   cup grated Parmesan cheese
- ½   tsp. garlic powder
- ¼   tsp. pepper
- 3   cups cubed cooked chicken breast
- 2   cups torn romaine
- ¾   cup Caesar salad croutons, coarsely chopped
- 6   whole wheat tortillas (8 in.), room temperature

In a large bowl, combine the salad dressing, cheese, garlic powder and pepper. Add the chicken, romaine and croutons. Spoon ⅔ cup chicken mixture down the center of each tortilla; roll up.

1 WRAP: 337 cal., 12g fat (2g sat. fat), 57mg chol., 730mg sod., 29g carb. (2g sugars, 4g fiber), 27g pro. **DIABETIC EXCHANGES:** 3 lean meat, 2½ starch, ½ fat.

CHICKEN PARMESAN BURGERS

A restaurant-quality burger that's topped with marinara and loaded with cheese—what's not to love? Fresh basil adds even more flavor if you're feeling adventurous.
—*Brooke Petras, Alpine, CA*

- -

Takes: 30 min. • **Makes:** 4 servings

3	Tbsp. olive oil, divided
1	small onion, finely chopped
2	garlic cloves, minced
¾	cup marinara sauce, divided
½	cup finely chopped or shredded part-skim mozzarella cheese
½	cup dry bread crumbs
1	tsp. Italian seasoning
1	tsp. dried oregano
½	tsp. salt
½	tsp. pepper
1	lb. ground chicken
4	slices part-skim mozzarella cheese
4	hamburger buns, split and toasted
¼	cup shredded Parmesan cheese Fresh basil leaves, optional

1. In a large skillet, heat 1 Tbsp. olive oil over medium-high heat. Add onion; cook and stir until tender, about 3 minutes. Add minced garlic; cook 1 minute longer. Remove from heat; cool slightly.

2. In a large bowl, combine ¼ cup marinara sauce, chopped mozzarella cheese, bread crumbs, seasonings and onion mixture. Add chicken; mix lightly but thoroughly. With wet hands, shape into four ½-in.-thick patties.

3. In the same skillet, heat remaining 2 Tbsp. oil over medium heat. Cook burgers until a thermometer reads 165°, 4-5 minutes on each side. Top with sliced mozzarella cheese; cook, covered, until cheese is melted, 1-2 minutes.

4. Serve in buns; top with remaining ½ cup marinara sauce, Parmesan cheese and, if desired, basil leaves.

1 BURGER: 603 cal., 33g fat (10g sat. fat), 108mg chol., 1275mg sod., 41g carb. (8g sugars, 3g fiber), 38g pro.

BROCCOLI CHEDDAR SOUP

This classic doesn't need to be made in big batches to be good. Here's proof that a small yield portion serves up the same big flavor.
—*Cheryl McRae, West Valley, UT*

- -

Takes: 20 min. • **Makes:** 2 servings

- ¼ cup chopped onion
- ¼ cup butter, cubed
- ¼ cup all-purpose flour
- ¼ tsp. salt
- ¼ tsp. pepper
- 1½ cups 2% milk
- ¾ cup chicken broth
- 1 cup cooked chopped fresh or frozen broccoli
- ½ cup shredded cheddar cheese

1. In a small saucepan, saute onion in butter until tender. Stir in the flour, salt and pepper until blended; gradually add milk and broth. Bring to a boil; cook and stir until thickened, about 2 minutes.

2. Add broccoli. Cook and stir until heated through. Remove from the heat; stir in cheese until melted.

1 CUP: 494 cal., 37g fat (24g sat. fat), 116mg chol., 1145mg sod., 26g carb. (11g sugars, 2g fiber), 16g pro.

SLOPPY JOES SANDWICHES

You'll love this quick, easy and economical dish. Brown sugar adds a touch of sweetness, both for traditional sandwiches on buns or as a down-home topping for rice, biscuits or baked potatoes.
—*Laurie Hauser, Rochester, NY*

- -

Takes: 30 min. • **Makes:** 4 servings

- 1 lb. ground beef
- 1 cup ketchup
- ¼ cup water
- 2 Tbsp. brown sugar
- 2 tsp. Worcestershire sauce
- 2 tsp. prepared mustard
- ½ tsp. garlic powder
- ½ tsp. onion powder
- ½ tsp. salt
- 4 hamburger buns, split

In a large skillet, cook beef over medium heat until no longer pink; drain. Stir in the ketchup, water, brown sugar, Worcestershire sauce, mustard, garlic powder, onion powder and salt. Bring to a boil. Reduce heat; cover and simmer for 15-20 minutes. Serve on buns.

1 SANDWICH: 439 cal., 16g fat (6g sat. fat), 75mg chol., 1360mg sod., 46g carb. (17g sugars, 2g fiber), 27g pro.

BBQ BACON PULLED CHICKEN SANDWICHES

This simple recipe tastes amazing. We prefer putting mayo on the bun and adding cheddar or Muenster cheese, lettuce, tomato and onion. Several of us put ranch dressing on our sandwiches, too.
—*Jennifer Darling, Ventura, CA*

Prep: 20 min. • **Cook:** 3 hours
Makes: 12 servings

1   bottle (18 oz.) barbecue sauce
½   cup amber beer or root beer
¼   cup cider vinegar
2   green onions, chopped
2   Tbsp. dried minced onion
2   Tbsp. Dijon mustard
2   Tbsp. Worcestershire sauce
4   garlic cloves, minced
1   Tbsp. dried parsley flakes
2   lbs. boneless skinless chicken breasts
12   hamburger buns, split and toasted
24   cooked bacon strips
12   lettuce leaves

1. In a large bowl, combine first 9 ingredients. Place chicken in a greased 4- or 5-qt. slow cooker; pour sauce over top. Cook, covered, on low until tender, 3-4 hours.
2. Remove chicken; shred with 2 forks. Return chicken to slow cooker; heat through. Serve on buns with bacon and lettuce.
1 SANDWICH: 401 cal., 12g fat (4g sat. fat), 65mg chol., 1175mg sod., 43g carb. (19g sugars, 2g fiber), 28g pro.

FIREHOUSE CHILI

As one of the cooks at the firehouse, I used to prepare meals for 10 men. This chili was among their favorites.
—*Richard Clements, San Dimas, CA*

Prep: 20 min. • **Cook:** 1½ hours
Makes: 16 servings (4 qt.)

2   Tbsp. canola oil
4   lbs. lean ground beef (90% lean)
2   medium onions, chopped
1   medium green pepper, chopped
4   cans (16 oz. each) kidney beans, rinsed and drained
3   cans (28 oz. each) stewed tomatoes, cut up
1   can (14½ oz.) beef broth
3   Tbsp. chili powder
2   Tbsp. ground coriander
2   Tbsp. ground cumin
4   garlic cloves, minced
1   tsp. dried oregano

In a Dutch oven, heat canola oil over medium heat. Brown beef in batches, crumbling meat, until no longer pink; drain and set aside. Add onions and green pepper; cook until tender. Return meat to Dutch oven. Stir in remaining ingredients. Bring to a boil. Reduce heat; simmer, covered, until flavors are blended, about 1½ hours.
1 CUP: 354 cal., 12g fat (4g sat. fat), 71mg chol., 657mg sod., 32g carb. (10g sugars, 8g fiber), 31g pro. **DIABETIC EXCHANGES:** 3 lean meat, 2 starch.

FAVORITE ITALIAN BEEF SANDWICHES

I'm a paramedic and firefighter, and easy slow-cooked recipes like this one suit my unpredictable schedule. My husband, children and the hungry bunch at the firehouse love these robust sandwiches that have a little zip.
—*Kris Swihart, Perrysburg, OH*

Prep: 20 min. • **Cook:** 8 hours
Makes: 12 servings

- 1 jar (11½ oz.) pepperoncini
- 1 boneless beef chuck roast (3½ to 4 lbs.)
- ¼ cup water
- 1¾ tsp. dried basil
- 1½ tsp. garlic powder
- 1½ tsp. dried oregano
- 1¼ tsp. salt
- ¼ tsp. pepper
- 1 large onion, sliced and quartered
- 12 hard rolls, split

1. Drain the pepperoncini, reserving liquid. Remove and discard stems of peppers; set peppers aside. Cut chuck roast into large chunks; place a third of the meat in a 5-qt. slow cooker. Add water.
2. In a small bowl, combine the seasonings; sprinkle half over beef. Layer with half the remaining meat, then the onion and pepperoncini. Pour pepperoncini liquid over the top. Add remaining meat to slow cooker; sprinkle with remaining seasonings.
3. Cover and cook on low until the meat is tender, 8-9 hours. Shred beef with 2 forks. Using a slotted spoon, serve the beef and peppers on hard rolls.
NOTE: Look for pepperoncini (pickled peppers) in the pickle and olive section of your grocery store.
1 SANDWICH: 376 cal., 15g fat (5g sat. fat), 86mg chol., 1132mg sod., 27g carb. (3g sugars, 2g fiber), 31g pro.

GUMBO IN A JIFFY

Here's yummy in a bowl. My husband loves the kick that Italian sausage gives this quick gumbo, and it's a cinch to assemble.
—*Amy Flack, Homer City, PA*

Takes: 20 min. • **Makes:** 6 servings (1½ qt.)

- 1 pkg. (12 oz.) smoked sausage
- 1 can (14½ oz.) diced tomatoes with green peppers and onions, undrained
- 1 can (14½ oz.) chicken broth
- ½ cup water
- 1 cup uncooked instant rice
- 1 can (7 oz.) whole kernel corn, drained
  Sliced green onions, optional

In a large saucepan, cook sliced sausage until browned on both sides. Stir in the tomatoes, broth and water; bring to a boil. Stir in rice and corn; cover and remove from the heat. Let stand for 5 minutes. If desired, top with sliced green onions.
1 CUP: 204 cal., 6g fat (2g sat. fat), 30mg chol., 884mg sod., 23g carb. (6g sugars, 2g fiber), 13g pro. **DIABETIC EXCHANGES:** 1½ lean meat, 1½ vegetable, 1 starch.

BETTER THAN EGG SALAD

Tofu takes on the taste and texture of classic egg salad in this quick-to-fix sandwich.
—*Lisa Renshaw, Kansas City, MO*

Takes: 20 min. • **Makes:** 4 servings

- ¼ cup reduced-fat mayonnaise
- ¼ cup chopped celery
- 2 green onions, chopped
- 2 Tbsp. sweet pickle relish
- 1 Tbsp. Dijon mustard
- ¼ tsp. ground turmeric
- ¼ tsp. salt
- ⅛ tsp. cayenne pepper
- 1 pkg. (12.3 oz.) silken firm tofu, cubed
- 8 slices whole wheat bread
- 4 lettuce leaves
  Coarsely ground pepper, optional

Mix first the 8 ingredients; stir in tofu. Line 4 slices of bread with lettuce. Top with tofu mixture. If desired, sprinkle with pepper; close sandwiches.
1 SANDWICH: 266 cal., 9g fat (2g sat. fat), 5mg chol., 692mg sod., 31g carb. (7g sugars, 4g fiber), 14g pro. **DIABETIC EXCHANGES:** 2 starch, 1 lean meat, 1 fat.

THE BEST EVER GRILLED CHEESE SANDWICH

Spreading a mixture of mayo and butter on the bread creates a delightfully crispy crust with the well-loved, wonderful flavor of butter one expects on a grilled cheese sandwich.
—*Josh Rink, Milwaukee, WI*

Takes: 25 min. • **Makes:** 4 servings

- 6 Tbsp. butter, softened, divided
- 8 slices sourdough bread
- 3 Tbsp. mayonnaise
- 3 Tbsp. finely shredded Manchego or Parmesan cheese
- ⅛ tsp. onion powder
- ½ cup shredded sharp white cheddar cheese
- ½ cup shredded Monterey Jack cheese
- ½ cup shredded Gruyere cheese
- 4 oz. Brie cheese, rind removed and sliced

1. Spread 3 Tbsp. butter on 1 side of bread slices. Toast bread, butter side down, in a large skillet or electric griddle over medium-low heat until golden brown, 2-3 minutes; remove. In a small bowl, mix mayonnaise, Manchego cheese, onion powder and remaining 3 Tbsp. butter. In another bowl, combine cheddar, Monterey Jack and Gruyere.
2. To assemble sandwiches, top toasted side of 4 bread slices with the sliced Brie. Sprinkle cheddar cheese mixture evenly over Brie. Top with the remaining bread slices, toasted side facing inward. Spread mayonnaise mixture on the outsides of each sandwich. Place in same skillet and cook until golden brown and cheese is melted, 5-6 minutes on each side. Serve
1 SANDWICH: 659 cal., 49g fat (27g sat. fat), 122mg chol., 1017mg sod., 30g carb. (3g sugars, 1g fiber), 24g pro.

1 FAVORITE 5 WAYS
Grilled Cheese

GRILLED CHEESE & PEPPERONI SANDWICH

Pizza lovers, rejoice! This super decadent sandwich comes fully loaded with pepperoni and five types of cheese!
—*Josh Rink, Milwaukee, WI*

Takes: 25 min. • **Makes:** 4 servings

- 6 Tbsp. butter, softened, divided
- 3 Tbsp. mayonnaise
- 3 Tbsp. finely shredded Manchego or Parmesan cheese
- ⅛ tsp. onion powder
- 8 slices sourdough bread
- 4 oz. Brie cheese, rind removed and sliced
- ½ cup shredded sharp white cheddar cheese
- ½ cup shredded Monterey Jack cheese
- ½ cup shredded Gruyere cheese
- 24 slices slices pepperoni

1. Spread 3 Tbsp. butter on 1 side of each slice of bread. Place bread, butter side down, in a large cast-iron skillet or electric griddle over medium-low heat until golden brown, 2-3 minutes; remove. In a small bowl, combine the cheddar, Monterey Jack and Gruyere. In another bowl, mix together remaining 3 Tbsp. butter, mayonnaise, Manchego cheese and onion powder.

2. To assemble sandwiches, top toasted side of 4 bread slices with pepperoni; add sliced Brie. Sprinkle cheddar cheese mixture evenly over Brie. Top with remaining bread slices, toasted side facing inwards. Spread the butter-mayonnaise mixture on the outsides of each sandwich. Place in same skillet and cook until golden brown and cheese is melted, 5-6 minutes on each side. Serve immediately.

1 SANDWICH: 719 cal., 55g fat (29g sat. fat), 134mg chol., 1207mg sod., 30g carb. (3g sugars, 1g fiber), 27g pro.

SUN-DRIED TOMATO GRILLED CHEESE SANDWICH

Grilled cheese is a quick and easy meal. I love experimenting with different combinations of ingredients to take it up a notch.
—*Jess Apfe, Berkeley, CA*

Takes: 30 min. • **Makes:** 4 servings

- ½ cup oil-packed sun-dried tomatoes
- ¼ cup grated Parmesan cheese
- ¼ cup chopped fresh basil
- 2 Tbsp. olive oil
- 1 tsp. balsamic vinegar
- 1 garlic clove, crushed
- ⅛ tsp. salt
- ⅛ tsp. pepper
- 8 slices sourdough bread
- 1¼ cups shredded part-skim mozzarella cheese
- ½ cup crumbled goat cheese
- ¼ cup fresh arugula
- 2 Tbsp. chopped roasted sweet red pepper
- 3 Tbsp. butter, melted

1. Place the first 8 ingredients in a food processor; process until blended.

2. Spread over each of 4 bread slices; top with cheeses, arugula, roasted red pepper and remaining bread. Brush outsides of sandwiches with butter.

3. On a griddle, toast sandwiches over medium heat until golden brown and cheese is melted, 3-4 minutes per side.

1 SANDWICH: 491 cal., 31g fat (14g sat. fat), 67mg chol., 942mg sod., 37g carb. (4g sugars, 3g fiber), 19g pro.

GRILLED CHEESE & PEPPER SANDWICHES

Here's a tasty veggie-filled sandwich that's perfect for one or two. It's a colorful, healthy twist on traditional grilled cheese...and especially good on rye bread.
—*Arline Hofland, Deer Lodge, MT*

Takes: 20 min. • **Makes:** 2 servings

1	Tbsp. olive oil
½	cup chopped onion
½	cup chopped green pepper
½	cup chopped sweet red pepper
2	tsp. chopped seeded jalapeno pepper
4	slices rye bread with caraway seeds
¾	cup shredded Monterey Jack cheese
1	Tbsp. butter, softened

1. In a skillet, heat oil over medium-high heat; saute onion and peppers until tender. Divide between 2 bread slices. Top with cheese and remaining bread. Spread the outsides of sandwiches with butter.
2. In a large skillet, toast sandwiches over medium heat until golden brown and cheese is melted, 2-3 minutes per side.
NOTE: Wear disposable gloves when cutting hot peppers; the oils can burn skin. Avoid touching your face.
1 SANDWICH: 470 cal., 28g fat (13g sat. fat), 53mg chol., 690mg sod., 39g carb. (7g sugars, 6g fiber), 17g pro.

GRILLED CHEESE, HAM & APPLE SANDWICH

Try my stepped-up version of a classic ham and cheese. Melty cheeses, crisp apples and smoky ham make for the ultimate combination.
—*Josh Rink, Milwaukee, WI*

Takes: 25 min. • **Makes:** 4 servings

6	Tbsp. butter, softened, divided
8	slices sourdough bread
3	Tbsp. mayonnaise
3	Tbsp. finely shredded Manchego or Parmesan cheese
⅛	tsp. onion powder
½	cup shredded sharp white cheddar cheese
½	cup shredded Monterey Jack cheese
½	cup shredded Gruyere cheese
4	oz. Brie cheese, rind removed and sliced
12	slices deli ham
1	thinly sliced tart apple

1. Spread 3 Tbsp. butter on 1 side of bread slices. Toast bread, butter side down, in a large skillet or electric griddle over medium-low heat until golden brown, 2-3 minutes; remove. In a small bowl, mix together mayonnaise, Manchego cheese, onion powder and remaining 3 Tbsp. butter. In another bowl, combine the cheddar, Monterey Jack and Gruyere cheeses.
2. To assemble the sandwiches, top toasted side of 4 bread slices with sliced Brie. Sprinkle cheddar cheese mixture evenly over Brie. Layer ham and apple slices over Brie; top with remaining bread slices, toasted side facing inward. Spread mayonnaise mixture on the outsides of each sandwich. Place in same skillet and cook until golden brown and cheese is melted, 5-6 minutes on each side. Serve immediately.
1 SANDWICH: 725 cal., 50g fat (27g sat. fat), 141mg chol., 1415mg sod., 37g carb. (9g sugars, 2g fiber), 32g pro.

GOURMET GRILLED CHEESE WITH DATE-BACON JAM

This sandwich doubles up on melty cheese, but the star of the show is the sweet and salty date-bacon jam. It makes for a truly grown-up version of the childhood classic. Try it on rustic country bread to make it even heartier.
—*Kathy Cooper, Tucson, AZ*

- -

Prep: 1 hour + cooling • **Cook:** 5 min.
Makes: 4 servings

½ lb. bacon strips, diced
1 cup finely chopped sweet onion
1 garlic clove, minced
6 oz. pitted dates, chopped
¾ cup water
¼ cup cider vinegar
⅛ tsp. salt
⅛ tsp. pepper

SANDWICHES
½ **cup shredded cheddar cheese**
1 **round (8 oz.) Brie cheese, rind removed and softened**
8 **slices sourdough bread**
2 **Tbsp. butter, softened**

1. In a large skillet, cook bacon over medium heat until crisp, stirring occasionally. Remove with a slotted spoon; drain on paper towels. Discard all but 2 Tbsp. drippings.
2. Add onion to drippings; cook and stir over medium heat until softened. Reduce heat to medium-low; cook, stirring occasionally, until onion is deep golden brown and caramelized, 35-40 minutes, adding garlic during the last 5 minutes of cooking.
3. Return cooked bacon to skillet and add the next 5 ingredients. Stir well. Reduce heat; simmer, covered, 30 minutes, stirring occasionally. Cool.

4. For sandwiches, combine cheeses, mixing well. Layer 4 slices of bread with the cheese mixture and 2 Tbsp. date-bacon jam; top with remaining bread. Spread outsides of sandwiches with butter. In a nonstick skillet, toast sandwiches over medium-low heat until golden brown and cheese is melted, 2-3 minutes per side. Cover and refrigerate remaining jam; save for another use.
1 SANDWICH: 572 cal., 33g fat (19g sat. fat), 97mg chol., 1015mg sod., 45g carb. (14g sugars, 3g fiber), 25g pro.

TEST KITCHEN TIP
This date-bacon jam freezes well, so we recommend doubling the recipe. Freeze the leftovers and you'll be ready to make this grilled cheese whenever the mood strikes.

Side Dishes, Salads & More

Round out your dinner menu with some help from these tasty sides, salads and condiments. With so many options, you're guaranteed to find the perfect accompaniment for your meal.

HEIRLOOM TOMATO SALAD

Here's a simple yet elegant dish that always pleases my guests. Not only is it tasty, but it is healthy, too. Select a mix of different colored tomatoes for a pretty presentation.
—*Jessie Apfel, Berkeley, CA*

- -

Prep: 20 min. + chilling • **Makes:** 6 servings

- 2 cups cut-up heirloom tomatoes
- 1 cup multicolored cherry tomatoes, halved
- 2 cups fresh baby spinach
- ½ cup sliced red onion

DRESSING

- 3 Tbsp. olive oil
- 2 Tbsp. white balsamic vinegar
- 1 garlic clove, minced
- ½ tsp. salt
- ¼ tsp. dried basil
- ¼ tsp. dried oregano
- ¼ tsp. dried rosemary, crushed
- ¼ tsp. dried thyme
- ¼ tsp. pepper
- ⅛ tsp. rubbed sage

Place tomatoes, spinach and onion in a large bowl. Whisk together dressing ingredients; toss with salad. Refrigerate, covered, 2 hours. Serve with a slotted spoon.

⅔ CUP: 75 cal., 5g fat (1g sat. fat), 0 chol., 161mg sod., 7g carb. (4g sugars, 2g fiber), 1g pro. **DIABETIC EXCHANGES:** 1 vegetable, 1 fat.

READER REVIEW

"I made this for a family reunion and got rave reviews. I barely got a bite of it to taste. I kept to the exact recipe except I did add in a handful of those tiny baby fresh mozzarella balls (bought at my local Italian market). Was a very good spring/summer salad and I plan on making it again soon (and will be sure to get my share)."

CEEGE, TASTEOFHOME.COM

COWBOY CALICO BEANS

These beans are a tradition when my girlfriends and I go up to northern Wisconsin for a girls' weekend. The husbands and kids are left at home, but the slow cooker comes with us!
—*Julie Butsch, Hartland, WI*

Prep: 30 min. • **Cook:** 4 hours
Makes: 8 servings

- 1 lb. lean ground beef (90% lean)
- 1 large sweet onion, chopped
- ½ cup packed brown sugar
- ¼ cup ketchup
- 3 Tbsp. cider vinegar
- 2 Tbsp. yellow mustard
- 1 can (16 oz.) butter beans, drained
- 1 can (16 oz.) kidney beans, rinsed and drained
- 1 can (15 oz.) pork and beans
- 1 can (15¼ oz.) lima beans, rinsed and drained

1. In a large skillet, cook beef and onion over medium heat until meat is no longer pink; drain.

2. Transfer to a 3-qt. slow cooker. Combine the brown sugar, ketchup, vinegar and mustard; add to meat mixture. Stir in the beans. Cover and cook on low until heated through, 4-5 hours.

¾ CUP: 326 cal., 5g fat (2g sat. fat), 35mg chol., 808mg sod., 52g carb. (22g sugars, 10g fiber), 22g pro.

GLAZED SWEET POTATOES

The fresh sweet potatoes Mom grew in her garden disappeared fast when she served them in this dish that features a sweet glaze. She still makes sweet potatoes this way and they're now a hit with the grandkids, too.
—*Rosemary Pryor, Pasadena, MD*

Prep: 30 min. • **Bake:** 30 min.
Makes: 5 servings

- 2 lbs. sweet potatoes or 2 cans (15¾ oz. each) sweet potatoes, drained
- ¼ cup butter, cubed
- ¼ cup maple syrup
- ¼ cup packed brown sugar
- ¼ tsp. ground cinnamon

1. If using fresh sweet potatoes, place in a large saucepan or Dutch oven; cover with water. Bring to a boil. Reduce heat; cover and cook for 25-40 minutes or until tender. Drain; cool slightly and peel. Cut into chunks.

2. Preheat oven to 350°. Place the sweet potatoes in a 2-qt. baking dish. In a small saucepan, combine butter, syrup, brown sugar and cinnamon; bring to a boil, stirring constantly. Pour over potatoes.

3. Bake, uncovered, 30-40 minutes or until heated through.

1 CUP: 352 cal., 9g fat (6g sat. fat), 24mg chol., 96mg sod., 66g carb. (39g sugars, 6g fiber), 3g pro.

TEST KITCHEN TIP
The sweet glaze in this recipe is also delicious on roasted carrots and butternut squash. For the best flavor, use pure maple syrup. Typical pancake syrups sold at most stores contain ingredients like corn syrup and artificial maple extract.

DILLY ZUCCHINI CASSEROLE

Whenever I take this time-saving casserole to a potluck or gathering, I seldom bring any home. If I have fresh dill on hand, I'll substitute a couple tablespoons for the dill weed.
—*Esther Kilborn, Bridgton, ME*

Prep: 15 min. • **Bake:** 25 min.
Makes: 5 servings

- 1 cup biscuit/baking mix
- ½ cup grated Parmesan cheese
- 1 Tbsp. dill weed
- 1 tsp. salt
- ⅛ tsp. pepper
- 4 large eggs, lightly beaten
- ½ cup canola oil
- 3 cups chopped zucchini
- 1 large onion, chopped

1. In a large bowl, combine the biscuit mix, Parmesan cheese, dill, salt and pepper. Add eggs and oil. Stir in zucchini and onion until blended. Pour mixture into a greased 1½-qt. baking dish.
2. Bake, uncovered, at 375° for 25-30 minutes or until golden brown.
1 PIECE: 410 cal., 32g fat (7g sat. fat), 176mg chol., 978mg sod., 21g carb. (4g sugars, 2g fiber), 11g pro.

LAYERED SALAD FOR A CROWD

This salad is a favorite with my three sons. I took it to a luncheon honoring our school district's food service manager, and she asked for the recipe. I like to make the dressing the day before so the flavors blend together.
—*Linda Ashley, Leesburg, GA*

Takes: 20 min. • **Makes:** 20 servings

- 1 cup mayonnaise
- ¼ cup 2% milk
- 2 tsp. dill weed
- ½ tsp. seasoning blend
- 1 bunch romaine, torn
- 2 medium carrots, grated
- 1 cup chopped red onion
- 1 medium cucumber, sliced
- 1 pkg. (10 oz.) frozen peas, thawed
- 1½ cups shredded cheddar cheese
- 8 bacon strips, cooked and crumbled

1. For dressing, in a small bowl, whisk the mayonnaise, milk, dill and seasoning blend.
2. In a 4-qt. clear glass serving bowl, layer the romaine, carrots, onion and cucumber (do not toss). Pour dressing over the top; sprinkle with peas, cheese and bacon. Cover and refrigerate until serving.
NOTE: This recipe was tested with Nature's Seasons seasoning blend by Morton. Look for it in the spice aisle.
⅔ CUP: 151 cal., 13g fat (4g sat. fat), 16mg chol., 216mg sod., 5g carb. (2g sugars, 1g fiber), 4g pro.

LOADED RED POTATO CASSEROLE

The flavor of this potato casserole reminds me of the potato skins many restaurants offer as an appetizer.
—*Charlane Gathy, Lexington, KY*

- -

Prep: 25 min. • **Bake:** 20 min.
Makes: 8 servings

- 16   small red potatoes (about 1¾ lbs.)
- ½   cup 2% milk
- ¼   cup butter, cubed
- ½   tsp. pepper
- ⅛   tsp. salt
- 1½   cups shredded cheddar cheese, divided
- ½   cup crumbled cooked bacon
- 1   cup sour cream
- 2   Tbsp. minced fresh chives

1. Preheat oven to 350°. Place potatoes in a 6-qt. stockpot; add water to cover. Bring to a boil. Reduce heat; cook, uncovered, until tender, 15-20 minutes. Drain; return to pot.
2. Mash potatoes, gradually adding milk, butter, pepper and salt. Spread into a greased 3-qt. baking dish; sprinkle with 1 cup cheese and bacon. Dollop with sour cream; sprinkle with chives and remaining cheese.
3. Bake, uncovered, until heated through and cheese is melted, 20-25 minutes.
¾ CUP: 187 cal., 12g fat (7g sat. fat), 23mg chol., 245mg sod., 15g carb. (2g sugars, 1g fiber), 6g pro.

READER REVIEW

"My husband and guests loved this! I didn't change anything. Definitely a keeper and I highly recommend it."

DEMCCOY, TASTEOFHOME.COM

BLACK-EYED PEAS & HAM

Every New Year's Day we celebrate with these slow-cooked black-eyed peas, sure to bring good luck for the coming year.
—*Dawn Legler, Fort Morgan, CO*

Prep: 20 min. + soaking • **Cook:** 5 hours
Makes: 12 servings

- 1 pkg. (16 oz.) dried black-eyed peas, rinsed and sorted
- ½ lb. fully cooked boneless ham, finely chopped
- 1 medium onion, finely chopped
- 1 medium sweet red pepper, finely chopped
- 5 bacon strips, cooked and crumbled
- 1 large jalapeno pepper, seeded and finely chopped
- 2 garlic cloves, minced
- 1½ tsp. ground cumin
- 1 tsp. reduced-sodium chicken bouillon granules
- ½ tsp. salt
- ½ tsp. cayenne pepper
- ¼ tsp. pepper
- 6 cups water
  Minced fresh cilantro, optional
  Hot cooked rice

1. Soak peas according to package directions.
2. Transfer peas to a 6-qt. slow cooker; add the next 12 ingredients. Cover and cook on low until peas are tender, 5-7 hours. Sprinkle with cilantro if desired. Serve with rice.
NOTE: Wear disposable gloves when cutting hot peppers; the oils can burn skin. Avoid touching your face.
¾ CUP: 170 cal., 3g fat (1g sat. fat), 13mg chol., 386mg sod., 24g carb. (5g sugars, 7g fiber), 13g pro. **DIABETIC EXCHANGES:** 1½ starch, 1 lean meat.

CAULIFLOWER BROCCOLI SALAD

I have nine children, so I love finding recipes we all enjoy. This salad has been to as many family gatherings as I have. It holds well, and leftovers are still tasty a day later.
—*Linda Kangas, Outlook, SK*

Prep: 15 min. + chilling • **Makes:** 20 servings

- 1 medium head cauliflower, broken into florets (about 7½ cups)
- 1 medium bunch broccoli, cut into florets (about 4 cups)
- 2 cups seedless red grapes
- 6 green onions with tops, sliced
- 2 cups shredded part-skim mozzarella cheese
- 2 cups mayonnaise
- ¼ cup grated Parmesan cheese
- 2 Tbsp. sugar
- 2 Tbsp. white vinegar
- ½ to 1 lb. sliced bacon, cooked and crumbled
    Leaf lettuce, optional

1. In a large bowl, combine the cauliflower, broccoli, grapes, onions and mozzarella cheese. Combine mayonnaise, Parmesan cheese, sugar and vinegar; pour over vegetable mixture and toss to coat.

2. Cover and refrigerate at least 2 hours. Just before serving, stir in bacon. If desired, line serving bowl with lettuce leaves; transfer salad to serving bowl. If desired, garnish with additional grapes.

¾ CUP: 248 cal., 22g fat (4g sat. fat), 19mg chol., 269mg sod., 8g carb. (6g sugars, 2g fiber), 6g pro.

HOMEMADE LEMON CURD

Lemon curd is a scrumptious spread for scones, biscuits or other baked goods. You can find it in larger grocery stores alongside the jams and jellies or with baking supplies, but I like making it from scratch.
—*Mark Hagen, Milwaukee, WI*

Prep: 20 min. + chilling • **Makes:** 1⅔ cups

- 3 large eggs
- 1 cup sugar
- ½ cup lemon juice (about 2 lemons)
- ¼ cup butter, cubed
- 1 Tbsp. grated lemon zest

In a small heavy saucepan over medium heat, whisk the eggs, sugar and lemon juice until blended. Add butter and lemon zest; cook, whisking constantly, until mixture is thickened and coats the back of a metal spoon. Transfer to a small bowl; cool 10 minutes. Refrigerate, covered, until cold.

2 TBSP.: 110 cal., 5g fat (3g sat. fat), 52mg chol., 45mg sod., 16g carb. (16g sugars, 0 fiber), 2g pro.

ASIAGO MASHED CAULIFLOWER

Asiago cheese and fresh parsley help turn this healthier alternative to mashed potatoes into a flavorful side dish that won't leave you feeling weighed down.
—Colleen Delawder, Herndon, VA

- -

Takes: 30 min. • **Makes:** 4 servings

- 1 medium head cauliflower, cut into 1-in. pieces
- 1 tsp. sea salt, divided
- 4 oz. cream cheese, softened
- ½ cup shredded Asiago cheese
- 2 Tbsp. unsalted butter
- 2 Tbsp. coarsely chopped fresh parsley
- ¼ tsp. pepper

1. Place cauliflower and ½ tsp. sea salt in a large saucepan; add water to cover. Bring to a boil. Cook, covered, until very tender, 12-15 minutes. Drain; cool slightly.
2. Transfer to a food processor. Add cream cheese, Asiago cheese, butter, parsley, pepper and remaining sea salt. Process until blended.
½ CUP: 239 cal., 20g fat (12g sat. fat), 56mg chol., 530mg sod., 10g carb. (4g sugars, 3g fiber), 9g pro.

CORN STUFFING BALLS

My mom had many winning recipes, and this was one of our family's favorites. I can still picture these corn stuffing balls encircling the large meat platter piled high with one of her delicious entrees.
—Audrey Groe, Lake Mills, IA

- -

Prep: 20 min. • **Bake:** 30 min.
Makes: 12 servings

- 6 cups herb-seasoned stuffing croutons
- 1 cup chopped celery
- ½ cup chopped onion
- ¾ cup butter, divided
- 1 can (14¾ oz.) cream-style corn
- 1 cup water
- 1½ tsp. poultry seasoning
- ¾ tsp. salt
- ¼ tsp. pepper
- 3 large eggs yolks, beaten

Place croutons in a large bowl and set aside. In a skillet, saute celery and onion in ½ cup butter. Add corn, water, poultry seasoning, salt and pepper; bring to a boil. Remove from the heat; cool for 5 minutes. Pour over the croutons. Add egg yolks and mix gently. Shape ½ cupfuls into balls; flatten slightly. Place in a greased 15x10x1-in. baking pan. Melt remaining butter; drizzle over stuffing balls. Bake, uncovered, at 375° 30 minutes or until lightly browned.
1 SERVING: 365 cal., 16g fat (7g sat. fat), 84mg chol., 1233mg sod., 47g carb. (4g sugars, 3g fiber), 10g pro.

WILD RICE STUFFING

I haven't made any other kind of stuffing since trying this recipe from my sister. It's so moist and tasty. When a big bowlful starts circulating around the table, happy smiles get even bigger!
—*Connie Olson, Green River, WY*

- -

Prep: 2¼ hours • **Bake:** 25 min.
Makes: 8 servings

     Turkey giblets
4   cups water
1   pkg. (6 oz.) long grain
     and wild rice mix
1   celery rib, chopped
1   small onion, chopped
½   cup butter
2½ cups crushed seasoned stuffing
1½ cups chicken broth

1. Remove liver from giblets if desired. Place giblets and water in a saucepan. Cover and simmer for 2 hours or until tender.
2. Meanwhile, prepare rice according to the package directions. In a small skillet, saute chopped celery and onion in butter; add to rice. Drain and dice giblets. Stir stuffing, broth and giblets into rice.
3. Spoon into an ungreased 1½-qt. baking dish. Bake, uncovered, at 350° for 25-30 minutes or until heated through.
¾ CUP: 279 cal., 13g fat (8g sat. fat), 97mg chol., 806mg sod., 31g carb. (2g sugars, 2g fiber), 8g pro.

READER REVIEW

"Always get rave reviews with this side dish at our Thanksgiving table (made without the giblets). Even people who don't like stuffing go back for seconds with this recipe."
ARGYLLCA, TASTEOFHOME.COM

EASY GRILLED SQUASH

Here's my favorite way to prepare butternut squash. It's great alongside grilled steak or chicken. As a bonus, butternut squash is full of vitamin A.
—*Esther Horst, Monterey, TN*

- -

Takes: 20 min. • **Makes:** 4 servings

3   Tbsp. olive oil
2   garlic cloves, minced
¼   tsp. salt
¼   tsp. pepper
1   small butternut squash, peeled and
     cut lengthwise into ½-in. slices

1. In a small bowl, combine oil, garlic, salt and pepper. Brush over squash slices.
2. Grill squash, covered, over medium heat or broil 4 in. from the heat for 4-5 minutes on each side or until tender.
2 SLICES: 178 cal., 10g fat (1g sat. fat), 0 chol., 156mg sod., 23g carb. (5g sugars, 7g fiber), 2g pro. **DIABETIC EXCHANGES:** 1½ starch, 1½ fat.

CRISPY FRIED ONION RINGS

These crispy burger toppers add an extra element to already-fantastic burgers. They're also perfect for giving your salads a little crunch.
—*Taste of Home Test Kitchen*

- -

Takes: 25 min. • **Makes:** 12 servings

½   cup all-purpose flour
½   cup water
1   large egg, lightly beaten
1   tsp. seasoned salt
½   tsp. baking powder
1   large onion, very thinly sliced
     Oil for deep-fat frying

In a shallow bowl, whisk the first 5 ingredients. Separate onion slices into rings. Dip rings into batter. In a deep-fat fryer, heat 1 in. oil to 375°. Fry onion rings in batches for 1-1½ minutes on each side or until golden brown. Drain on paper towels. Serve immediately.
½ CUP: 71 cal., 5g fat (0 sat. fat), 18mg chol., 150mg sod., 5g carb. (1g sugars, 0 fiber), 1g pro.

CLASSIC COBB SALAD

Making this salad is a lot like planting a garden. I place each ingredient in nice, neat sections, just as I do with seedlings.
—Patricia Kile, Elizabethtown, PA

Takes: 20 min. • **Makes:** 4 servings

- 6 cups torn iceberg lettuce
- 2 medium tomatoes, chopped
- 1 medium ripe avocado, peeled and chopped
- ¾ cup diced fully cooked ham
- 2 hard-boiled large eggs, chopped
- ¾ cup diced cooked turkey
- 1¼ cups sliced fresh mushrooms
- ½ cup crumbled blue cheese
  Salad dressing of choice
  Optional: Sliced ripe olives and lemon wedges

Place lettuce on a platter or in a large serving bowl. Arrange remaining ingredients in rows or sections as desired. Serve with dressing of choice; if desired, serve with sliced ripe olives and lemon wedges.

1 SERVING: 260 cal., 15g fat (5g sat. fat), 148mg chol., 586mg sod., 10g carb. (5g sugars, 4g fiber), 23g pro. **DIABETIC EXCHANGES:** 3 lean meat, 2 vegetable, 2 fat.

ANGELA LIVELY
Conroe, TX

BACON PEA SALAD

My husband loves peas. My middle son isn't the biggest fan, but he loves bacon. So I decided to combine the two, and it was perfect! This salad is an awesome side dish, especially for picnics and barbecues.
—Angela Lively, Conroe, TX

Prep: 10 min. + chilling • **Makes:** 6 servings

- 4 cups frozen peas (about 16 oz.), thawed
- ½ cup shredded sharp cheddar cheese
- ½ cup ranch salad dressing
- ⅓ cup chopped red onion
- ¼ tsp. salt
- ¼ tsp. pepper
- 4 bacon strips, cooked and crumbled

Combine the first 6 ingredients; toss to coat. Refrigerate, covered, at least 30 minutes. Stir in bacon before serving.

¾ CUP: 218 cal., 14g fat (4g sat. fat), 17mg chol., 547mg sod., 14g carb. (6g sugars, 4g fiber), 9g pro.

CRANBERRY WALDORF SALAD

Cranberries grow in the coastal area about 50 miles from our home. As soon as they're available, I pull out the recipe for this salad.
—Faye Huff, Longview, WA

Prep: 40 min. + chilling • **Makes:** 12 servings

- 2 cups fresh or frozen cranberries, halved
- ¾ cup sugar
- 3 cups miniature marshmallows
- 2 cups chopped apples
- ½ cup chopped nuts
- ¾ cup pineapple tidbits, drained
- 1 cup halved green grapes
- 1 cup heavy whipping cream, whipped

Combine cranberries and sugar; let stand for 30 minutes. Add next 5 ingredients and mix well. Gently fold in whipped cream; chill.

¾ CUP: 226 cal., 11g fat (5g sat. fat), 27mg chol., 15mg sod., 34g carb. (28g sugars, 2g fiber), 2g pro.

GRANDMA'S COLLARD GREENS

My grandmother was famous for her collard greens. Eating them with a slice of buttermilk cornbread is pure bliss.
—*Sherri Williams, Crestview, FL*

- -

Prep: 30 min. • **Cook:** 2 hours
Makes: 6 servings

- 3 Tbsp. lard or shortening, divided
- 1 large onion, chopped
- 6 garlic cloves, minced
- 1½ lbs. smoked ham hocks
- 6 cups water
- 2 tsp. seasoned salt
- 1 to 3 tsp. crushed red pepper flakes
- 1 large bunch collard greens (about 2 lbs.), coarsely chopped
- 1½ cups white wine
- ¼ tsp. sugar

1. In a 6-qt. stockpot, heat 1 Tbsp. lard over medium heat. Add onion and garlic; cook and stir until tender. Add the ham hocks, water, seasoned salt and pepper flakes. Bring to a boil. Reduce heat; simmer, uncovered, until meat is tender, 55-60 minutes.
2. Add collard greens, wine, sugar and remaining lard. Return to a boil. Reduce heat; simmer, uncovered, 55-60 minutes or until greens are very tender. Remove meat from bones; finely chop and return to pan. Discard bones. Serve with a slotted spoon.

1 CUP: 204 cal., 9g fat (3g sat. fat), 19mg chol., 849mg sod., 13g carb. (3g sugars, 7g fiber), 10g pro.

CHEDDAR & CHIVE MASHED POTATOES

My husband swears my cheddar mashed potatoes are the world's best. I always keep some stocked in the freezer. Sometimes I dollop individual servings in muffin cups and freeze them that way for easy reheating later.
—*Cyndy Gerken, Naples, FL*

- -

Prep: 45 min. + chilling • **Bake:** 1 hour
Makes: 16 servings

- 5 lbs. Yukon Gold potatoes, peeled and cut into 1-in. pieces (about 10 cups)
- 1 cup butter, cubed
- 1 cup sour cream
- 2 tsp. salt
- ¾ tsp. pepper
- ½ cup heavy whipping cream
- 1½ cups shredded cheddar cheese
- 1½ cups shredded Monterey Jack cheese
- ¼ cup grated Parmesan cheese
- 2 Tbsp. minced fresh chives

TOPPINGS
- 1 cup shredded cheddar cheese
- 1 can (6 oz.) french-fried onions

1. Place potatoes in a 6-qt. stockpot; add water to cover. Bring to a boil. Reduce heat to medium; cook, uncovered, until tender, 10-15 minutes. Drain; transfer to a large bowl.
2. Add butter, sour cream, salt and pepper; beat until blended. Beat in whipping cream. Stir in cheeses and chives. Transfer potato mixture to a 13x9-in. baking dish. Refrigerate, covered, overnight.
3. To serve, preheat oven to 350°. Remove potatoes from refrigerator while oven heats.
4. Bake, covered, 45 minutes, stirring after 30 minutes. Sprinkle with toppings; bake, uncovered, until heated through, about 15 minutes.

¾ CUP: 474 cal., 32g fat (18g sat. fat), 70mg chol., 693mg sod., 37g carb. (3g sugars, 2g fiber), 11g pro.

TEST KITCHEN TIP
Remove the potatoes from the refrigerator while the oven preheats to take some of the chill off both the potatoes and the baking dish. If you put a cold dish directly into a hot oven, the heat can cause it to crack.

L ❄

SPINACH PESTO

Serve this vibrant pesto on pasta, pizza, veggies, sandwiches, scrambled eggs and other favorites. Omit the fresh oregano if you don't have any on hand.
—Susan Westerfield, Albuquerque, NM

- -

Takes: 15 min. • **Makes:** 2 cups

  2 **cups fresh baby spinach**
  2 **cups loosely packed basil leaves**
  1 **cup grated Romano cheese**
  2 **Tbsp. fresh oregano**
  2 **tsp. minced garlic**
  ½ **tsp. salt**
  ½ **cup chopped walnuts, toasted**
  1 **Tbsp. lemon juice**
  2 **tsp. grated lemon zest**
  1 **cup olive oil**
     Hot cooked pasta

1. Place the first 6 ingredients in a food processor; cover and pulse until chopped. Add the walnuts, lemon juice and zest; cover and process until blended. While processing, gradually add oil in a steady stream.

2. Serve desired amount of pesto with pasta. Transfer remaining pesto to ice cube trays. Cover and freeze up to 1 month.

TO USE FROZEN PESTO: Thaw in the refrigerator for 3 hours. Serve with pasta.

2 TBSP.: 177 cal., 18g fat (4g sat. fat), 8mg chol., 205mg sod., 1g carb. (0 sugars, 1g fiber), 4g pro.

POTLUCK ANTIPASTO PASTA SALAD

I love trying new recipes, and this one for pasta salad tops all other varieties I've tried. With beans, cheese, sausage and vegetables, it's a hearty complement to any meal.
—*Bernadette Nelson, Arcadia, CA*

- -

Takes: 30 min. • **Makes:** 18 servings

- 1   pkg. (16 oz.) penne pasta
- 1   can (15 oz.) garbanzo beans or chickpeas, rinsed and drained
- 1   medium sweet red or green pepper, julienned
- 2   plum tomatoes, halved lengthwise and sliced
- 1   bunch green onions, sliced
- 4   oz. Monterey Jack cheese, julienned
- 4   oz. part-skim mozzarella cheese, julienned
- 4   oz. brick or provolone cheese, julienned
- 4   oz. thinly sliced hard salami, julienned
- 3   oz. thinly sliced pepperoni
- 1   can (2¼ oz.) sliced ripe olives, drained
- 1   to 2 Tbsp. minced chives

BASIL VINAIGRETTE

- ⅔   cup canola oil
- ⅓   cup red wine vinegar
- 3   Tbsp. minced fresh basil or 1 Tbsp. dried basil
- 1   garlic clove, minced
- ¼   tsp. salt

1. Cook pasta according to the package directions; rinse with cold water and drain. In a large bowl, combine the pasta, beans, vegetables, cheeses, meats, olives and chives.
2. In a small bowl, whisk the vinaigrette ingredients. Pour over salad; toss to coat. Cover and refrigerate. Toss before serving.
1 CUP: 248 cal., 18g fat (5g sat. fat), 24mg chol., 431mg sod., 13g carb. (2g sugars, 2g fiber), 9g pro.

SWEET & SOUR SQUASH SALAD

This salad always goes over well with all ages, and it's a good way to get kids to eat squash.
—*Opal Shipman, Levelland, TX*

Prep: 20 min. + chilling • **Makes:** 6 servings

- ¾ cup sugar
- ½ cup cider vinegar
- ¼ cup olive oil
- 2 Tbsp. ranch salad dressing mix
- ¼ to ½ tsp. pepper
- ⅛ tsp. salt
- 2 medium zucchini, thinly sliced
- 2 medium yellow summer squash, thinly sliced
- 2 celery ribs, chopped
- 1 cup chopped red onion
- ½ cup chopped green pepper
- ½ cup chopped sweet red pepper

1. For dressing, whisk the first 6 ingredients until sugar is dissolved. Place vegetables in a large bowl; toss with dressing.

2. Refrigerate, covered, until cold. Serve with a slotted spoon.

¾ CUP: 241 cal., 10g fat (1g sat. fat), 0 chol., 703mg sod., 38g carb. (30g sugars, 2g fiber), 2g pro.

CRUMB-TOPPED MACARONI & CHEESE

Everyone loves this grown-up mac and cheese. It's also tasty with sharp cheddar and cream cheese instead of Gruyere and mascarpone. Throw in some crispy bacon for a twist.
—*Jennifer Standing, Taos, NM*

Prep: 30 min. • **Bake:** 15 min.
Makes: 8 servings

- 2 cups uncooked elbow macaroni
- ½ cup butter, divided
- ½ tsp. crushed red pepper flakes
- ¼ cup all-purpose flour
- 1½ cups whole milk
- 2 cups shredded Gruyere cheese or Swiss cheese
- 1 carton (8 oz.) mascarpone cheese
- 4½ tsp. Dijon mustard
- ¼ tsp. salt
- ⅛ tsp. pepper
- ¾ cup panko bread crumbs
- 1 Tbsp. Italian seasoning

1. Preheat oven to 425°. In a 6-qt. stockpot, cook macaroni according to the package directions for al dente; drain noodles and return to the stockpot.

2. Meanwhile, in a medium saucepan, heat ¼ cup butter and pepper flakes over medium heat until butter is melted. Stir in flour until smooth; gradually whisk in milk. Bring to a boil, stirring constantly; cook and stir until thickened, 1-2 minutes.

3. Stir in Gruyere, mascarpone, mustard, salt and pepper until blended. Add the sauce to macaroni, tossing to combine. Transfer to a greased 13x9-in. baking dish.

4. Melt remaining butter. Add panko and Italian seasoning; toss to coat. Sprinkle over macaroni. Bake, uncovered, until topping is golden brown, 10-15 minutes.

¾ CUP: 473 cal., 36g fat (21g sat. fat), 102mg chol., 487mg sod., 23g carb. (3g sugars, 1g fiber), 16g pro.

DELI-STYLE PASTA SALAD

Spiral pasta is the base for this tongue-tingling make-ahead salad. It has lots of fresh and satisfying ingredients topped with a flavorful dressing. It's terrific to serve to company or take to a potluck.

—*Joyce McLennan, Algonac, MI*

Prep: 20 min. + chilling • **Makes:** 12 servings

- 7 oz. tricolor spiral pasta
- 6 oz. thinly sliced hard salami, julienned
- 6 oz. provolone cheese, cubed
- 1 can (2¼ oz.) sliced ripe olives, drained
- 1 small red onion, thinly sliced
- 1 small zucchini, halved and thinly sliced
- ½ cup chopped green pepper
- ½ cup chopped sweet red pepper
- ¼ cup minced fresh parsley
- ¼ cup grated Parmesan cheese
- ½ cup olive oil
- ¼ cup red wine vinegar
- 1 garlic clove, minced
- 1½ tsp. ground mustard
- 1 tsp. dried basil
- 1 tsp. dried oregano
- ¼ tsp. salt
  Dash pepper
- 2 medium tomatoes, cut into wedges

1. Cook the pasta according to the package directions; rinse in cold water and drain. Place in a large bowl and add the next 9 ingredients.
2. In a jar with tight-fitting lid, combine the oil, vinegar, garlic, mustard, basil, oregano, salt and pepper; shake well.
3. Pour over salad; toss to coat. Cover and chill for 8 hours or overnight. Toss before serving. Garnish with tomatoes.

1 CUP: 273 cal., 18g fat (6g sat. fat), 25mg chol., 536mg sod., 17g carb. (3g sugars, 1g fiber), 11g pro.

GARLIC CREAMED SPINACH

This creamed spinach goes with just about anything. Try it with pasta, roasted pork or baked chicken.

—*Debbie Glasscock, Conway, AR*

Takes: 20 min. • **Makes:** 4 servings

- 1 Tbsp. olive oil
- 1 small onion, chopped
- 2 pkg. (10 oz. each) frozen chopped spinach, thawed and squeezed dry
- 2 garlic cloves, minced
- 8 oz. cream cheese, softened
- ¼ cup 2% milk
- ½ tsp. salt
- ½ tsp. pepper

In a large skillet, heat oil over medium-high heat. Add onion; cook and stir until tender, 5-7 minutes. Add spinach and garlic; cook 2 minutes longer. Stir in remaining ingredients; cook until cream cheese is melted.
½ CUP: 279 cal., 24g fat (12g sat. fat), 57mg chol., 579mg sod., 11g carb. (4g sugars, 5g fiber), 9g pro.

TEST KITCHEN TIP
When a recipe calls for frozen spinach, thawed and squeezed dry, place it in a salad spinner and give it a few whirls. It makes it easy work of getting rid of the excess water.

CAULIFLOWER AU GRATIN

Vegetable and nonvegetable lovers alike will fall for this healthy riff on au gratin potatoes. Sometimes I substitute broccoli for all or half the cauliflower, and it tastes just as good!
—*Jacki Ricci, Ely, NV*

- -

Takes: 30 min. • **Makes:** 8 servings

6	Tbsp. butter, cubed
4	oz. cooked ham, chopped
1	to 2 garlic cloves, minced
1	head cauliflower, broken into florets
1½	cups heavy whipping cream
2	Tbsp. all-purpose flour
¼	tsp. salt
¼	tsp. pepper
	Dash cayenne pepper
1½	cups shredded Swiss cheese
2	to 3 Tbsp. minced fresh parsley

1. Preheat broiler. Meanwhile, in a large skillet, heat butter over medium heat. Add ham and garlic; saute for 2 minutes. Add cauliflower, and cook just until crisp-tender. Combine the cream and flour; stir into skillet and blend well. Add salt, pepper and cayenne pepper. Cook and stir until thickened and bubbly; cook and stir 1 minute longer.

2. Pour into a 2-qt. baking dish and sprinkle with cheese. Broil until top is lightly browned, 2-4 minutes. Sprinkle with minced parsley. Serve immediately.

¾ CUP: 351 cal., 32g fat (20g sat. fat), 100mg chol., 362mg sod., 7g carb. (3g sugars, 2g fiber), 11g pro.

> **TEST KITCHEN TIP**
> For an added boost of nutrition and a pop of color, add ½ lb. chopped asparagus or frozen peas along with the cauliflower.

APPLE-FETA TOSSED SALAD

A friend of mine shared this recipe with me after I raved about the delightful salad at dinner. I have served it for years now, and no matter where I take it, I have to bring along copies of the recipe to hand out.
—*Marlene Clark, Apple Valley, CA*

- -

Takes: 30 min. • **Makes:** 10 servings

2	Tbsp. butter
1	Tbsp. sugar
⅛	tsp. pepper
1	cup walnut halves

DRESSING

⅓	cup olive oil
3	Tbsp. white wine vinegar
1½	tsp. Dijon mustard
2	garlic cloves, minced
½	tsp. sugar
¼	tsp. dried oregano
⅛	tsp. salt
⅛	tsp. dried parsley flakes
⅛	tsp. pepper
2	Tbsp. finely chopped onion

SALAD

5	cups torn romaine
5	cups torn red leaf lettuce
1	medium green apple, chopped
1	medium red apple, chopped
½	to 1 cup crumbled feta cheese

1. Preheat oven to 350°. In a small skillet, melt butter over medium heat; stir in sugar and pepper. Add the walnuts; toss to coat. Spread evenly onto a baking sheet. Bake until lightly browned, about 15 minutes, stirring every 5 minutes. Cool on wire rack.

2. Place dressing ingredients in a blender; cover and process until blended. Place salad ingredients in a large bowl; toss with dressing. Top with walnuts. Serve immediately.

1 CUP: 191 cal., 17g fat (4g sat. fat), 9mg chol., 127mg sod., 8g carb. (5g sugars, 2g fiber), 3g pro.

PENNSYLVANIA DUTCH CUCUMBERS

My mom's side of the family was of German and Irish heritage. Settling in Pennsylvania, they adopted some of the cooking and customs of the Pennsylvania Dutch. Mom loved this Dutch dish of crisp homegrown cucumbers. Today it's how I crave garden salad.
—*Shirley Joan Helfenbein, Lapeer, MI*

Prep: 30 min. + chilling • **Makes:** 6 servings

- 3 to 4 small cucumbers
- 1 tsp. salt
- 1 medium onion, thinly sliced into rings
- ½ cup sour cream
- 2 Tbsp. white vinegar
- 1 Tbsp. minced chives
- ½ tsp. dill seed
- ¼ tsp. pepper
  Pinch sugar
  Lettuce leaves, optional
  Tomato slices, optional

1. Peel cucumbers; slice paper-thin into a bowl. Sprinkle with salt; cover and refrigerate for 3-4 hours.

2. Rinse and drain cucumbers. Pat gently to press out excess liquid. In a bowl, combine cucumbers and onion; set aside. In a small bowl, combine sour cream, vinegar, chives, dill seed, pepper and sugar.

3. Just before serving, add the dressing to cucumbers; toss to coat. Arrange lettuce and tomatoes in a serving bowl if desired. Top with prepared cucumbers.

1 CUP: 61 cal., 3g fat (2g sat. fat), 13mg chol., 406mg sod., 5g carb. (2g sugars, 1g fiber), 2g pro.

TWICE-BAKED CHEDDAR POTATO CASSEROLE

Bacon, cheddar and sour cream turn ordinary potatoes into an extraordinary casserole. It's one of our family's beloved mainstays for the holidays and other special occasions.
—*Kyle Cox, Scottsdale, AZ*

Prep: 70 min. • **Bake:** 15 min.
Makes: 12 servings

- 8 medium baking potatoes (about 8 oz. each)
- ½ cup butter, cubed
- ⅔ cup sour cream
- ⅔ cup 2% milk
- 1 tsp. salt
- ¾ tsp. pepper
- 10 bacon strips, cooked and crumbled, divided
- 2 cups shredded cheddar cheese, divided
- 4 green onions, chopped, divided

1. Preheat oven to 425°. Scrub potatoes; pierce several times with a fork. Bake until tender, 45-60 minutes. Remove from oven; reduce oven setting to 350°.

2. When potatoes are cool enough to handle, cut each potato lengthwise in half. Scoop out pulp and place in a large bowl; discard shells. Mash pulp with butter; stir in sour cream, milk, salt and pepper.

3. Reserve ¼ cup crumbled bacon for topping. Gently fold remaining bacon, 1 cup cheese and half the green onions into potato mixture (do not overmix).

4. Transfer to a greased 11x7-in. baking dish. Top with the remaining cheese and green onions; sprinkle with reserved bacon. Bake until heated through and cheese is melted, 15-20 minutes.

⅔ CUP: 301 cal., 19g fat (11g sat. fat), 57mg chol., 517mg sod., 22g carb. (3g sugars, 2g fiber), 10g pro.

APPLE WALNUT SLAW

After a co-worker shared this recipe with me, it became one of my favorites. Apples, walnuts and raisins are a fun way to dress up coleslaw.
—*Joan Hallford, North Richland Hills, TX*

- -

Takes: 15 min.
Makes: 12 servings

- ¾ cup mayonnaise
- ¾ cup buttermilk
- 4 to 5 Tbsp. sugar
- 4½ tsp. lemon juice
- ¾ tsp. salt
- ¼ to ½ tsp. pepper
- 6 cups shredded cabbage (about 1 small head)
- 1½ cups shredded carrots (2-3 medium carrots)
- ⅓ cup finely chopped red onion
- 1 cup coarsely chopped walnuts, toasted
- ¾ cup raisins
- 2 medium apples, chopped

1. Whisk together the first 6 ingredients. In a large bowl, combine vegetables, walnuts and raisins; toss with dressing. Fold in apples.
2. Refrigerate, covered, until serving.
NOTE: To toast nuts, bake in a shallow pan in a 350° oven for 5-10 minutes or cook in a skillet over low heat until lightly browned, stirring occasionally.
¾ CUP: 233 cal., 17g fat (2g sat. fat), 2mg chol., 264mg sod., 21g carb. (14g sugars, 3g fiber), 3g pro.

BANANA SPLIT FLUFF

This pretty pink mixture, rich with yummy fruit and nuts, is sure to disappear in a hurry. It's a sweet and speedy treat that can be served as a dessert or salad.
—*Anne Powers, Munford, AL*

- -

Takes: 10 min. • **Makes:** 10 servings

- 1 can (14 oz.) sweetened condensed milk
- 1 carton (12 oz.) frozen whipped topping, thawed
- 1 can (21 oz.) cherry pie filling
- 3 medium firm bananas, cut into chunks
- 1 can (8 oz.) crushed pineapple, drained
- ½ cup chopped nuts

In a large bowl, combine the milk and whipped topping until well blended. Fold in pie filling, bananas, pineapple and nuts.
¾ CUP: 374 cal., 13g fat (8g sat. fat), 13mg chol., 62mg sod., 58g carb. (49g sugars, 2g fiber), 5g pro.

BASIC BUTTERMILK SALAD DRESSING

Serving salad to a crowd? Skip the bottled store-bought dressing and make your own. This handy recipe makes a full quart of creamy, delicious dressing to toss with your favorite greens and veggies.
—*Patricia Mele, Lower Burrell, PA*

- -

Takes: 5 min. • **Makes:** 32 servings (1 qt.)

- 2 cups mayonnaise
- 2 cups buttermilk
- 1 Tbsp. onion powder
- 1 Tbsp. dried parsley flakes
- 1½ tsp. garlic powder
- ½ tsp. salt
- ½ tsp. celery salt
- ¼ tsp. pepper

Whisk together all ingredients. Refrigerate, covered, until serving.
2 TBSP.: 98 cal., 10g fat (2g sat. fat), 2mg chol., 155mg sod., 1g carb. (1g sugars, 0 fiber), 1g pro. **DIABETIC EXCHANGES:** 2 fat.

Hearty Main Dishes

Whether you choose cherished dishes passed down for generations or modern twists on the classics, you and your loved ones will come back to these hearty dinner favorites time and again.

5i

BAKED HAM WITH PINEAPPLE

I first learned the technique for cooking ham with pineapple for a themed dinner my husband and I hosted. Since it was widely known as the symbol of hospitality, pineapple was the star ingredient on our menu and on this lovely baked ham.

—*JoAnn Fox, Johnson City, TN*

Prep: 10 min. • **Bake:** 2 hours
Makes: 20 servings

- 1 **fully cooked bone-in ham (6 to 8 lbs.)**
  Whole cloves
- 1 **can (20 oz.) sliced pineapple**
- ½ **cup packed brown sugar**
- 12 **maraschino cherries**

Place ham in roasting pan. Score the surface with shallow diagonal cuts, making diamond shapes; insert cloves into diamonds. Cover and bake ham at 325° for 1½ hours. Drain pineapple, reserving ¼ cup juice. Combine brown sugar and reserved pineapple juice; pour over ham. Arrange pineapple slices and cherries on ham. Bake, uncovered, 30-45 minutes longer or until a thermometer reads 140° and the ham is heated through.

3 OZ. COOKED HAM: 219 cal., 13g fat (5g sat. fat), 48mg chol., 924mg sod., 8g carb. (8g sugars, 0 fiber), 17g pro.

TEST KITCHEN TIP
Dark brown sugar contains more molasses than light or golden brown sugar. While brown sugars are generally interchangeable in most recipes, choose dark brown sugar if you prefer a bolder flavor. The sweetness of pineapple in this recipe is an especially good way to bring out all the best and savory flavors you get with ham.

SHRIMP PASTA ALFREDO

My son loves any recipe with Alfredo sauce. When he cooked as a bachelor, shrimp pasta was one of his first recipes. Now his children ask for it.
—*Gail Lucas, Olive Branch, MS*

- -

Takes: 25 min. • **Makes:** 4 servings

- 3 cups uncooked bow tie pasta
- 2 cups frozen peas
- 1 lb. peeled and deveined cooked medium shrimp, tails removed
- 1 jar (15 oz.) Alfredo sauce
- ¼ cup shredded Parmesan cheese

1. In a Dutch oven, cook pasta according to package directions, adding peas during the last 3 minutes of cooking; drain and return to pan.

2. Stir in shrimp and sauce; heat through over medium heat, stirring occasionally. Sprinkle with cheese.

2 CUPS: 545 cal., 16g fat (9g sat. fat), 206mg chol., 750mg sod., 60g carb. (5g sugars, 6g fiber), 41g pro.

PRESSURE-COOKER MUSHROOM POT ROAST

Packed with wholesome veggies and tender beef, this is a wow-worthy entree that will delight all ages. Serve mashed potatoes alongside to soak up every last drop of the beefy gravy.
—*Angie Stewart, Topeka, KS*

- -

Prep: 25 min. • **Cook:** 65 min. + releasing
Makes: 10 servings

- 1 boneless beef chuck roast (3 to 4 lbs.)
- ½ tsp. salt
- ¼ tsp. pepper
- 1 Tbsp. canola oil
- 1½ cups dry red wine or reduced-sodium beef broth
- 1½ lbs. sliced fresh shiitake mushrooms
- 2½ cups thinly sliced onions
- 1½ cups reduced-sodium beef broth
- 1 can (8 oz.) tomato sauce
- ¾ cup chopped peeled parsnips
- ¾ cup chopped celery
- ¾ cup chopped carrots
- 8 garlic cloves, minced
- 2 bay leaves
- 1½ tsp. dried thyme
- 1 tsp. chili powder
- ¼ cup cornstarch
- ¼ cup water
  Mashed potatoes
  Chopped fresh parsley, optional

1. Halve roast; sprinkle with salt and pepper. Select saute or browning setting on a 6-qt. electric pressure cooker. Adjust for medium heat; add 1½ tsp. oil. When oil is hot, brown a roast half on all sides. Remove; repeat with remaining beef and 1½ tsp. oil. Add wine to pressure cooker. Cook 2 minutes, stirring to loosen browned bits from pan. Press cancel. Return beef to pressure cooker.

2. Add mushrooms, onions, broth, tomato sauce, parsnips, celery, carrots, garlic, bay leaves, thyme and chili powder. Lock lid; close pressure-release valve. Adjust to pressure-cook on high for 60 minutes. Let pressure release naturally for 10 minutes; quick-release any remaining pressure. A thermometer inserted in beef should read at least 160°.

3. Remove meat and vegetables to a serving platter and keep warm. Discard bay leaves. Skim fat from cooking juices; transfer back to the pressure cooker. In a small bowl, mix cornstarch and water until smooth; stir into cooking juices. Select saute setting and adjust for low heat. Simmer, stirring constantly, until thickened, 1-2 minutes. Serve with mashed potatoes, meat and vegetables. If desired, top with chopped parsley.

FREEZE OPTION: Place roast and vegetables in freezer containers; top with the cooking juices. Cool and freeze. To use, partially thaw in refrigerator overnight. Heat through in a covered saucepan, stirring gently and adding a little broth if necessary.

4 OZ. COOKED BEEF WITH ⅔ CUP VEGETABLES AND ½ CUP GRAVY: 316 cal., 15g fat (5g sat. fat), 89mg chol., 373mg sod., 16g carb. (4g sugars, 4g fiber), 30g pro.
DIABETIC EXCHANGES: 4 lean meat, 2 vegetable, 1½ fat.

CHICKEN BURRITOS

This mouthwatering southwestern recipe makes enough for two casseroles, so you can enjoy one today and freeze the other for a busy weeknight. These burritos are super to have on hand for quick meals or to take to potlucks.
—*Sonya Nightingale, Burley, ID*

- -

Prep: 20 min. • **Bake:** 35 min.
Makes: 2 casseroles (6 servings each)

- 6 Tbsp. butter
- 1 large onion, chopped
- ¼ cup chopped green pepper
- ½ cup all-purpose flour
- 3 cups chicken broth
- 1 can (10 oz.) diced tomatoes and green chiles, undrained
- 1 tsp. ground cumin
- 1 tsp. chili powder
- ½ tsp. garlic powder
- ½ tsp. salt
- 2 Tbsp. chopped jalapeno pepper, optional
- 1 can (15 oz.) chili with beans
- 1 pkg. (8 oz.) cream cheese, cubed
- 8 cups cubed cooked chicken
- 24 flour tortillas (6 in.), warmed
- 6 cups shredded Colby-Monterey Jack cheese
  Salsa, optional

1. Preheat oven to 350°. In a Dutch oven, heat butter over medium-high heat. Add onion and pepper; cook and stir until tender. Stir in flour until blended; gradually stir in broth. Bring to a boil; cook and stir 2 minutes. Reduce the heat; stir in the tomatoes, seasonings and, if desired, jalapeno. Cook 5 minutes. Add chili and cream cheese; stir until cream cheese is melted. Stir in chicken.

2. Spoon about ½ cup filling across center of each tortilla; sprinkle each with ¼ cup Colby-Monterey Jack cheese. Fold bottom and sides over filling and roll up. Place tortillas in 2 greased 13x9-in. baking dishes.

3. Bake, covered, 35-40 minutes or until heated through. If desired, serve with salsa.

FREEZE OPTION: Cool unbaked casseroles; cover and freeze. To use, partially thaw in the refrigerator overnight. Remove casseroles from refrigerator 30 minutes before baking. Preheat oven to 350°. Cover casserole with foil; bake as directed, increasing baking time to 50-55 minutes or until heated through and a thermometer inserted in center reads 160°.

NOTE: Wear disposable gloves when cutting hot peppers; the oils can burn skin. Avoid touching your face.

2 BURRITOS: 760 cal., 44g fat (23g sat. fat), 177mg chol., 1608mg sod., 40g carb. (2g sugars, 2g fiber), 51g pro.

SPAGHETTI PORK CHOPS

Tender pork chops are simmered to perfection in a tangy sauce and then served over pasta. This was one of my mother's favorite recipes.
—*Ellen Gallavan, Midland, MI*

- -

Prep: 20 min. • **Cook:** 6 hours
Makes: 6 servings

- 3 cans (8 oz. each) tomato sauce
- 1 can (10¾ oz.) condensed tomato soup, undiluted
- 1 small onion, finely chopped
- 1 bay leaf
- 1 tsp. celery seed
- ½ tsp. Italian seasoning
- 6 bone-in pork loin chops (8 oz. each)
- 2 Tbsp. olive oil
- 9 oz. uncooked spaghetti

1. In a 5-qt. slow cooker, combine the tomato sauce, soup, onion, bay leaf, celery seed and Italian seasoning.

2. In a large skillet, brown pork chops in oil. Add to the slow cooker. Cover and cook on low until meat is tender, 6-8 hours. Discard bay leaf.

3. Cook the spaghetti according to package directions; drain. Serve pork chops and sauce over spaghetti.

1 PORK CHOP WITH ⅔ CUP SPAGHETTI: 587 cal., 25g fat (8g sat. fat), 111mg chol., 792mg sod., 46g carb. (8g sugars, 4g fiber), 44g pro.

LILY JULOW
Lawrenceville, GA

GARLIC-BUTTER STEAK

This quick and easy skillet entree is definitely restaurant quality and sure to become a staple at your house, too!
—*Lily Julow, Lawrenceville, GA*

Takes: 20 min. • **Makes:** 2 servings

2 Tbsp. butter, softened, divided
1 tsp. minced fresh parsley
½ tsp. minced garlic
¼ tsp. reduced-sodium soy sauce
1 beef flat iron steak or boneless top sirloin steak (¾ lb.)
⅛ tsp. salt
⅛ tsp. pepper

1. Mix 1 Tbsp. butter, parsley, garlic and soy sauce.

2. Sprinkle steak with salt and pepper. In a large skillet, heat remaining butter over medium heat. Add steak; cook until meat reaches desired doneness (for medium-rare, a thermometer should read 135°; medium, 140°; medium-well, 145°), 4-7 minutes per side. Serve with garlic butter.

4 OZ. COOKED BEEF WITH 2 TSP. GARLIC BUTTER: 316 cal., 20g fat (10g sat. fat), 124mg chol., 337mg sod., 0 carb. (0 sugars, 0 fiber), 32g pro.

SOUTHERN SHRIMP & GRITS

Expecting company? Serve your guests this southern specialty. Sometimes called breakfast shrimp, this comforting dish is welcome morning, noon or night.
—*Mandy Rivers, Lexington, SC*

Prep: 15 min. • **Cook:** 20 min.
Makes: 4 servings

- 2 cups reduced-sodium chicken broth
- 2 cups 2% milk
- ⅓ cup butter, cubed
- ¾ tsp. salt
- ½ tsp. pepper
- ¾ cup uncooked old-fashioned grits
- 1 cup shredded cheddar cheese

SHRIMP

- 8 thick-sliced bacon strips, chopped
- 1 lb. uncooked medium shrimp, peeled and deveined
- 3 garlic cloves, minced
- 1 tsp. Cajun or blackened seasoning
- 4 green onions, chopped

1. In a large saucepan, bring the broth, milk, butter, salt and pepper to a boil. Slowly stir in grits. Reduce heat. Cover and cook until thickened, 12-14 minutes, stirring occasionally. Stir in cheddar cheese until melted. Set aside and keep warm.

2. In a large skillet, cook chopped bacon over medium heat until crisp. Remove to paper towels with a slotted spoon; drain, reserving 4 tsp. drippings. Saute the shrimp, garlic and seasoning in drippings until shrimp turn pink. Serve with grits and sprinkle with onions.

1 CUP GRITS WITH ½ CUP SHRIMP MIXTURE: 674 cal., 42g fat (22g sat. fat), 241mg chol., 1845mg sod., 33g carb. (7g sugars, 1g fiber), 41g pro.

> **TEST KITCHEN TIP**
> To quickly peel fresh garlic, gently crush the clove with the flat side of a large knife blade to loosen the peel. If you don't have a large knife, you can crush the garlic with a small can.

EASY PEPPER STEAK

Green peppers, tomatoes and tender beef strips combine in this simple stir-fry. Toss in red or orange bell peppers for some of the green for extra color.
—Carolyn Butterfield, Atkinson, NE

Prep: 10 min. • **Cook:** 55 min.
Makes: 4 servings

1	lb. beef top round steak, cut into ¼-in. x 2-in. strips
1	Tbsp. paprika
2	Tbsp. butter
1	can (10½ oz.) beef broth
2	garlic cloves, minced
2	medium green peppers, cut into strips
1	cup thinly sliced onion
2	Tbsp. cornstarch
2	Tbsp. reduced-sodium soy sauce
⅓	cup cold water
2	fresh tomatoes, peeled and cut into wedges
	Cooked rice

1. Sprinkle meat with paprika. In a large skillet, melt butter over medium-high heat. Brown beef. Add broth and garlic. Simmer, covered, for 30 minutes. Add green peppers and onion. Cover and continue to simmer for 5 minutes.
2. Combine cornstarch, soy sauce and water; stir into meat mixture. Cook and stir until thickened. Gently stir in tomatoes and heat through. Serve over rice.
1 SERVING: 317 cal., 10g fat (0 sat. fat), 46mg chol., 405mg sod., 35g carb. (0 sugars, 2g fiber), 21g pro. **DIABETIC EXCHANGES:** 2½ lean meat, 1½ starch, 1½ vegetable, ½ fat.

SUNDAY PORK ROAST

There's nothing like a well-seasoned pork roast. Mom would prepare this delectable dish for our family, friends and customers at the three restaurants she and Dad owned. The herb rub and vegetables give it a remarkable flavor.
—Sandi Pichon, Memphis, TN

Prep: 20 min. • **Bake:** 1 hour 10 min. + standing
Makes: 12 servings

2	medium onions, chopped
2	medium carrots, chopped
1	celery rib, chopped
4	Tbsp. all-purpose flour, divided
1	bay leaf, finely crushed
½	tsp. dried thyme
1¼	tsp. salt, divided
1¼	tsp. pepper, divided
1	boneless pork loin roast (3 to 4 lbs.)
⅓	cup packed brown sugar

1. Preheat oven to 350°. Place vegetables on bottom of a shallow roasting pan. Mix 2 Tbsp. flour, bay leaf, thyme, and 1 tsp. each salt and pepper; rub over roast. Place the roast on top of vegetables, fat side up. Add 1 cup water to the pan.
2. Roast 1 hour, basting once with pan juices if desired. Sprinkle brown sugar over roast. Roast for 10-15 minutes longer or until a thermometer reads 140°. (Temperature of the roast will continue to rise another 5-10° upon standing.)
3. Remove roast to a platter. Tent with foil; let stand 15 minutes before slicing.
4. Strain drippings from roasting pan into a measuring cup; skim fat. Add enough water to the drippings to measure 1½ cups.
5. In a small saucepan over medium heat, whisk remaining flour and ⅓ cup water until smooth. Gradually whisk in drippings mixture and remaining salt and pepper. Bring to a boil over medium-high heat, stirring constantly; cook and stir 2 minutes or until thickened. Serve roast with gravy.
FREEZE OPTION: Freeze cooled sliced pork and gravy in freezer containers. To use, partially thaw in refrigerator overnight. Heat through in a covered saucepan, gently stirring and adding a little broth or water if necessary.
3 OZ. COOKED PORK WITH ABOUT 2 TBSP. GRAVY: 174 cal., 5g fat (2g sat. fat), 57mg chol., 280mg sod., 8g carb. (6g sugars, 0 fiber), 22g pro. **DIABETIC EXCHANGES:** 3 lean meat, ½ starch.

2 pkg. (24 oz. each) frozen
  cheese ravioli, thawed
1 cup shredded Parmesan cheese
18 slices provolone cheese, cut in half
6 cups shredded Monterey Jack cheese
5 large tomatoes, sliced

1. In a Dutch oven, bring the first 5 ingredients to a boil. Reduce heat; simmer, uncovered, for 20 minutes or until desired thickness is achieved, stirring often.
2. In a large skillet, cook sausage over medium heat until no longer pink; drain. Stir in raisins and Italian seasoning; add to sauce. In the same skillet, saute mushrooms and onion until moisture has evaporated. Stir into sauce. In a large bowl, combine the eggs, ricotta, spinach and grated Parmesan cheese; set aside.
3. In each of 2 greased 13x9-in. baking dishes, layer 1⅓ cups sauce, half a package of ravioli, 1⅓ cups sauce, ¼ cup shredded Parmesan cheese, 6 half slices provolone cheese, 1 cup Monterey Jack cheese and 2½ cups spinach mixture.
4. Top each with 6 half slices provolone cheese, 1 cup Monterey Jack cheese, 1⅓ cups sauce, remaining ravioli and sauce, ¼ cup shredded Parmesan cheese, 6 half slices provolone cheese, sliced tomatoes and remaining Monterey Jack cheese (dishes will be full).
5. Cover and bake at 375° for 45 minutes. Uncover; bake 10-15 minutes longer or until a thermometer reads 160°. Let stand for 15 minutes before serving.
1 PIECE: 483 cal., 24g fat (13g sat. fat), 102mg chol., 1081mg sod., 36g carb. (13g sugars, 4g fiber), 31g pro.

SPEEDY SALMON PATTIES

When I was a girl growing up on the farm, my mom often fixed these nicely seasoned patties when we were working late in the field. They're also tasty with chopped green peppers added to the mixture.
—*Bonnie Evans, Cameron, NC*

Takes: 25 min. • **Makes:** 3 servings

⅓ cup finely chopped onion
1 large egg, beaten
5 saltines, crushed
½ tsp. Worcestershire sauce
¼ tsp. salt
⅛ tsp. pepper
1 can (14¾ oz.) salmon, drained, bones and skin removed
2 tsp. butter

1. In a large mixing bowl, combine the first 6 ingredients. Crumble salmon over mixture and mix well. Shape into 6 patties.
2. In a large skillet over medium heat, fry the patties in butter for 3-4 minutes on each side or until set and golden brown.
2 PATTIES: 288 cal., 15g fat (4g sat. fat), 139mg chol., 1063mg sod., 5g carb. (1g sugars, 0 fiber), 31g pro.

WORTH IT LASAGNA

I break out this lasagna recipe whenever I need something special to feed a crowd. It has such an abundance of tasty ingredients. Often, I'll serve one pan to guests and freeze the other for a family meal later.
—*Joan Broxholme, Boulder City, NV*

Prep: 1 hour • **Bake:** 55 min. + standing
Makes: 2 casseroles (12 servings each)

2 jars (24 oz. each) meatless spaghetti sauce
1 can (14½ oz.) diced tomatoes, drained
½ cup Burgundy wine
2 Tbsp. brown sugar
3 garlic cloves, minced
2 lbs. Italian turkey sausage links, casings removed
¾ cup raisins
2 tsp. Italian seasoning
1½ lbs. sliced fresh mushrooms
1 medium onion, chopped
2 large eggs, lightly beaten
2 cartons (15 oz. each) ricotta cheese
1 pkg. (10 oz.) frozen chopped spinach, thawed and squeezed dry
1 cup grated Parmesan cheese

TURKEY-STUFFED BELL PEPPERS

This lactose-free meal is so tasty, you won't even miss having real cheddar cheese. Round out the dinner with a salad or a side of rice.
—*Judy Hand-Truitt, Birmingham, AL*

- -

Prep: 30 min. • **Bake:** 20 min.
Makes: 5 servings

5	medium green, red or yellow peppers
2	tsp. olive oil
1¼	lbs. extra-lean ground turkey (99% lean)
1	large onion, chopped
1	garlic clove, minced
2	tsp. ground cumin
1	tsp. Italian seasoning
½	tsp. salt
½	tsp. pepper
2	medium tomatoes, finely chopped
1¾	cups shredded cheddar-flavored lactose-free or other cheese
1½	cups soft bread crumbs
¼	tsp. paprika

1. Preheat oven to 325°. Cut the peppers lengthwise in half; remove seeds. Place in a 15x10x1-in. pan coated with cooking spray.
2. In a large skillet, heat oil over medium-high heat. Cook and crumble turkey with onion, garlic and seasonings over medium-high heat until meat is no longer pink, 6-8 minutes. Cool slightly. Stir in tomatoes, cheese and bread crumbs.
3. Fill with turkey mixture. Sprinkle with paprika. Bake, uncovered, until heated through and filled peppers are tender, 20-25 minutes.
NOTE: Some bread crumbs are made with milk. To ensure this recipe is lactose-free, read the label or ask your baker.
2 STUFFED PEPPER HALVES: 323 cal., 10g fat (0 sat. fat), 45mg chol., 771mg sod., 20g carb. (6g sugars, 4g fiber), 40g pro. **DIABETIC EXCHANGES:** 5 lean meat, 2 vegetable, 1 starch, ½ fat.

SENATE BEAN POTPIE

The flavors from a classic Senate bean soup inspired this hearty potpie with a cornbread topping.
—*Janice Elder, Charlotte, NC*

- -

Prep. 30 min. • **Bake:** 20 min. + standing
Makes: 6 servings

2	Tbsp. canola oil
2	medium carrots, chopped
2	celery ribs, chopped
1	medium onion, chopped
1½	cups cubed fully cooked ham
3	Tbsp. all-purpose flour
1	can (14½ oz.) chicken broth
2	cans (15½ oz. each) navy or great northern beans, rinsed and drained
¼	tsp. salt
¼	tsp. pepper
1	pkg. (8½ oz.) cornbread/muffin mix
½	cup 2% milk
1	large egg, lightly beaten
2	green onions, finely chopped
¼	cup minced fresh parsley
2	Tbsp. butter, melted

1. Preheat oven to 425°. In a 10-in. ovenproof skillet, heat oil over medium-high heat. Add the carrots, celery and onion; cook and stir 6-8 minutes or until tender. Add ham. Stir in flour until blended; gradually stir in broth. Bring to a boil, stirring constantly; cook and stir 1-2 minutes or until thickened.
2. Add beans, salt and pepper; return to a boil. In a small bowl, combine muffin mix, milk, egg, green onions, parsley and melted butter; stir just until blended. Spoon evenly over bean mixture (dish will be full).
3. Bake 20-25 minutes or until the topping is golden brown. Let stand 15 minutes.
1 SERVING: 513 cal., 17g fat (5g sat. fat), 66mg chol., 1619mg sod., 67g carb. (12g sugars, 12g fiber), 24g pro.

CHICKEN WITH PEACH-AVOCADO SALSA

This super fresh dinner is pure summer—juicy peaches, creamy avocado, grilled chicken and a kick of hot sauce and lime. Make the salsa ahead of time to get it on the table even quicker.
—*Shannon Norris, Cudahy, WI*

Takes: 30 min. • **Makes:** 4 servings

- 1 medium peach, peeled and chopped
- 1 medium ripe avocado, peeled and cubed
- ½ cup chopped sweet red pepper
- 3 Tbsp. finely chopped red onion
- 1 Tbsp. minced fresh basil
- 1 Tbsp. lime juice
- 1 tsp. hot pepper sauce
- ½ tsp. grated lime zest
- ¾ tsp. salt, divided
- ½ tsp. pepper, divided
- 4 boneless skinless chicken breast halves (6 oz. each)

1. For salsa, in a small bowl, combine the peaches, avocado, red pepper, onion, basil, lime juice, hot sauce, lime zest, ¼ tsp. salt and ¼ tsp. pepper.

2. Sprinkle chicken with remaining salt and pepper. On a lightly greased grill rack, grill chicken, covered, over medium heat for 5 minutes. Turn; grill until a thermometer reads 165°, 7-9 minutes longer. Serve with fresh salsa.

1 CHICKEN BREAST HALF WITH ½ CUP SALSA: 265 cal., 9g fat (2g sat. fat), 94mg chol., 536mg sod., 9g carb. (4g sugars, 3g fiber), 36g pro. **DIABETIC EXCHANGES:** 5 lean meat, 1 fat, ½ starch.

PORK VEGGIE STIR-FRY

Even kids find this colorful combo of vegetables, pork strips, seasonings and peanuts appealing. Serve it over rice for a main dish that needs no sides.
—*Laurel Reisinger, Saskatoon, SK*

Takes: 20 min. • **Makes:** 6 servings

- 3 cups sliced cauliflower
- 3 Tbsp. vegetable oil, divided
- 2 medium carrots, julienned
- 1 can (15 oz.) whole baby corn, rinsed and drained
- ½ cup frozen peas, thawed
- 1 lb. boneless pork, cut into thin strips
- 2 green onions, thinly sliced
- 2 garlic cloves, minced
- 1 Tbsp. minced fresh gingerroot
- ½ to 1 tsp. chili powder
- 1 cup water
- ¼ cup soy sauce
- 4 tsp. honey
- 2 tsp. chicken bouillon granules
- 4 tsp. cornstarch
- 2 Tbsp. cold water
- ¼ cup salted peanuts
  Hot cooked rice, optional

1. In a skillet or wok, stir-fry cauliflower in 2 Tbsp. oil for 3 minutes. Add carrots; stir-fry for 2 minutes. Add corn and peas; stir-fry until vegetables are crisp-tender. Remove from pan; keep warm.

2. Stir-fry pork in remaining oil for 2 minutes. Add onions, garlic, ginger and chili powder; stir-fry until pork is no longer pink. Remove; keep warm.

3. Combine 1 cup water, soy sauce, honey and bouillon in same pan. Combine cornstarch and cold water; gradually add to pan. Bring to a boil; cook and stir until thickened, 2 minutes.

4. Return vegetables and pork mixture to pan; heat through. Stir in peanuts. If desired, serve with rice.

1 SERVING: 277 cal., 14g fat (3g sat. fat), 45mg chol., 1131mg sod., 16g carb. (8g sugars, 4g fiber), 22g pro.

GARDEN-FRESH GRILLED VEGGIE PIZZA

I have four gardens and, between them, I grow a pretty good spread of veggies. I created this loaded-up pizza as a fun summer appetizer using some of my best garden goodies.

—Dianna Wara, Washington, IL

Prep: 30 min. • **Grill:** 15 min.
Makes: 6 servings

- 3 Tbsp. olive oil
- 3 garlic cloves, minced
- 3 medium tomatoes, cut into ½-in. slices
- 1 large sweet red pepper, halved, stemmed and seeded
- 1 small zucchini, cut lengthwise into ¼-in. slices
- 1 small onion, cut crosswise into ½-in. slices
- 1 tsp. coarsely ground pepper
- 1 prebaked 12-in. pizza crust
- ⅓ cup spreadable garden vegetable cream cheese
- 8 slices smoked provolone cheese, divided
- ½ cup minced fresh basil, divided
- ¼ cup shredded carrots
- 1 Tbsp. minced fresh oregano
- 1 tsp. minced fresh thyme

1. Mix oil and garlic; brush onto both sides of vegetables. Sprinkle with pepper. Grill, covered, over medium heat until tender, 4-5 minutes per side for pepper and onion, 3-4 minutes per side for zucchini, 2-3 minutes per side for tomatoes.
2. Coarsely chop pepper, onion and zucchini. Spread pizza crust with cream cheese; layer with 4 slices provolone and tomato slices. Sprinkle with ¼ cup basil, carrots, oregano and thyme. Top with grilled vegetables, then remaining cheese.
3. Grill pizza, covered, over medium heat until bottom is golden brown and cheese is melted, 5-7 minutes. Top with remaining basil.
1 SLICE: 395 cal., 22g fat (8g sat. fat), 23mg chol., 618mg sod., 36g carb. (6g sugars, 3g fiber), 16g pro.

SOUTHERN FRIED CHICKEN STRIPS

What's not to love with these crowd-pleasing golden fried chicken strips? A hint of garlic makes them irresistible.

—Genise Krause, Sturgeon Bay, WI

Prep: 30 min. • **Cook:** 5 min./batch
Makes: 6 servings

- 1 large egg
- ½ cup buttermilk
- 1 cup all-purpose flour
- 1½ tsp. garlic powder
- 1½ tsp. pepper
- ½ tsp. salt
- ½ tsp. paprika
- 2 lbs. chicken tenderloins
  Oil for deep-fat frying
- 2 Tbsp. grated Parmesan cheese

1. In a shallow bowl, whisk egg and buttermilk. In a separate shallow bowl, combine the flour, garlic powder, pepper, salt and paprika. Dip chicken in egg mixture, then flour mixture.
2. In an electric skillet, heat oil to 375°. Fry chicken, a few pieces at a time, for 2-3 minutes on each side or until no longer pink. Drain on paper towels. Sprinkle with cheese.
5 OZ. COOKED CHICKEN: 327 cal., 11g fat (2g sat. fat), 126mg chol., 320mg sod., 18g carb. (2g sugars, 1g fiber), 39g pro.

DIANNA WARA
Washington, IL

LEMON-PARSLEY BAKED COD

After trying a few cod recipes, this was the first fish recipe that got two thumbs-up from my family of meat lovers. The tangy lemon gives the cod some oomph.
—*Trisha Kruse, Eagle, ID*

- -

Takes: 30 min. • **Makes:** 4 servings

3	Tbsp. lemon juice
3	Tbsp. butter, melted
¼	cup all-purpose flour
½	tsp. salt
¼	tsp. paprika
¼	tsp. lemon-pepper seasoning
4	cod fillets (6 oz. each)
2	Tbsp. minced fresh parsley
2	tsp. grated lemon zest

1. Preheat oven to 400°. In a shallow bowl, mix lemon juice and butter. In a separate shallow bowl, mix flour and seasonings. Dip fillets in lemon juice mixture, then in flour mixture to coat both sides; shake off excess.

2. Place in a 13x9-in. baking dish coated with cooking spray. Drizzle with remaining lemon juice mixture. Bake 12-15 minutes or until fish just begins to flake easily with a fork. Mix parsley and lemon zest; sprinkle over fish.

1 FILLET: 232 cal., 10g fat (6g sat. fat), 87mg chol., 477mg sod., 7g carb. (0 sugars, 0 fiber), 28g pro. **DIABETIC EXCHANGES:** 4 lean meat, 2 fat, ½ starch.

TEST KITCHEN TIP
Use freshly squeezed lemon juice when preparing this dish. Bottled juice, which is from concentrate, won't provide the same bright, fresh flavor. Purchase 4 lemons to get the job done.

LASAGNA CUPS

I love lasagna and garlic bread, so it only made sense to put them together in these fun little cups. Enjoy one as an appetizer or two for a complete meal.
—*Angelique Douglas, Maryville, IL*

- -

Prep: 40 min. • **Bake:** 15 min.
Makes: 16 lasagna cups

- 3 **individual lasagna noodles**
- ½ **lb. ground turkey or beef**
- 1 **cup meatless pasta sauce**
- ⅓ **cup 2% cottage cheese**
- ¼ **tsp. garlic powder**
- 2 **tubes (8 oz. each) refrigerated crescent rolls**
- 2 **cups shredded Italian cheese blend or cheddar cheese**
- 1 **cup grape tomatoes, halved**

1. Preheat oven to 375°. Cook lasagna noodles according to the package directions. Drain and rinse with water; cut each noodle into 6 squares.

2. In a large skillet, cook and crumble ground turkey over medium heat until no longer pink, 5-7 minutes. Stir in sauce, cottage cheese and garlic powder; bring to a boil. Remove from the heat.

3. Unroll both tubes of crescent dough; separate each into 8 triangles. Press each triangle onto bottom and up sides of a greased muffin cup. Layer each with 1 Tbsp. cheese, 1 noodle piece and 1 rounded Tbsp. meat sauce (discard extra noodle pieces). Sprinkle with remaining cheese.

4. Bake on a lower oven rack until crust is golden brown, 15-20 minutes. Let stand 5 minutes before removing from pan. Top with tomatoes.

2 LASAGNA CUPS: 412 cal., 21g fat (9g sat. fat), 39mg chol., 839mg sod., 34g carb. (7g sugars, 1g fiber), 18g pro.

APPLE & HERB ROASTED TURKEY

My daughter loves to help me make this moist roasted turkey with herbs. Her job is to hand Mommy the ingredients—if she doesn't eat the apples first!
—*Kimberly Jackson, Gay, GA*

Prep: 20 min. • **Bake:** 3 hours + standing
Makes: 14 servings

- ¼ cup minced fresh sage
- ¼ cup minced fresh rosemary
- 1 turkey (14 lbs.)
- 1 medium apple, quartered
- 1 medium onion, halved
- 1 celery rib, halved
- ½ cup butter, melted
- ½ cup apple jelly, warmed

1. Combine sage and rosemary. With fingers, carefully loosen skin from the turkey breast; rub herbs under skin. Secure skin to underside of breast with toothpicks.

2. Place breast side up on a rack in a roasting pan. Stuff turkey with apple, onion and celery. Brush with butter.

3. Bake, uncovered, at 325° for 3-3½ hours or until a thermometer reads 180°, basting occasionally with the pan drippings. (Cover loosely with foil if turkey browns too quickly.) Brush with apple jelly. Cover turkey and let stand for 15 minutes before removing toothpicks and carving.

8 OZ. COOKED TURKEY: 626 cal., 31g fat (11g sat. fat), 262mg chol., 222mg sod., 10g carb. (9g sugars, 0 fiber), 72g pro.

SO-TENDER SWISS STEAK

We requested this fork-tender Swiss steak with a rich gravy a lot when I was growing up. Mom took pride in preparing scrumptious, hearty meals like this for our family and guests.
—*Linda McGinty, Parma, OH*

Prep: 30 min. • **Bake:** 2 hours
Makes: 8 servings

- ¼ cup all-purpose flour
- ½ tsp. salt
- ¼ tsp. pepper
- 2 lbs. beef top round steak, cut into serving-size pieces
- 2 Tbsp. canola oil
- 1 medium onion, thinly sliced
- 2 cups water
- 2 Tbsp. Worcestershire sauce

GRAVY

- ¼ cup all-purpose flour
- ¼ tsp. salt
- ⅛ tsp. pepper
- 1¼ cups beef broth or water
   Hot cooked noodles or mashed potatoes, optional

1. Preheat oven to 325°. In a large shallow dish, combine flour, salt and pepper. Pound steak with a mallet to tenderize. Toss meat, a few pieces at a time, in flour mixture to coat.

2. In an ovenproof Dutch oven, brown steak in oil on both sides. Arrange the onion slices between layers of meat. Add the water and Worcestershire sauce.

3. Cover and bake 2-2½ hours or until meat is very tender. Remove to a serving platter and keep warm.

4. For gravy, in a small bowl, combine flour, salt, pepper and broth until smooth; stir into pan juices. Bring to a boil over medium heat; cook and stir 2 minutes or until thickened. Serve steak and gravy with noodles or mashed potatoes, if desired.

FREEZE OPTION: Freeze cooled beef mixture in freezer containers. To use, partially thaw in refrigerator overnight. Heat through in a covered saucepan, gently stirring and adding a little broth or water if necessary.

1 SERVING: 213 cal., 7g fat (2g sat. fat), 64mg chol., 424mg sod., 9g carb. (1g sugars, 1g fiber), 27g pro.

⏱ 15-MINUTE MEAT LOAF

15-MINUTE MEAT LOAF

I combined a few tasty meat loaf recipes to create this flavorful version, which my husband loves. And because it's made in the microwave, the entree is ideal for busy nights.

—Deb Thompson, Lincoln, NE

- -

Takes: 15 min. • **Makes:** 4 servings

- 1   large egg, lightly beaten
- 5   Tbsp. ketchup, divided
- 2   Tbsp. prepared mustard
- ½   cup dry bread crumbs
- 2   Tbsp. onion soup mix
- ¼   tsp. salt
- ¼   tsp. pepper
- 1   lb. ground beef
- ¼   cup sugar
- 2   Tbsp. brown sugar
- 2   Tbsp. cider vinegar

1. In a large bowl, combine the egg, 2 Tbsp. ketchup, mustard, bread crumbs, dry soup mix, salt and pepper. Crumble beef over mixture and mix well. Shape into an oval loaf.
2. Place in a shallow 1-qt. microwave-safe dish. Cover and microwave on high 10-12 minutes or until no pink remains and a thermometer reads 160°; drain.
3. Meanwhile in a small bowl, combine the sugars, vinegar and remaining ketchup; drizzle over meat loaf. Cover and microwave on high for 2-3 minutes longer or until heated through. Let stand for 10 minutes before slicing.
4 OZ.: 375 cal., 13g fat (5g sat. fat), 94mg chol., 960mg sod., 38g carb. (0 sugars, 1g fiber), 27g pro. **DIABETIC EXCHANGES:** 3 lean meat, 2½ starch.

CHICKEN PICCATA WITH LEMON SAUCE

Once you've tried this tangy dish, you won't hesitate to make it for company. Seasoned with Parmesan and parsley, the chicken cooks up golden brown, then is drizzled with a light lemon sauce.

—Susan Pursell, Fountain Valley, CA

- -

Prep: 25 min. • **Cook:** 25 min.
Makes: 8 servings

- 8   boneless skinless chicken breast halves (4 oz. each)
- ½   cup egg substitute
- 2   Tbsp. plus ¼ cup dry white wine or chicken broth, divided
- 5   Tbsp. lemon juice, divided
- 3   garlic cloves, minced
- ⅛   tsp. hot pepper sauce
- ½   cup all-purpose flour
- ½   cup grated Parmesan cheese
- ¼   cup minced fresh parsley
- ½   tsp. salt
- 3   tsp. olive oil, divided
- 2   Tbsp. butter

1. Flatten chicken to ¼-in. thickness. In a shallow dish, combine the egg substitute, 2 Tbsp. wine, 2 Tbsp. lemon juice, garlic and hot pepper sauce. In another shallow dish, combine the flour, Parmesan cheese, parsley and salt. Coat chicken with flour mixture, dip in egg substitute mixture, then coat again with flour mixture.
2. In a large nonstick skillet, brown 4 chicken breast halves in 1½ tsp. oil for 3-5 minutes on each side or until juices run clear. Remove and keep warm. Drain pan drippings. Repeat with remaining chicken and oil. Remove and keep warm.
3. In the same pan, melt butter. Add the remaining wine and lemon juice. Bring to a boil. Boil, uncovered, until sauce is reduced by a fourth. Drizzle over chicken.
1 CHICKEN BREAST HALF: 232 cal., 9g fat (4g sat. fat), 75mg chol., 346mg sod., 8g carb. (1g sugars, 0 fiber), 27g pro. **DIABETIC EXCHANGES:** 3 lean meat, 1 fat, ½ starch.

SEASONED TACO MEAT

I work at a restaurant, and that is where I stumbled upon this recipe for classic taco meat—no store-bought packet required! Everyone in town loves the blend of different seasonings, and now the secret's out!
—Denise Mumm, Dixon, IA

Prep: 10 min. • **Cook:** 35 min.
Makes: 6 cups

- 3   lbs. ground beef
- 2   large onions, chopped
- 2   cups water
- 5   Tbsp. chili powder
- 2   tsp. salt
- 1   tsp. ground cumin
- ¾   tsp. garlic powder
- ¼   to ½ tsp. crushed red pepper flakes

In a large cast-iron skillet or Dutch oven, cook beef and onion over medium heat until the meat is no longer pink; drain. Add the water and seasonings. Bring to a boil. Reduce heat; simmer, uncovered, until water is evaporated, about 15 minutes. Fill tacos or enchiladas, or use meat to top pizza or baked potatoes.

¼ CUP: 113 cal., 7g fat (3g sat. fat), 35mg chol., 277mg sod., 2g carb. (1g sugars, 1g fiber), 10g pro.

**1 FAVORITE
5 WAYS**
Taco Meat

1

🕐

LAYERED TACO SALAD

I invented this taco salad to satisfy my kids' taco cravings. This recipe calls for ground beef, but it's equally good when topped with seasoned ground turkey or chicken.
—*Betty Nickels, Tampa, FL*

- -

Takes: 15 min. • **Makes:** 6 servings

- 1 **cup salsa**
- 1 **Tbsp. lime juice**
- 6 **oz. baked tortilla chips
  (about 70 chips)**
- 12 **cups chopped iceberg lettuce**
- 6 **plum tomatoes, seeded and chopped**
- 1 **can (15 oz.) black beans,
  rinsed and drained**
- 1½ **cups shredded reduced-fat
  Mexican cheese blend**
- 1 **large sweet yellow or red
  pepper, thinly sliced**
- 2 **cups seasoned taco meat,
  heated through**
- 1 **medium red onion, thinly sliced**
- ⅓ **cup fat-free sour cream**

In a small bowl, mix salsa and lime juice. Arrange tortilla chips on a serving platter; layer with lettuce, tomatoes, beans, cheese, yellow pepper, taco meat, onion, salsa mixture and sour cream. Serve immediately.

1 SERVING: 442 cal., 14g fat (6g sat. fat), 69mg chol., 925mg sod., 52g carb. (9g sugars, 7g fiber), 31g pro.

> **TEST KITCHEN TIP**
> To make this salad even healthier, use spinach or lettuce as a base instead of tortilla chips. Add more veggies and skip or reduce the cheese and sour cream.

BEEF NACHO PIE

I like to spend time in my garden, so I look for recipes that don't require hours in the kitchen. This southwestern pie is quick and makes a tasty meal with a garden-fresh salad.
—*Doris Gill, Sargent, NE*

Prep: 20 min. • **Bake:** 20 min.
Makes: 8 servings

- 2 cups seasoned taco meat
- 1 can (8 oz.) tomato sauce
- 1 tube (8 oz.) refrigerated crescent rolls
- 1½ cups crushed nacho-flavored tortilla chips, divided
- 1 cup sour cream
- 1 cup shredded Mexican cheese blend

1. In a large skillet, combine seasoned taco meat and tomato sauce over medium heat. Bring to a boil. Reduce heat; simmer, uncovered, for 5 minutes.
2. Meanwhile, separate crescent dough into 8 triangles; place in a greased 9-in. pie plate with points toward the center. Press onto the bottom and up the sides to form a crust; seal perforations.
3. Sprinkle 1 cup chips over crust. Top with meat mixture. Carefully spread sour cream over meat mixture. Sprinkle with cheese and remaining chips. Bake at 350° 20-25 minutes until cheese is melted and crust is golden brown. Let stand for 5 minutes before cutting.
1 PIECE: 391 cal., 25g fat (9g sat. fat), 55mg chol., 765mg sod., 24g carb. (5g sugars, 1g fiber), 17g pro.

TATER TOT-CHOS

Playing with food is loads of fun when you have Tater Tots and taco toppings. Let kids build their own for smiles all around.
—*Eleanor Mielke, Mitchell, SD*

Takes: 20 min. • **Makes:** 6 servings

- 4 cups frozen miniature Tater Tots
- 2 cups seasoned taco meat, heated through
- ½ cup shredded cheddar cheese
- 2 cups shredded lettuce
- ¼ cup sliced ripe olives, optional
- ¼ cup taco sauce
- ½ cup sour cream

Bake Tater Tots according to package directions. To serve, top Tater Tots with seasoned taco meat, cheese, lettuce and, if desired, olives. Serve with taco sauce and sour cream.
1 SERVING: 375 cal., 23g fat (9g sat. fat), 70mg chol., 828mg sod., 27g carb. (4g sugars, 2g fiber), 18g pro.

MEXICAN TACO BAKE

This casserole makes a delicious change of pace from ordinary pasta casseroles. The corkscrew noodles? They make it fun!
—*Joy Smith, Bigfork, MT*

Prep: 10 min. • **Bake:** 30 min.
Makes: 6 servings

- 2 cups seasoned taco meat
- 1 can (15 oz.) tomato sauce
- ¼ cup chopped green pepper
- 1 tsp. garlic powder
- 1 tsp. dried oregano
- 8 oz. uncooked spiral pasta, cooked and drained
- 1 cup shredded cheddar cheese, divided
- ½ cup sour cream

1. In a large skillet, combine seasoned taco meat and tomato sauce over medium heat. Bring to a boil. Reduce heat; simmer, uncovered, for 5 minutes.
2. Meanwhile, combine the pasta, ½ cup cheese and sour cream. Spoon into a greased 2-qt. baking dish. Top with meat mixture and remaining cheese. Bake, uncovered, at 350° for 30 minutes or until heated through.
1 SERVING: 434 cal., 20g fat (9g sat. fat), 70mg chol., 1034mg sod., 39g carb. (3g sugars, 3g fiber), 25g pro.

CHEDDAR BEEF ENCHILADAS

I created these enchiladas to satisfy several picky eaters in our house. They were an instant hit and are now requested at least once a week. I especially like that we can enjoy this meal twice by freezing half for a busy day.
—*Stacy Cizek, Conrad, IA*

Prep: 15 min. • **Bake:** 20 min.
Makes: 2 casseroles (3 servings each)

- 2 cups seasoned taco meat, heated through
- 2 cups cooked rice
- 1 can (16 oz.) refried beans
- 2 cups shredded cheddar cheese, divided
- 12 flour tortillas (8 in.), warmed
- 1 jar (16 oz.) salsa
- 1 can (10¾ oz.) condensed cream of chicken soup, undiluted

1. In a large bowl, combine taco meat and rice. Spread about 2 Tbsp. refried beans, ¼ cup beef mixture and 1 Tbsp. cheese down the center of each tortilla; roll up. Place seam side down in 2 greased 13x9-in. baking dishes.
2. Combine salsa and soup; pour down the center of enchiladas. Sprinkle with remaining cheddar cheese.
3. Bake 1 casserole, uncovered, at 350° for 20-25 minutes or until heated through and cheese is melted. Cover and freeze remaining casserole up to 3 months.
FREEZE OPTION: Thaw in the refrigerator overnight. Cover and bake at 350° for 30 minutes. Uncover; bake 5-10 minutes longer or until heated through and cheese is melted.
2 ENCHILADAS: 840 cal., 33g fat (14g sat. fat), 88mg chol., 2242mg sod., 95g carb. (4g sugars, 7g fiber), 37g pro.

Casserole Entrees

It's time to cozy up to casseroles. From signature layered dishes passed down from Grandma to fun new twists on old faves, these recipes are the ones our readers love to make and share.

ITALIAN PASTA BAKE

I make this whenever I need to bring a dish to pass. Fresh sliced tomatoes add a nice touch that you often don't find in typical meat, pasta and tomato casseroles.
—*Karla Johnson, East Helena, MT*

- -

Prep: 40 min. • **Bake:** 25 min.
Makes: 8 servings

2	lbs. ground beef
1	large onion, chopped
2	garlic cloves, minced
1	jar (24 oz.) spaghetti sauce
1	can (14½ oz.) diced tomatoes, undrained
1	can (4 oz.) mushroom stems and pieces, drained
1	tsp. Italian seasoning
3	cups uncooked medium pasta shells
3	plum tomatoes, sliced
¾	cup shredded provolone cheese
¾	cup shredded part-skim mozzarella cheese

1. In a large skillet, cook beef and onion over medium heat until no longer pink. Add garlic; cook 1 minute longer. Drain. Stir in spaghetti sauce, diced tomatoes, mushrooms and Italian seasoning. Bring to a boil. Reduce the heat; simmer, uncovered, 20 minutes.
2. Meanwhile, preheat oven to 350°. Cook pasta according to package directions; drain. Add to beef mixture and gently stir in sliced plum tomatoes.
3. Transfer to an ungreased 13x9-in. baking dish. Sprinkle with cheeses. Bake until bubbly and heated through, 25-30 minutes.
1½ CUPS: 489 cal., 20g fat (8g sat. fat), 80mg chol., 702mg sod., 45g carb. (10g sugars, 5g fiber), 32g pro.

TEST KITCHEN TIP
The best way to cut through the skin of a tomato is with a serrated, not straight-edged, knife. Cut a tomato vertically, from stem end to blossom end, for slices that will be less juicy and hold their shape better.

QUICK TATER TOTS BAKE

I make this dish when I need to get supper on the table and time is tight. If we have unexpected company, I just double the ingredients and use a 13x9-in. pan. I call it my Please Stay Casserole!
—*Jean Ferguson, Elverta, CA*

- -

Prep: 15 min. • **Bake:** 30 min
Makes: 4 servings

- ¾ to 1 lb. ground beef or turkey
- 1 small onion, chopped
  Salt and pepper to taste
- 1 pkg. (16 oz.) frozen Tater Tots potatoes
- 1 can (10¾ oz.) condensed cream of mushroom soup, undiluted
- ⅔ cup 2% milk or water
- 1 cup shredded cheddar cheese

1. Preheat oven to 350°. In a large skillet, cook beef and onion over medium heat until meat is no longer pink; drain. Season with salt and pepper.
2. Transfer to a greased 2-qt. baking dish. Top with potatoes. Combine soup and milk; pour over potatoes. Sprinkle with cheese. Bake, uncovered, 30-40 minutes or until heated through.
1½ CUPS: 570 cal., 35g fat (12g sat. fat), 87mg chol., 1357mg sod., 37g carb. (5g sugars, 0g fiber), 26g pro.

TLC (THANKSGIVING LEFTOVER CASSEROLE)

Turkey, stuffing and veggies come together into a fabulous casserole made from leftovers. There's comfort in every bite.
—*Barbara Lento, Houston, PA*

- -

Prep: 20 min. + standing • **Bake:** 65 min.
Makes: 8 servings

- 4 cups seasoned stuffing cubes
- 4 cups cubed cooked turkey
- 2 celery ribs, finely chopped
- 1 cup frozen peas
- 1 cup fresh or frozen cranberries
- ½ cup chopped sweet onion
- ¼ cup all-purpose flour
- 4 large eggs
- 3 cups 2% milk
- 1 can (8¼ oz.) cream-style corn
- ½ tsp. salt
- ½ tsp. pepper
- 2 Tbsp. butter
- ⅓ cup coarsely chopped pecans

1. Preheat oven to 350°. Layer the first 6 ingredients in a greased 13x9-in. baking dish. In a large bowl, whisk flour, eggs and milk until smooth. Add corn, salt and pepper; mix well. Pour over top; let stand 15 minutes. Dot with butter and sprinkle with pecans.
2. Cover and bake 35 minutes. Uncover and bake 30-35 minutes or until a knife inserted in the center comes out clean.
1½ CUPS: 415 cal., 15g fat (5g sat. fat), 173mg chol., 768mg sod., 38g carb. (9g sugars, 4g fiber), 32g pro. **DIABETIC EXCHANGES:** 3 lean meat, 2½ starch, 1½ fat.

CHEESY FIESTA BEEF CASSEROLE

I've tweaked this recipe over the years to get it just right. The result is a delicious and quick weeknight meal. Feel free to spice it up with jalapenos, if you prefer a little heat.
—*Joan Hallford, North Richland Hills, TX*

- -

Prep: 25 min. • **Cook:** 15 min.
Makes: 8 servings

- 1 lb. ground beef
- 1 medium onion, chopped
- 1 can (15 oz.) black beans, rinsed and drained
- 1 cup picante sauce
- ½ tsp. chili powder
- 1 can (10½ oz.) reduced-fat reduced-sodium condensed cream of chicken soup, undiluted
- 1 can (10 oz.) diced tomatoes and green chiles, undrained
- 1 can (4 oz.) chopped green chiles
- 1 pkg. (9¾ oz.) nacho-flavored tortilla chips or plain tortilla chips, crushed
- 1 cup shredded sharp cheddar cheese
- 1 cup shredded Monterey Jack cheese
  Optional: Cubed avocado and sour cream

1. In a large skillet, cook beef and onion over medium heat until the beef is no longer pink, 6-8 minutes, breaking up beef into crumbles; drain. Stir in the beans, picante sauce and chili powder.

2. In a bowl, combine soup, tomatoes and green chiles. In a lightly greased 2½-qt. baking dish, layer half the chips, beef mixture, soup mixture and cheeses. Repeat layers.

3. Microwave on medium-high, uncovered, until heated through and cheese is melted, about 12 minutes. If desired, top with avocado and sour cream.

1¼ CUPS: 477 cal., 26g fat (9g sat. fat), 63mg chol., 1119mg sod., 37g carb. (4g sugars, 5g fiber), 23g pro.

SIX-LAYER DINNER

I originally came across a five-layer version of this dish at a university extension program. I increased the ground beef and added the celery, which pleased my family's palates.
—*Charlotte McDaniel, Williamsville, IL*

- -

Prep: 5 min. • **Cook:** 1 hour 20 min.
Makes: 6 servings

- 1½ lbs. ground beef
- 2 medium onions, thinly sliced
- 3 medium potatoes, peeled and thinly sliced
- 1 large green pepper, chopped
- 1½ tsp. salt
- ½ tsp. pepper
- 2 celery ribs, chopped
- 1 can (14½ oz.) stewed tomatoes
- ¼ tsp. dried basil

1. In a Dutch oven, cook beef over medium heat until no longer pink; drain. Layer beef with onions, potatoes and green pepper, seasoning each layer lightly with salt and pepper. Top with celery, tomatoes and basil.

2. Bring to a boil. Reduce the heat; cover and simmer until the vegetables are tender, 1 hour.

1 SERVING: 330 cal., 13g fat (5g sat. fat), 70mg chol., 795mg sod., 29g carb. (7g sugars, 2g fiber), 24g pro.

JOAN HALLFORD
North Richland Hills, TX

SOUTHWESTERN TURKEY BAKE

I make this as a sneaky way to get my nieces (and husband) to eat their vegetables. The creamy entree will fill you up fast.
—*Crystal Kolady, Henrietta, NY*

- -

Prep: 20 min. • **Bake:** 25 min.
Makes: 12 servings

- 2 **large onions, chopped**
- 2 **jalapeno peppers, seeded and chopped**
- 2 **Tbsp. butter**
- 6 **cups cubed cooked turkey**
- 2 **cans (10¾ oz. each) condensed cream of chicken soup, undiluted**
- 2 **cups sour cream**
- 1 **pkg. (10 oz.) frozen chopped spinach, thawed and squeezed dry**
- 2 **cups shredded Monterey Jack cheese**
- 1 **pkg. (9¾ oz.) nacho-flavored tortilla chips, crushed**
- 4 **green onions, sliced**

1. Preheat oven to 350°. In a Dutch oven, saute onions and jalapenos in butter until tender. Stir in turkey, soup, sour cream and spinach. In a greased 13x9-in. baking dish, layer half the turkey mixture, cheese and tortilla chips. Repeat layers.

2. Bake, uncovered, 25-30 minutes or until bubbly. Let stand 5 minutes before serving. Sprinkle with green onions.

NOTE: Wear disposable gloves when cutting hot peppers; the oils can burn skin. Avoid touching your face.

1 PIECE: 464 cal., 28g fat (12g sat. fat), 106mg chol., 773mg sod., 23g carb. (3g sugars, 3g fiber), 30g pro.

GERMAN SCHNITZEL & POTATOES WITH GORGONZOLA CREAM

I lived in Germany for five years and developed a fondness for traditional schnitzel. It's a labor of love, so I came up with this easy, clever way to make it in a slow cooker.
—*Beth Taylor, Pleasant Grove, UT*

Prep: 20 min. • **Cook:** 4 hours
Makes: 4 servings

- 1 pork tenderloin (1 lb.)
- 1 cup dry bread crumbs
- 2 lbs. medium Yukon Gold potatoes, peeled and cut into ¼-in. slices
- 2 cups heavy whipping cream
- ⅔ cup crumbled Gorgonzola cheese
- 1 tsp. salt
- ¼ cup minced fresh Italian parsley
  Lemon wedges

1. Cut tenderloin into 12 slices. Pound with a meat mallet to ¼-in. thickness. Place 4 slices in a 3- or 4-qt. slow cooker. Layer with ¼ cup bread crumbs and a third of the potatoes.

Repeat the layers twice; top with remaining bread crumbs.

2. In a small bowl, combine cream, Gorgonzola and salt. Pour over pork mixture; cook on low, covered, until meat and potatoes are tender, 4-6 hours. Sprinkle with parsley; serve with lemon wedges.

3 SLICES PORK WITH 1 CUP POTATO MIXTURE: 926 cal., 54g fat (33g sat. fat), 216mg chol., 1132mg sod., 73g carb. (9g sugars, 5g fiber), 38g pro.

> **TEST KITCHEN TIP**
> Austrians are often credited with inventing schnitzel, a thin slice of breaded meat that's often fried. It's since been incorporated into many European cuisines. Eliminate the mess of frying by making schnitzel in the slow cooker. Add 1-2 tsp. of your favorite dried herbs to the bread crumbs to customize.

CHURCH SUPPER HOT DISH

This recipe was published in my mom's church cookbook, and now it has made an appearance in my church cookbook, too! Apparently it was too good to miss a generation. I often make this to take to potlucks.

—*Norma Turner, Haslett, MI*

Prep: 40 min. • **Bake:** 30 min.
Makes: 8 servings

- 1 lb. ground beef
- 2 cups sliced peeled potatoes
- 2 cups finely chopped celery
- ¾ cup finely chopped carrots
- ¼ cup finely chopped green pepper
- ¼ cup finely chopped onion
- 2 Tbsp. butter
- 1 cup water
- 2 cans (10¾ oz. each) condensed cream of mushroom soup, undiluted
- 1 can (5 oz.) chow mein noodles, divided
- 1 cup shredded cheddar cheese

1. Preheat oven to 350°. In a large skillet, cook beef over medium heat until no longer pink; drain and set aside.
2. In same skillet, saute potatoes, celery, carrots, green pepper and onion in butter 5 minutes. Add the water; cover and simmer 10 minutes or until vegetables are tender. Stir in soup and cooked ground beef until blended.
3. Sprinkle half the chow mein noodles into a greased shallow 2-qt. baking dish. Spoon meat mixture over noodles. Cover and bake 20 minutes. Top with cheese and remaining noodles. Bake, uncovered, 10 minutes longer or until heated through.
1 SERVING: 339 cal., 20g fat (9g sat. fat), 53mg chol., 537mg sod., 25g carb. (2g sugars, 3g fiber), 16g pro.

5i

WEEKNIGHT LASAGNA

My husband and I love lasagna, but it can be time-consuming to build all the layers, and we always end up with too much. Using frozen ravioli solves everything.

—*Pamela Nicholson, Festus, MO*

Prep: 15 min. • **Bake:** 45 min.
Makes: 6 servings

- 1 jar (24 oz.) pasta sauce
- 1 pkg. (25 oz.) frozen meat or cheese ravioli
- 1½ cups shredded part-skim mozzarella cheese
- 3 cups fresh baby spinach

1. Preheat oven to 350°. In a small saucepan, heat sauce 5-7 minutes over medium heat or just until simmering, stirring occasionally.
2. Spread ½ cup pasta sauce into a greased 11x7-in. baking dish. Layer with half the ravioli, 1½ cups spinach, ½ cup cheese and half the remaining sauce; repeat layers. Sprinkle with remaining cheese.
3. Bake, uncovered, 45-50 minutes or until edges are bubbly and cheese is melted. Let stand 5 minutes before serving.
1 CUP: 344 cal., 10g fat (5g sat. fat), 26mg chol., 850mg sod., 45g carb. (10g sugars, 5g fiber), 17g pro. **DIABETIC EXCHANGES:** 3 starch, 2 medium-fat meat.

CHICKEN CHILES RELLENOS CASSEROLE

I took my husband's love for Mexican food and his love for casseroles and combined the two for one amazing dish. This cornbread-topped chicken with poblanos and chiles satisfies our craving for dinner at a Mexican restaurant.
—Erica Ingram, Lakewood, OH

Prep: 20 min. • **Bake:** 35 min. + standing
Makes: 8 servings

- 2 Tbsp. butter
- 2 poblano peppers, seeded and coarsely chopped
- 1 small onion, finely chopped
- 2 Tbsp. all-purpose flour
- 1 tsp. ground cumin
- 1 tsp. smoked paprika
- ¼ tsp. salt
- ⅔ cup 2% milk
- 1 pkg. (8 oz.) cream cheese, cubed
- 2 cups shredded pepper jack cheese
- 2 cups coarsely shredded rotisserie chicken
- 1 can (4 oz.) chopped green chiles
- 2 pkg. (8½ oz. each) cornbread/muffin mix

1. Preheat oven to 350°. In a large skillet, heat butter over medium-high heat. Add peppers and onion; cook and stir until peppers are tender, 4-6 minutes.
2. Stir in flour and seasonings until blended; gradually stir in milk. Bring to a boil, stirring constantly; cook and stir until thickened, about 1 minute. Stir in cream cheese until blended. Add pepper jack, chicken and green chiles; heat through, stirring to combine. Transfer to a greased 11x7-in. baking dish.
3. Prepare cornbread batter according to package directions. Spread over chicken mixture. Bake, uncovered, until golden brown and a toothpick inserted in topping comes out clean, 35-40 minutes. Let stand 10 minutes before serving.
1 SERVING: 610 cal., 34g fat (16g sat. fat), 151mg chol., 987mg sod., 51g carb. (16g sugars, 5g fiber), 27g pro.

TORTILLA PIE

My husband and I enjoy this southwestern take on lasagna because it's not as dense or heavy as traditional layered dishes made with pasta. Our two daughters enjoy the mild flavor.
—Lisa King, Caledonia, MI

Takes: 30 min. • **Makes:** 4 servings

- ½ lb. lean ground beef (90% lean)
- ½ cup chopped onion
- 2 garlic cloves, minced
- 1 tsp. chili powder
- ½ tsp. ground cumin
- 1 can (14½ oz.) Mexican diced tomatoes, drained
- ¾ cup reduced-fat ricotta cheese
- ¼ cup shredded part-skim mozzarella cheese
- 3 Tbsp. minced fresh cilantro, divided
- 4 whole wheat tortillas (8 in.)
- ½ cup shredded cheddar cheese

1. Preheat oven to 400°. In a large skillet, cook and crumble beef with onion and garlic over medium heat until meat is no longer pink, 4-6 minutes. Stir in the spices and tomatoes. Bring to a boil; remove from heat. In a small bowl, mix ricotta cheese, mozzarella cheese and 2 Tbsp. cilantro.
2. Place 1 tortilla in a 9-in. round baking pan coated with cooking spray. Layer with half the meat sauce, 1 tortilla, ricotta mixture, another tortilla and remaining meat sauce. Top with the remaining tortilla; sprinkle with cheddar cheese and remaining cilantro.
3. Bake, covered, until heated through,
1 SERVING: 356 cal., 14g fat (6g sat. fat), 65mg chol., 574mg sod., 32g carb. (7g sugars, 5g fiber), 25g pro. **DIABETIC EXCHANGES:** 3 medium-fat meat, 2 starch.

MEATBALLS SAUSAGE DINNER

One day I was having trouble deciding what to make for dinner, so I combined a mix of items I had in my refrigerator and freezer. To my surprise, everyone loved it!
—*Elizabeth Martz, Pleasant Gap, PA*

Prep: 25 min. • **Bake:** 40 min.
Makes: 8 servings

- 3 cups frozen broccoli florets, thawed
- 2 medium potatoes, peeled and cubed
- 3 medium carrots, sliced
- 1 medium onion, chopped
- 1 lb. smoked kielbasa or Polish sausage, halved and cut into 1-in. pieces
- ½ lb. lean ground beef
- 1 can (14½ oz.) beef broth
  Lemon-pepper seasoning to taste

Preheat oven to 350°. Combine broccoli, potatoes, carrots and onion. Transfer to a greased 13x9-in. baking dish. Sprinkle with sausage. Shape beef into 1-in. balls; arrange over top. Pour beef broth over casserole; sprinkle with lemon-pepper seasoning. Bake, uncovered, until meatballs are no longer pink, about 40 minutes.

Note: Prepare a brownie mix and pop it into the oven when the Meatball Sausage Dinner is done. Dessert will bake while you're eating. Serve the brownies with vanilla ice cream.

1 SERVING: 289 cal., 19g fat (7g sat. fat), 55mg chol., 652mg sod., 14g carb. (4g sugars, 2g fiber), 14g pro.

READER REVIEW

"I didn't have ground beef, so instead I used beef stew meat cut into bite-sized pieces. This meal was fantastic! It was easy preparation, baked itself, and all we had to do was dish it out and eat it. It was a huge hit. In fact, my husband went back for thirds. Needless to say there wasn't much in the way of leftovers!"

SUZISUZUKI, TASTEOFHOME.COM

SWEET POTATO ENCHILADA STACK

Mexican flavors abound in this enchilada stack. It's jam-packed with black beans and sweet potato and topped with plenty of cheese.
—*Taste of Home Test Kitchen*

Prep: 20 min. • **Bake:** 20 min.
Makes: 6 servings

- 1 large sweet potato, peeled and cut into ½-in. cubes
- 1 Tbsp. water
- 1 lb. ground beef
- 1 medium onion, chopped
- 1 can (15 oz.) black beans, rinsed and drained
- 1 can (10 oz.) enchilada sauce
- 2 tsp. chili powder
- ½ tsp. dried oregano
- ½ tsp. ground cumin
- 3 flour tortillas (8 in.)
- 2 cups shredded cheddar cheese

1. In a large microwave-safe bowl, combine sweet potato and water. Cover and microwave on high for 4-5 minutes or until potato is almost tender.

2. Meanwhile, in a large skillet, cook beef and onion over medium heat until the meat is no longer pink; drain. Stir in the beans, enchilada sauce, chili powder, oregano, cumin and sweet potato; heat through.

3. Place a flour tortilla in a greased 9-in. deep-dish pie plate; layer with a third of the beef mixture and shredded cheese. Repeat layers twice. Bake at 400° for 20-25 minutes or until bubbly.

1 PIECE: 457 cal., 22g fat (12g sat. fat), 87mg chol., 804mg sod., 39g carb. (6g sugars, 6g fiber), 29g pro.

PORK SPANISH RICE

My family wasn't fond of pork roast until I used it in this yummy casserole. It's a keeper!
—*Betty Unrau, MacGregor, MB*

- -

Prep: 20 min. • **Bake:** 20 min.
Makes: 4 servings

- 1 medium green pepper, chopped
- 1 small onion, chopped
- 2 Tbsp. butter
- 1 can (14½ oz.) diced tomatoes, drained
- 1 cup chicken broth
- ½ tsp. salt
- ¼ tsp. pepper
- 1¾ cups cubed cooked pork
- 1 cup uncooked instant rice
  Optional: Lime wedges and minced cilantro

1. In a large skillet, saute the green pepper and onion in butter until tender. Stir in diced tomatoes, broth, salt and pepper. Bring to a boil; stir in pork and rice.

2. Transfer to a greased 2-qt. baking dish. Cover and bake at 350° until rice is tender and liquid is absorbed, 20-25 minutes. Stir before serving. If desired, serve with lime wedges and top with minced cilantro.

1 CUP: 304 cal., 12g fat (6g sat. fat), 71mg chol., 756mg sod., 29g carb. (5g sugars, 3g fiber), 21g pro. **DIABETIC EXCHANGES:** 3 lean meat, 2 starch, 1½ fat.

SAUSAGE & SPINACH CRESCENT BAKE

A classic Florentine casserole boasts spinach and cheese. I make a comforting version with mozzarella, mushrooms and sausage. It's gone in the blink of an eye at our house.
—*Noelle Carle, Bristow, OK*

- -

Prep: 20 min. • **Bake:** 25 min. + standing
Makes: 8 servings

- 1 lb. bulk pork sausage
- 2 cups sliced fresh mushrooms
- 1 medium onion, chopped
- 2 garlic cloves, minced
- 1 pkg. (10 oz.) frozen chopped spinach, thawed and squeezed dry
- 1 cup shredded part-skim mozzarella cheese
- 4 oz. cream cheese, softened
- 1 cup half-and-half cream
- 1 tube (8 oz.) refrigerated crescent rolls

1. Preheat oven to 350°. In a large skillet, cook sausage, mushrooms, onion and garlic over medium heat until sausage is no longer pink, breaking up sausage into crumbles, 6-8 minutes. Drain.

2. Add spinach, mozzarella cheese, cream cheese and cream to sausage mixture; cook and stir until blended. Transfer to a greased 13x9-in. baking dish.

3. Unroll crescent dough into 1 long rectangle; press perforations to seal. Place over sausage mixture. Bake, covered, 10 minutes. Bake, uncovered, until golden brown and filling is bubbly, 12-15 minutes longer. Let stand for 5-10 minutes before cutting.

1 PIECE: 401 cal., 29g fat (12g sat. fat), 70mg chol., 758mg sod., 18g carb. (5g sugars, 1g fiber), 15g pro.

MODERN TUNA CASSEROLE

I loved tuna casserole growing up and found myself craving it as an adult. However, the high fat and salt content in the original recipe were a turnoff, and it just didn't taste as good as I remembered. I reconfigured the recipe to include more vegetables and reduced-sodium broth—the result was delicious!
—*Rebecca Blanton, St. Helena, CA*

Prep: 20 min. • **Cook:** 20 min.
Makes: 6 servings

- 3 Tbsp. butter, divided
- 4 medium carrots, chopped
- 1 medium onion, chopped
- 1 medium sweet red pepper, chopped
- 1 cup sliced baby portobello mushrooms
- 2 cans (5 oz. each) albacore white tuna in water, drained and flaked
- 2 cups fresh baby spinach
- 1 cup frozen peas
- 3 cups uncooked spiral pasta
- 1 Tbsp. all-purpose flour
- ⅔ cup reduced-sodium chicken broth
- ⅓ cup half-and-half cream
- ½ cup shredded Parmesan cheese
- ¾ tsp. salt
- ¼ tsp. pepper

1. In a large skillet, heat 1 Tbsp. butter over medium-high heat. Add carrots, onion, red pepper and mushrooms. Cook and stir until tender, 8-10 minutes. Add tuna, spinach and peas; cook until the spinach is just wilted, 2-3 minutes.

2. Meanwhile, cook pasta according to the package directions for al dente. Drain pasta, reserving 1 cup pasta water. In a large bowl, place pasta and tuna mixture; toss to combine. Wipe skillet clean.

3. In the same skillet, melt remaining butter over medium heat. Stir in flour until smooth; gradually whisk in broth and cream. Bring to a boil, stirring constantly; cook and stir until thickened, adding reserved pasta water if needed, 1-2 minutes. Stir in cheese, salt and pepper. Pour over pasta; toss to coat.

1¾ CUPS: 372 cal., 11g fat (6g sat. fat), 47mg chol., 767mg sod., 44g carb. (7g sugars, 5g fiber), 23g pro. **DIABETIC EXCHANGES:** 3 lean meat, 2½ starch, 1½ fat, 1 vegetable.

CHICKEN FLORENTINE CASSEROLE

Creamy and comforting, this chicken and spinach bake is sure to be a hit at dinnertime. The toasty bread crumb topping delivers a bit of a crunch.
—*Dori Jackson, Gulf Breeze, FL*

Prep: 20 min. • **Bake:** 40 min.
Makes: 6 servings

- 2 cups uncooked elbow macaroni
- 3 cups shredded cooked chicken
- 1 can (10¾ oz.) condensed cream of mushroom soup, undiluted
- 2 cups shredded Swiss cheese
- 1 pkg. (10 oz.) frozen creamed spinach, thawed
- ½ cup mayonnaise
- ¼ cup loosely packed minced fresh basil
- 1 tsp. garlic powder
- ½ tsp. dried thyme
- ½ tsp. pepper
- ½ cup seasoned bread crumbs
- 2 Tbsp. butter, melted

1. Preheat oven to 350°. Cook macaroni according to package directions.

2. Meanwhile, in a large bowl, combine chicken, soup, cheese, spinach, mayonnaise, basil, garlic powder, thyme and pepper.

3. Drain macaroni; gently stir into chicken mixture. Transfer to an ungreased 2½-qt. baking dish. Toss bread crumbs and butter; sprinkle over casserole.

4. Bake, uncovered, until bubbly, 40-45 minutes.

1½ CUPS: 539 cal., 36g fat (13g sat. fat), 111mg chol., 1006mg sod., 17g carb. (4g sugars, 2g fiber), 36g pro.

DOUBLE-CRUST PIZZA CASSEROLE

After my husband and I got married, this biscuit pizza solved the what's-for-dinner problem. As our family grew, I just made bigger and bigger batches. It never disappoints!
—*Pat Crane, Pine City, NY*

Prep: 20 min. • **Bake:** 20 min.
Makes: 12 servings

- 2 lbs. lean ground beef (90% lean)
- 2 cans (15 oz. each) pizza sauce, divided
- 2 tsp. dried oregano
- 3 cups biscuit/baking mix
- 1¼ cups 2% milk
- 1 large egg, lightly beaten
- 2 cups shredded part-skim mozzarella cheese
- 1 cup sliced fresh mushrooms
- 1 medium green pepper, chopped
- 1 medium onion, chopped
- ¼ cup grated Parmesan cheese
- 1 plum tomato, chopped

1. Preheat oven to 400°. In a large skillet, cook beef over medium heat until no longer pink, 8-10 minutes, breaking into crumbles; drain. Stir in 1 can pizza sauce and oregano. Bring to a boil. Reduce heat; simmer, uncovered, until slightly thickened, 5-6 minutes, occasionally. Remove from heat.

2. In a large bowl, combine biscuit mix, milk and egg; stir just until moistened. Spread half the batter onto bottom of a greased 13x9-in. baking pan. Spread with remaining pizza sauce. Top with mozzarella cheese, mushrooms, pepper, onion and beef mixture. Spoon remaining batter over top; sprinkle with Parmesan cheese.

3. Bake, uncovered, until golden brown, 20-25 minutes. Sprinkle with tomato. Let stand 5 minutes before serving.

1 PIECE: 369 cal., 16g fat (7 g sat. fat), 78mg chol., 710mg sod., 30g carb. (4g sugars, 3g fiber), 26g pro.

SLOPPY JOE UNDER A BUN

I usually keep a can of sloppy joe sauce in the pantry because our kids love sloppy joes. But I don't always have buns on hand. With this fun casserole, we can enjoy the flavor they adore any time.
—Trish Bloom, Ray, MI

- -

Prep: 15 min. • **Bake:** 25 min.
Makes: 8 servings

- 1½ lbs. ground beef
- 1 can (15½ oz.) sloppy joe sauce
- 2 cups shredded cheddar cheese
- 2 cups biscuit/baking mix
- 2 large eggs, lightly beaten
- 1 cup 2% milk
- 1 Tbsp. sesame seeds

1. In a large skillet, cook beef over medium heat until no longer pink; drain. Stir in sloppy joe sauce. Transfer to a lightly greased 13x9-in. baking dish; sprinkle with cheese.

2. In a large bowl, combine the biscuit mix, eggs and milk just until blended. Pour over cheese; sprinkle with sesame seeds. Bake, uncovered, at 400° for 25 minutes or until golden brown.

1 SERVING: 423 cal., 23g fat (12g sat. fat), 129mg chol., 961mg sod., 26g carb. (6g sugars, 1g fiber), 27g pro.

READER REVIEW

"I love this recipe! I've used it for years! It takes the mess out of sloppy joes. I can even hide veggies, like bell peppers, onions and carrots, in the hamburger mix. Great recipe!"

AARDVARKSIS, TASTEOFHOME.COM

HAM & VEGGIE CASSEROLE

I've paired ham with broccoli and cauliflower for years. This comforting casserole is one of my favorite ways to showcase this trio.
—*Sherri Melotik, Oak Creek, WI*

Takes: 30 min. • **Makes:** 4 servings

- 1 pkg. (16 oz.) frozen broccoli florets
- 1 pkg. (16 oz.) frozen cauliflower
- 2 tsp. plus 2 Tbsp. butter, divided
- ¼ cup seasoned bread crumbs
- 2 Tbsp. all-purpose flour
- 1½ cups 2% milk
- ¾ cup shredded sharp cheddar cheese
- ½ cup grated Parmesan cheese
- 1½ cups cubed fully cooked ham (about 8 oz.)
- ¼ tsp. pepper

1. Preheat oven to 425°. Cook broccoli and cauliflower according to package directions; drain.
2. Meanwhile, in a small skillet, melt 2 tsp. butter. Add bread crumbs; cook and stir over medium heat until lightly toasted, 2-3 minutes. Remove from heat.
3. In a large saucepan, melt the remaining butter over medium heat. Stir in flour until smooth; gradually whisk in milk. Bring to a boil, stirring constantly; cook and stir 1-2 minutes or until thickened. Remove from heat; stir in cheeses until blended. Stir in the ham, pepper and vegetables.
4. Transfer to a greased 8-in. square baking dish. Sprinkle with the toasted bread crumbs. Bake, uncovered, until heated through, 10-15 minutes.
1½ CUPS: 420 cal., 23g fat (13g sat. fat), 89mg chol., 1233mg sod., 25g carb. (10g sugars, 6g fiber), 28g pro.

VEGETABLE BEEF CASSEROLE

This easy one-dish recipe has been a family favorite ever since my husband's aunt passed it down to me many years ago. I recommend using whatever vegetables you have on hand. A simple salad is a nice accompaniment.
—*Evangeline Rew, Manassas, VA*

Prep: 20 min. • **Bake:** 1¼ hours + standing
Makes: 6 servings

- 3 medium potatoes, sliced
- 3 carrots, sliced
- 3 celery ribs, sliced
- 2 cups cut fresh or frozen cut green beans
- 1 medium onion, chopped
- 1 lb. lean ground beef (90% lean)
- 1 tsp. dried thyme
- 1 tsp. salt
- 1 tsp. pepper
- 4 medium tomatoes, peeled, seeded and chopped
- 1 cup shredded cheddar cheese

1. In a 3-qt. casserole dish, layer half the potatoes, carrots, celery, green beans and onion. Crumble half the uncooked beef over vegetables. Sprinkle with ½ tsp. each thyme, salt and pepper. Repeat layers.
2. Top with tomatoes. Cover and bake at 400° for 15 minutes. Reduce heat to 350°; bake about 1 hour longer or until vegetables are tender and meat is no longer pink. Sprinkle with cheddar cheese; cover and let stand until cheese is melted.
1 SERVING: 326 cal., 13g fat (6g sat. fat), 66mg chol., 607mg sod., 30g carb. (7g sugars, 6g fiber), 23g pro.

MOM'S MACARONI & CHEESE

The wonderful homemade goodness of this creamy macaroni and cheese makes it a staple side dish in my mother's kitchen—and in mine, too. It has tender noodles and a crowd-pleasing golden crumb topping.
—*Maria Costello, Monroe, NC*

Prep: 30 min. • **Bake:** 30 min.
Makes: 6 servings

- 1½ cups uncooked elbow macaroni
- 5 Tbsp. butter, divided
- 3 Tbsp. all-purpose flour
- ½ tsp. salt
- ¼ tsp. pepper
- 1½ cups whole milk
- 1 cup shredded cheddar cheese
- 2 oz. cubed Velveeta
- 2 Tbsp. dry bread crumbs

1. Cook macaroni according to package directions. Meanwhile, in a saucepan, melt 4 Tbsp. butter over medium heat. Stir in the flour, salt and pepper until smooth. Gradually add the milk. Bring to a boil; cook and stir for 2 minutes or until thickened. Reduce the heat. Add the cheeses, stirring until the cheese is melted. Drain macaroni.
2. Transfer macaroni to a greased 1½-qt. baking dish. Pour cheese sauce over macaroni; mix well. Melt the remaining butter; add the bread crumbs. Sprinkle over the top. Bake, uncovered, at 375° for 30 minutes or until heated through and topping is golden brown.
1 SERVING: 309 cal., 20g fat (13g sat. fat), 60mg chol., 569mg sod., 22g carb. (4g sugars, 1g fiber), 11g pro.

LEMONY CHICKEN & RICE

I couldn't tell you who loves this casserole the most. Because every time I serve it, it gets raves! Occasionally I even get a phone call or email from a friend requesting the recipe, and it's certainly a favorite for my grown children and 15 grandchildren.
—*Maryalice Wood, Langley, BC*

Prep: 15 min. + marinating • **Bake:** 55 min.
Makes: 2 casseroles (4 servings each)

- 2 cups water
- ½ cup reduced-sodium soy sauce
- ¼ cup lemon juice
- ¼ cup olive oil
- 2 garlic cloves, minced
- 2 tsp. ground ginger
- 2 tsp. pepper
- 16 bone-in chicken thighs, skin removed (about 6 lbs.)
- 2 cups uncooked long grain rice
- 4 Tbsp. grated lemon zest, divided
- 2 medium lemons, sliced

1. In a large shallow dish, combine the first 7 ingredients. Add chicken; turn to coat and cover. Refrigerate 4 hours or overnight.
2. Preheat oven to 325°. Spread 1 cup rice into each of 2 greased 13x9-in. baking dishes. Top each with 1 Tbsp. lemon zest, 8 chicken thighs and half the marinade. Top with sliced lemons.
3. Bake casserole, covered, 40 minutes. Bake, uncovered, until a thermometer inserted in chicken reads 170°-175°, 15-20 minutes longer. Sprinkle with remaining lemon zest.
2 CHICKEN THIGHS WITH ¾ CUP RICE MIXTURE: 624 cal., 26g fat (6g sat. fat), 173mg chol., 754mg sod., 41g carb. (1g sugars, 1g fiber), 53g pro.

DEBORAH SMITH
DeWitt, NE

FOLD-OVER TORTILLA BAKE

Here's something a little different to shake up taco night. But don't reserve this zippy dish for a weeknight—it's perfect for potlucks and serving company, too.
—*Deborah Smith, DeWitt, NE*

Prep: 20 min. • **Bake:** 20 min.
Makes: 6 servings

- 1 lb. ground beef
- 1 cup chopped onion
- 2 cans (14½ oz. each) stewed tomatoes
- 1 cup enchilada sauce
- 1 to 2 tsp. ground cumin
- ½ tsp. salt
- ¼ tsp. pepper
- 12 flour or corn tortillas (6 in.)
- 6 oz. cream cheese, softened
- 1 can (4 oz.) chopped green chiles, drained
- 1 cup shredded Monterey Jack cheese
  Minced fresh cilantro, optional

1. In a large skillet, cook ground beef and onion until beef is no longer pink; drain. Stir in the stewed tomatoes, enchilada sauce and seasonings. Bring to a boil. Reduce the heat and simmer, covered, for 5 minutes. Pour half the meat sauce into a 13x9-in. baking dish. Set aside.

2. Wrap the stack of tortillas in foil; warm at 350° for 8-10 minutes. Spread warm tortillas with cream cheese and top with chiles. Fold tortillas in half. Arrange folded tortillas over meat sauce; pour remaining sauce over top.

3. Cover and bake at 350° for 15 minutes. Sprinkle with cheese; bake until the cheese is melted, about 5 minutes longer. If desired, top with cilantro.

2 TORTILLAS: 473 cal., 25g fat (10g sat. fat), 69mg chol., 1138mg sod., 38g carb. (7g sugars, 2g fiber), 27g pro.

WINTER VEGETABLE SHEPHERD'S PIE

We love comfort food during the holidays and in cold weather...but as good as they are, these dishes aren't always healthy. I came up with this healthier take on classic shepherd's pie. Topped with creamy mashed squash, potatoes and carrots, it checks all the boxes.
—*Ann Sheehy, Lawrence, MA*

Prep: 55 min. • **Bake:** 30 min. + standing
Makes: 8 servings

- 3 cups cubed peeled butternut squash (1-in. pieces)
- 1 large potato, peeled and cut into 1-in. cubes (about 2 cups)
- 2 medium carrots, thinly sliced
- 2 cups vegetable broth
- ½ tsp. plus ¾ tsp. salt, divided
- ¾ tsp. pepper, divided
- 2 lbs. ground turkey
- 1 large onion, chopped
- 1 Tbsp. olive oil
- ¾ lb. sliced fresh mushrooms
- 3 garlic cloves, minced
- ½ cup white wine
- 1 tsp. dried thyme
- ¼ cup all-purpose flour
- 2 cups frozen peas (about 8 oz.)

1. Preheat oven to 350°. Place the first 4 ingredients in a large saucepan; bring to a boil. Reduce the heat; simmer, covered, until vegetables are tender, 10-15 minutes. Drain vegetables, reserving broth. Mash vegetables until smooth, stirring in ½ tsp. salt and ¼ tsp. pepper.

2. In 2 batches, cook turkey and onion in a Dutch oven over medium-high heat until turkey is no longer pink, 5-7 minutes, breaking turkey into crumbles. Remove from pan.

3. In same pan, heat oil over medium-high heat; saute mushrooms until tender, 7-9 minutes. Add garlic; cook and stir 1 minute. Add wine, thyme and the remaining salt and pepper; bring to a boil, stirring to remove browned bits from pan. Cook until liquid is evaporated. Stir in the flour until blended; gradually stir in reserved broth. Bring to a boil; cook and stir until thickened. Stir in peas and turkey mixture; heat through.

4. Transfer to a greased 2½-qt. baking dish. Spread filling with mashed vegetables. Bake, uncovered, until the filling is bubbly, 30-35 minutes. Let stand 10 minutes before serving.

1 SERVING: 314 cal., 11g fat (2g sat. fat), 75mg chol., 654mg sod., 29g carb. (6g sugars, 5g fiber), 28g pro. **DIABETIC EXCHANGES:** 3 lean meat, 2 starch.

CHINESE BEEF CASSEROLE

Crispy chow mein noodles top this twist on chop suey. Make a new family favorite!
—*Willie DeWaard, Coralville, IA*

- -

Prep: 15 min. • **Bake:** 45 min.
Makes: 8 servings

- 2 lbs. ground beef
- 1 cup chopped onion
- 1 cup chopped celery
- 2 cans (10¾ oz. each) condensed cream of mushroom soup, undiluted
- 1 can (14 oz.) bean sprouts, undrained
- ¼ cup reduced-sodium soy sauce
- ½ tsp. pepper
- 1 cup uncooked long grain rice
- 1 can (8 oz.) sliced water chestnuts, drained
- 2 cups frozen peas, thawed
- 1 can (5 oz.) chow mein noodles

1. In a large skillet, cook beef, onion and celery over medium heat until meat is no longer pink; drain. Stir in the soup, bean sprouts, soy sauce and pepper. Bring to a boil. Pour into a greased 3-qt. baking dish. Stir in rice and water chestnuts.

2. Cover and bake at 350° for 30 minutes. Uncover; stir in peas and sprinkle with chow mein noodles. Bake 15-20 minutes longer or until heated through.

1 CUP: 461 cal., 18g fat (7g sat. fat), 59mg chol., 1233mg sod., 44g carb. (4g sugars, 5g fiber), 28g pro.

TACO NOODLE DISH

We were housebound during a snowstorm one winter, so I got creative and used ingredients we had on hand to come up with this zesty casserole. Later, I modified it so it has less fat and fewer calories.
—*Judy Munger, Warren, MN*

- -

Takes: 30 min. • **Makes:** 6 servings

- 3 cups uncooked wide egg noodles
- 2 lbs. lean ground turkey
- 1 envelope reduced-sodium taco seasoning
- 1 tsp. onion powder
- 1 tsp. chili powder
- ½ tsp. garlic powder
- 1 can (8 oz.) tomato sauce
- 1 can (4 oz.) chopped green chiles
- ½ cup water
- 1 cup shredded cheddar cheese

TOPPINGS
- 2 cups shredded lettuce
- 2 medium tomatoes, chopped
- ⅓ cup sliced ripe olives
- ½ cup taco sauce
- ½ cup fat-free sour cream

1. Preheat oven to 350°. Cook the noodles according to package directions for al dente and drain.

2. Meanwhile, in a large nonstick skillet, cook and crumble turkey over medium-high heat until no longer pink, 6-8 minutes; drain. Stir in the seasonings, tomato sauce, chiles and water; bring to a boil. Reduce heat; simmer, uncovered, 5 minutes.

3. Spread noodles in a 11x7-in. baking dish coated with cooking spray. Top with turkey mixture and sprinkle with shredded cheese. Bake, uncovered, until cheese is melted, 10-15 minutes.

4. Top the casserole with lettuce, tomatoes, olives and taco sauce. Serve with sour cream.

1 SERVING: 455 cal., 20g fat (7g sat. fat), 140mg chol., 954mg sod., 27g carb. (7g sugars, 3g fiber), 40g pro.

GREEK SPAGHETTI WITH CHICKEN

This Mediterranean-inspired spaghetti makes for a flavorful and satisfying dinner. Featuring chicken, spinach and two types of cheese, it's sure to please.
—*Melanie Dalbec, Inver Grove, MN*

Prep: 25 min. • **Bake:** 25 min.
Makes: 10 servings

- 1 pkg. (16 oz.) spaghetti, broken into 2-in. pieces
- 4 cups cubed cooked chicken breast
- 2 pkg. (10 oz. each) frozen chopped spinach, thawed and squeezed dry
- 2 cans (10¾ oz. each) condensed cream of chicken soup, undiluted
- 1 cup mayonnaise
- 1 cup sour cream
- 3 celery ribs, chopped
- 1 small onion, chopped
- ½ cup chopped green pepper
- 1 jar (2 oz.) diced pimientos, drained
- ½ tsp. lemon-pepper seasoning
- 1 cup shredded Monterey Jack cheese
- ½ cup soft bread crumbs
- ½ cup shredded Parmesan cheese

1. Cook spaghetti according to the package directions; drain. Return spaghetti to the saucepan. Stir in the chicken, spinach, soup, mayonnaise, sour cream, celery, onion, green pepper, pimientos and lemon-pepper.
2. Transfer to a greased 13x9-in. baking dish (dish will be full). Top with Monterey Jack cheese, bread crumbs and Parmesan cheese. Bake, uncovered, at 350° for 25-30 minutes or until heated through.
1⅓ CUPS: 601 cal., 32g fat (10g sat. fat), 85mg chol., 850mg sod., 44g carb. (4g sugars, 4g fiber), 31g pro.

CHICKEN BISCUIT BAKE

Golden biscuits cover this homespun dish laden with chicken, broccoli and cheese. My family requests this all-in-one dinner once a month.
—*Karen Weirick, Bourbon, IN*

Prep: 15 min. • **Bake:** 50 min.
Makes: 8 servings

- 1 can (10¾ oz.) condensed cream of chicken soup, undiluted
- ⅔ cup mayonnaise
- 2 to 3 tsp. Worcestershire sauce
- 4 cups cubed cooked chicken
- 3 cups chopped broccoli, cooked
- 1 medium onion, chopped
- 1 cup shredded cheddar cheese
- 2 tubes (12 oz. each) refrigerated buttermilk biscuits
- 2 large eggs
- ½ cup sour cream
- 2 tsp. celery seed
- 1 tsp. salt

1. In a large mixing bowl, combine the soup, mayonnaise and Worcestershire sauce. Stir in the chicken, broccoli and onion. Transfer to a greased 13x9-in. baking dish. Sprinkle with cheddar cheese. Cover and bake at 375° for 20 minutes.
2. Separate biscuits; cut each in half. Arrange, cut side down, over hot chicken mixture.
3. In a small bowl, combine the remaining ingredients; pour mixture over biscuits. Bake, casserole, uncovered, 28-32 minutes longer or until the biscuits are golden brown and completely baked.
1 SERVING: 527 cal., 31g fat (9g sat. fat), 150mg chol., 1245mg sod., 29g carb. (3g sugars, 3g fiber), 32g pro.

Slow-Cooker & Instant Pot® Dinners

Juggling a hectic schedule or simply trying to serve home-cooked meals regularly without losing your mind? Don't sweat it! Rely on the unbeatable magic of today's two hottest kitchen appliances—slow cookers and electric pressure cookers—to whip up hearty dinners that will earn their spot in your recipe collection as family favorites!

TERIYAKI BEEF ROAST

My dad and I created this pot roast with a hint of Japanese flair. It will make taste buds dance. Try it for a family dinner or to serve company.
—*Mary Flurkey, Golden, CO*

- -

Prep: 30 min. • **Cook:** 7 hours
Makes: 6 servings

4	medium potatoes, peeled and quartered
1½	cups fresh baby carrots
1	medium green pepper, seeded and cut into ½-in. strips
1	medium yellow onion, quartered
¼	cup all-purpose flour
1	boneless beef chuck roast (about 2 lbs.)
2	Tbsp. canola oil
8	oz. medium fresh mushrooms, cut into thick slices
¼	cup packed brown sugar
½	cup teriyaki sauce
2	tsp. ground ginger
1	tsp. beef base
1	tsp. dried oregano
1	tsp. pepper
2	to 3 green onions (green portion only), thinly sliced

1. Place potatoes, carrots, green pepper and onion in a 5- or 6-qt. slow cooker. Rub flour over roast. In a large skillet, heat oil over medium heat; brown roast on all sides. Transfer roast and drippings to slow cooker; arrange the mushrooms around roast and sprinkle roast with brown sugar.
2. Combine teriyaki sauce, ginger, beef base, oregano and pepper in a small bowl. Drizzle sauce slowly over mushrooms and roast.
3. Cook, covered, on low until roast is tender, 7-8 hours. Remove roast and vegetables to a serving platter; top with green onions. If desired, skim fat and thicken cooking juices for gravy; serve with roast.
NOTE: Look for beef base near the broth and bouillon.
1 SERVING: 494 cal., 19g fat (6g sat. fat), 98mg chol., 1024mg sod., 43g carb. (16g sugars, 3g fiber), 35g pro.

TEST KITCHEN TIP
Combine leftover meat and gravy and place on toasted buns for easy roast beef sandwiches.

PRESSURE-COOKER STUFFED PEPPERS

Here's a good-for-you entree that's also a meal-in-one classic. And it comes together in 20 minutes. Add a salad and dinner's done!
—*Michelle Gurnsey, Lincoln, NE*

Prep: 15 min. • **Cook:** 5 min. + releasing
Makes: 4 servings

- 4 medium sweet red peppers
- 1 can (15 oz.) black beans, rinsed and drained
- 1 cup shredded pepper jack cheese
- ¾ cup salsa
- 1 small onion, chopped
- ½ cup frozen corn
- ⅓ cup uncooked converted long grain rice
- 1¼ tsp. chili powder
- ½ tsp. ground cumin
  Reduced-fat sour cream, optional

1. Place trivet insert and 1 cup water in a 6-qt. electric pressure cooker.
2. Cut and discard tops from the peppers; remove seeds. In a large bowl, mix beans, cheese, salsa, onion, corn, rice, chili powder and cumin; spoon into peppers. Set peppers on trivet.
3. Lock lid and close pressure-release valve. Adjust to pressure-cook on high for 5 minutes. Let pressure release naturally. If desired, serve with sour cream.
1 STUFFED PEPPER: 333 cal., 10g fat (5g sat. fat), 30mg chol., 582mg sod., 45g carb. (8g sugars, 8g fiber), 15g pro. **DIABETIC EXCHANGES:** 2 starch, 2 lean meat, 2 vegetable, 1 fat.

SLOW-COOKER SALSA CHICKEN

This is a go-to recipe when I know I'll be having a busy day. My family loves salsa, so I came up with this recipe for something to throw into a slow cooker and simmer on low. We love it served over rice or noodles and topped with tortilla chips and sour cream.
—*Deborah Pennington, Cullman, AL*

Prep: 15 min. • **Cook:** 3 hours
Makes: 4 servings

- 4 boneless skinless chicken breast halves (6 oz. each)
- 1 jar (16 oz.) salsa
- 1¾ cups frozen corn, thawed
- 1 can (15 oz.) pinto beans, rinsed and drained
- 1 can (15 oz.) no-salt-added black beans, rinsed and drained
- 1 can (10 oz.) diced tomatoes and green chiles, undrained
- 1 tsp. sugar
- ½ tsp. salt
- ¼ tsp. pepper
  Optional: Hot cooked rice, cubed avocado, chopped fresh tomato, sliced green onions and lime wedges

Place chicken in a 4- or 5-qt. slow cooker. Top with salsa, corn, beans, diced tomatoes and chiles, sugar, salt and pepper. Cook, covered, on low until a thermometer inserted in the chicken reads 165°, 3-4 hours. If desired, serve with optional ingredients.
1 CHICKEN BREAST HALF WITH 1½ CUPS BEAN MIXTURE: 470 cal., 6g fat (1g sat. fat), 94mg chol., 1270mg sod., 55g carb. (8g sugars, 11g fiber), 47g pro.

JUDY BATSON
Tampa, FL

SPICY SEAFOOD STEW

The hardest part of this quick and easy recipe is peeling and dicing the potatoes— and you can even do that the night before. Just place the potatoes in water and store them in the refrigerator overnight to speed up assembly the next day.
—*Bonnie Marlow, Ottoville, OH*

- -

Prep: 30 min. • **Cook:** 4¾ hours
Makes: 9 servings (about 2 qt.)

2	lbs. potatoes, peeled and diced
1	lb. carrots, sliced
1	jar (24 oz.) pasta sauce
2	jars (6 oz. each) sliced mushrooms, drained
1½	tsp. ground turmeric
1½	tsp. minced garlic
1	tsp. cayenne pepper
¼	tsp. salt
1½	cups water
1	lb. sea scallops
1	lb. uncooked shrimp (31-40 per lb.), peeled and deveined

In a 5-qt. slow cooker, combine the first 8 ingredients. Cook, covered, on low until potatoes are tender, 4½-5 hours. Stir in water, scallops and shrimp. Cook, covered, until scallops are opaque and shrimp turn pink, 15-20 minutes longer.

1 CUP: 229 cal., 2g fat (0 sat. fat), 73mg chol., 803mg sod., 34g carb. (10g sugars, 6g fiber), 19g pro.

🎗 SPICY SAUSAGE FETTUCCINE

One time, I accidentally bought hot Italian sausage instead of mild. I tossed it in the slow cooker with mushrooms, tomatoes and wine, which mellowed out the heat. Now I buy the hot stuff on purpose!
—*Judy Batson, Tampa, FL*

- -

Prep: 25 min. • **Cook:** 6 hours
Makes: 8 servings

2	tsp. canola oil
8	hot Italian sausage links
½	lb. sliced fresh mushrooms
1	small sweet onion, chopped
2	garlic cloves, minced
1	can (14½ oz.) diced tomatoes with mild green chiles, undrained
½	cup beef stock
½	cup dry white wine or additional stock
1	pkg. (12 oz.) fettuccine or tagliatelle Grated Parmesan cheese, optional

1. In a large skillet, heat oil over medium heat; brown sausages on all sides. Transfer to a 3-qt. slow cooker, reserving drippings in pan.
2. In same skillet, saute mushrooms and onion in drippings over medium heat until tender, 4-5 minutes. Stir in the garlic; cook and stir 1 minute. Stir in diced tomatoes, stock and wine; pour over sausages. Cook, covered, on low 6-8 hours (a thermometer inserted in sausages should read at least 160°).
3. To serve, cook fettuccine according to package directions; drain. Remove sausages from slow cooker; cut into thick slices.
4. Skim fat from mushroom mixture. Add fettuccine and sausage; toss to combine. Serve in bowls. If desired, top with cheese.

1⅓ CUPS: 448 cal., 25g fat (7g sat. fat), 57mg chol., 817mg sod., 37g carb. (5g sugars, 3g fiber), 19g pro.

SLOW-COOKER MALAYSIAN CHICKEN

Malaysian food has influences from the Malays, Chinese, Indians, Thai, Portuguese and British. In this dish, Asian ingredients combine for maximum flavor, and the sweet potatoes help to thicken the sauce as the dish slowly cooks.
—*Suzanne Banfield, Basking Ridge, NJ*

- -

Prep: 20 min. • **Cook:** 5 hours
Makes: 6 servings

- 1   cup coconut milk
- 2   Tbsp. brown sugar
- 2   Tbsp. soy sauce
- 2   Tbsp. creamy peanut butter
- 1   Tbsp. fish sauce
- 2   tsp. curry powder
- 2   garlic cloves, minced
- ½   tsp. salt
- ½   tsp. pepper
- 1   can (14½ oz.) diced tomatoes, undrained
- 2   medium sweet potatoes, peeled and cut into ½-in. thick slices
- 2   lbs. boneless skinless chicken thighs
- 2   Tbsp. cornstarch
- 2   Tbsp. water

1. In a bowl, whisk the first 9 ingredients; stir in tomatoes. Place sweet potatoes in a 5- or 6-qt. slow cooker; top with the chicken. Pour tomato mixture over top. Cook, covered, on low until chicken is tender and a thermometer reads 170°, 5-6 hours.

2. Remove chicken and sweet potatoes; keep warm. Transfer cooking juices to a saucepan. In a small bowl, mix cornstarch and water until smooth; stir into cooking juices. Bring to a boil; cook and stir 1-2 minutes or until thickened. Serve sauce with chicken and sweet potatoes.

1 SERVING: 425 cal., 20g fat (10g sat. fat), 101mg chol., 964mg sod., 28g carb. (14g sugars, 4g fiber), 33g pro.

CALIFORNIA TAMALE PIE

When I serve this fun riff on a Mexican classic, I know I'll see smiles on the faces of everyone at my table. With this recipe, you can enjoy the taste and texture of traditional tamales, but without the time and extra work.
—*Patricia Nieh, Portola Valley, CA*

- -

Prep: 15 min. • **Cook:** 6 hours
Makes: 5 servings

- 1   cup beef broth
- ¾   cup cornmeal
- 1   lb. ground beef
- 1   tsp. chili powder
- ½   tsp. ground cumin
- 1   jar (16 oz.) chunky salsa
- 1   can (15¼ oz.) whole kernel corn, drained
- 1   can (15 oz.) black beans, rinsed and drained
- ¼   cup sliced ripe olives
- ½   cup shredded Monterey Jack cheese
  Optional toppings: Sour cream and fresh jalapeno pepper slices

1. In a 3-qt. slow cooker, combine broth and cornmeal. Let stand for 5 minutes. In a large skillet, cook beef over medium heat until no longer pink; drain. Stir in chili powder and cumin. Transfer to slow cooker. Stir in the salsa, corn, beans and olives. Cover and cook on low for 6-8 hours or until heated through.
2. Sprinkle with cheese. Cover and cook 5-10 minutes longer or until cheese is melted. Top with sour cream and jalapeno slices if desired.

1⅓ CUPS: 455 cal., 16g fat (6g sat. fat), 66mg chol., 1112mg sod., 45g carb. (7g sugars, 7g fiber), 27g pro.

GREEK ORZO CHICKEN

Take your first bite and set sail for a dinner-table tour of the sunny Greek isles. Sprinkle lemon zest on top for a little extra flair.
—*Angela Buchanan, Longmont, CO*

Prep: 15 min. • **Cook:** 5½ hours
Makes: 6 servings

- 6 bone-in chicken thighs, (about 2¼ lbs.), skin removed
- 1 cup sliced fresh carrots
- 1 cup chicken broth
- ¼ cup lemon juice
- 1 garlic clove, minced
- 1 tsp. dried oregano
- ½ tsp. salt
- 1 cup uncooked orzo pasta
- ½ cup sliced pitted green olives
- ¼ cup golden raisins
- ½ cup minced fresh parsley
- ½ cup crumbled feta cheese

1. In a 3-qt. slow cooker, combine the chicken, carrots, broth, lemon juice, garlic, oregano and salt. Cover and cook on low for 5-6 hours or until chicken is tender.

2. Stir in the orzo, olives and raisins. Cover and cook 30 minutes longer or until pasta is tender. Sprinkle with parsley and feta cheese.

1 CHICKEN THIGH WITH ½ CUP ORZO MIXTURE: 391 cal., 14g fat (4g sat. fat), 93mg chol., 783mg sod., 35g carb. (6g sugars, 2g fiber), 31g pro.

THAI-STYLE BRISKET

Here's a unique take on brisket that will have you hooked. Peanut butter, soy, crisp-tender veggies and zesty seasonings give it the authentic Thai flavor we crave.
—*Teri Lee Rasey, Cadillac, MI*

Prep: 1 hour • **Cook:** 8½ hours
Makes: 8 servings

- 1 fresh beef brisket (3 to 4 lbs.), cut in half
- 3 Tbsp. olive oil, divided
- 1 cup chunky peanut butter
- ⅔ cup soy sauce
- 4 tsp. sesame oil
- 1 Tbsp. minced fresh cilantro
- 1 Tbsp. lemon juice
- 1 tsp. garlic powder
- 1 tsp. crushed red pepper flakes
- 1 tsp. pepper
- 1 Tbsp. cornstarch
- 1 cup water
- 1¼ cups julienned carrots
- 1 medium sweet red pepper, sliced
- 1 medium green pepper, sliced
- ½ cup chopped green onions
- 1 cup unsalted peanuts, optional
  Hot cooked rice

1. In a large skillet over medium-high heat, brown brisket on both sides in 2 Tbsp. olive oil. Transfer meat and drippings to a 5-qt. slow cooker. Combine the peanut butter, soy sauce, sesame oil, cilantro, lemon juice, garlic, pepper flakes and pepper; pour over brisket. Cover and cook on low for 8-9 hours or until meat is tender.

2. Remove brisket and keep warm. Combine cornstarch and water until smooth; stir into cooking juices. Cover and cook on high for 30 minutes or until thickened. Meanwhile, in a large skillet or wok, stir-fry the carrots, peppers and onions in the remaining olive oil until crisp-tender. Add peanuts if desired. Stir cooking juices and stir into vegetable mixture.

3. Thinly slice meat across the grain. Place rice on a large serving platter; top with meat and vegetable mixture.

NOTE: This recipe is made with a fresh beef brisket, not corned beef.

1 SERVING: 505 cal., 31g fat (6g sat. fat), 72mg chol., 1455mg sod., 12g carb. (5g sugars, 4g fiber), 46g pro.

SLOW-COOKED BEEF ENCHILADAS

Enchiladas get a beefy boost of goodness from slow-cooked roast. When the meat is done, assemble with tortillas and bake. Top with lettuce and tomatoes if desired.
—Taste of Home Test Kitchen

Prep: 15 min. • **Cook:** 7¼ hours
Makes: 6 servings

- 1 boneless beef chuck roast (1¾ lbs.)
- 1 envelope taco seasoning
- 1 medium onion, chopped
- 1 cup beef broth
- 2 Tbsp. all-purpose flour
- 1 Tbsp. cold water
- 6 flour tortillas (8 in.)
- 1 can (4 oz.) chopped green chiles
- 1½ cups shredded Mexican cheese blend, divided
- 1 can (10 oz.) enchilada sauce
  Chopped lettuce and chopped tomatoes, optional

1. Rub roast with taco seasoning. Transfer to a greased 3-qt. slow cooker. Top with onion and broth. Cook, covered, on low 7-8 hours or until meat is tender. Remove roast; cool slightly. Reserve ½ cup cooking juices in a saucepan; discard remaining juices. Skim fat from reserved juices. Shred beef with 2 forks; return to slow cooker.

2. In a small bowl, mix flour and cold water until smooth; add to saucepan. Cook and stir 2 minutes or until thickened. Stir into meat mixture.

3. Preheat oven to 425°. Spoon ½ cup meat mixture off center on each tortilla; top with chiles and 2 Tbsp. cheese. Roll up and place in a greased 13x9-in. baking dish, seam side down. Top with enchilada sauce; sprinkle with remaining cheese. Bake, uncovered, 15-20 minutes or until cheese is melted. If desired, top with chopped lettuce and tomatoes.

1 ENCHILADA: 551 cal., 26g fat (11g sat. fat), 111mg chol., 1388mg sod., 40g carb. (3g sugars, 2g fiber), 38g pro.

ORANGE CHIPOTLE CHICKEN

The citrus in this delicious chicken dish keeps things fresh and lively. We're big on spice in our house, so sometimes I use two chipotle peppers.
—Deborah Biggs, Omaha, NE

Prep: 15 min. • **Cook:** 10 min.
Makes: 6 servings

- ½ cup plus 2 Tbsp. cold water, divided
- ½ cup thawed orange juice concentrate
- ¼ cup barbecue sauce
- 1 chipotle pepper in adobo sauce
- ¼ tsp. salt
- ¼ tsp. garlic powder
- 6 boneless skinless chicken breast halves (6 oz. each)
- ¼ cup chopped red onion
- 4 tsp. cornstarch
  Grated orange zest

1. Place ½ cup water, juice concentrate, barbecue sauce, chipotle pepper, salt and garlic powder in a blender; cover and process until blended.

2. Place chicken and onion in a 6-qt. electric pressure cooker; top with juice mixture. Lock lid; close pressure-release valve. Adjust to pressure-cook on high for 6 minutes.

3. Quick-release pressure. A thermometer inserted in chicken should read at least 165°. Remove the chicken from pressure cooker; keep warm. In a small bowl, mix cornstarch and remaining 2 Tbsp. water until smooth; gradually stir into pressure cooker. Select the saute setting and adjust for low heat. Simmer, stirring constantly, until thickened, 1-2 minutes. Spoon over chicken; top with orange zest.

1 CHICKEN BREAST WITH ¼ CUP SAUCE: 246 cal., 4g fat (1g sat. fat), 94mg chol., 315mg sod., 15g carb. (11g sugars, 1g fiber), 35g pro.

COUNTRY-STYLE BARBECUE RIBS

These ribs get a good sear under the broiler, then go into the slow cooker to become fall-apart tender. Enjoy them with great sides, or shredded on a bun. Either way, you'll agree they're the most amazing ribs you've ever had.
—Shannon Copley, Upper Arlington, OH

Prep: 15 min. • **Cook:** 3 hours
Makes: 10 servings

- 2   Tbsp. paprika
- 2   Tbsp. brown sugar
- 2   tsp. salt
- 2   tsp. garlic powder
- 2   tsp. chili powder
- 1   tsp. onion powder
- 1   tsp. ground chipotle pepper
- 1   tsp. pepper
- ¾   tsp. dried thyme
- 4   lbs. boneless country-style pork ribs
- 1   bottle (18 oz.) barbecue sauce
- ¾   cup amber beer or reduced-sodium chicken broth

1. Preheat broiler. Mix first 9 ingredients. Place pork ribs in a foil-lined 15x10x1-in. pan; rub generously with seasonings. Broil 4-5 in. from heat until browned, 2-3 minutes per side.
2. Transfer the ribs to a 5-qt. slow cooker. Whisk together barbecue sauce and beer; pour over ribs. Cook, covered, on low until tender, 3-4 hours.
3. Remove the ribs. Reserve 2 cups cooking juices; discard remaining juices. Skim the fat from reserved juices. Serve with ribs.
1 SERVING: 393 cal., 17g fat (6g sat. fat), 105mg chol., 1098mg sod., 26g carb. (20g sugars, 1g fiber), 33g pro.

> **TEST KITCHEN TIP**
> Country-style are the meatiest of all pork ribs. Look for highly marbled ribs; they might be labeled pork shoulder country-style ribs.

PRESSURE-COOKER CAJUN CHICKEN ALFREDO

This dish is true comfort food. The Cajun spice adds a nice heat to the creamy Alfredo sauce. And nothing beats having to clean only one pot. Add more or less seasoning depending on your preferred spice level. This recipe would also be tasty with shrimp or smoked sausage.
—Jennifer Stowell, Deep River, IA

Prep: 20 min. • **Cook:** 10 min.
Makes: 6 servings

- 2   Tbsp. olive oil, divided
- 2   medium green peppers, chopped
- 2   boneless skinless chicken breasts (6 oz. each), cubed
- 2   Tbsp. Cajun seasoning, divided
- 1   pkg. (16 oz.) bow tie pasta
- 3   cups chicken stock
- 2   cups water
- 2   cups heavy whipping cream
- 1   cup shredded Parmesan cheese

1. Select saute setting on a 6-qt. electric pressure cooker; adjust for medium heat; add 1 Tbsp. oil. When oil is hot, cook and stir peppers until crisp-tender, 3-4 minutes. Remove and keep warm. Heat remaining 1 Tbsp. oil. Add chicken and 1 Tbsp. Cajun seasoning. Cook and stir until browned, 3-4 minutes. Press cancel.
2. Add pasta, stock and water (do not stir). Lock lid; close pressure-release valve. Adjust to pressure cook on high for 6 minutes. Let the pressure release naturally for 3 minutes; quick-release any remaining pressure.
3. Select the saute setting, and adjust for low heat. Stir in the cream, Parmesan cheese, remaining 1 Tbsp. Cajun seasoning and the reserved peppers. Cook until heated through (do not boil).
1⅔ CUPS: 717 cal., 40g fat (22g sat. fat), 131mg chol., 935mg sod., 60g carb. (6g sugars, 3g fiber), 31g pro.

SHANNON COPLEY
Upper Arlington, OH

VEGETARIAN TORTILLA LASAGNA

You won't miss the meat in this savory delight. The layered main course is as tasty as it is impressive. Serve warm wedges alongside chips and salsa or a green salad.

—*Connie McDowell, Greenwood, DE*

Prep: 20 min. • **Cook:** 3 hours
Makes: 8 servings

- 1 can (14½ oz.) diced tomatoes with basil, oregano and garlic
- 1 cup chunky salsa
- 1 can (6 oz.) tomato paste
- ½ tsp. ground cumin
- 2 cans (15½ oz. each) hominy, rinsed and drained
- 1 can (15 oz.) no-salt-added black beans, rinsed and drained
- 3 flour tortillas (10 in.)
- 2 cups shredded Monterey Jack cheese
- ¼ cup sliced ripe olives

1. Cut three 25x3-in. strips of heavy-duty foil; crisscross so they resemble spokes of a wheel. Place strips on the bottom and up the sides of a round 5-qt. slow cooker. Coat strips with cooking spray.
2. In a large bowl, combine the tomatoes, salsa, tomato paste and cumin. Stir in hominy and beans. Place 1 tortilla on the bottom of slow cooker. Top with a third of the hominy mixture and cheese. Repeat layers twice. Sprinkle with olives. Cover and cook on low for 3-3½ hours or until heated through.
3. Using foil strips as handles, remove the lasagna to a platter. Let stand for 5 minutes before cutting into wedges.
1 SLICE: 335 cal., 12g fat (6g sat. fat), 25mg chol., 1166mg sod., 41g carb. (6g sugars, 8g fiber), 15g pro.

TANGY PORK CHOPS

When my husband and I had our first child, we turned to this convenient recipe often. I could start it during nap time and we'd enjoy an easy, satisfying dinner that night.
—*Karol Hines, Kitty Hawk, NC*

Prep: 15 min. • **Cook:** 5½ hours
Makes: 4 servings

- 4 bone-in pork loin chops
- ⅛ tsp. pepper
- 2 medium onions, chopped
- 2 celery ribs, chopped
- 1 large green pepper, sliced
- 1 can (14½ oz.) no-salt-added stewed tomatoes
- ½ cup ketchup
- 2 Tbsp. cider vinegar
- 2 Tbsp. brown sugar
- 2 Tbsp. Worcestershire sauce
- 1 Tbsp. lemon juice
- 1 tsp. beef bouillon granules
- 3 Tbsp. cornstarch
- 2 Tbsp. cold water
  Hot cooked rice or mashed potatoes, optional

1. Place chops in a 3-qt. slow cooker; sprinkle with pepper. Add the onions, celery, green pepper and tomatoes. Combine the ketchup, vinegar, brown sugar, Worcestershire sauce, lemon juice and bouillon; pour sauce over vegetables. Cover and cook on low until meat is tender, 5-6 hours.
2. Mix cornstarch and water until smooth; stir into liquid in slow cooker. Cover and cook on high until thickened, about 30 minutes. Serve with rice or mashed potatoes, if desired.
1 PORK CHOP: 349 cal., 9g fat (3g sat. fat), 86mg chol., 757mg sod., 34g carb. (24g sugars, 4g fiber), 32g pro.

3. For dumplings, whisk together flour, baking powder, salt and pepper in a large bowl. Stir in milk and butter to form a thick dough. Drop by ¼ cupfuls over the chicken mixture. Cook, covered, on low until bubbly and dumplings are set, 6-8 hours. Discard bay leaves. Remove slow-cooker insert and let stand, uncovered, for 15 minutes.

1 DUMPLING WITH 1 CUP SAUCE: 370 cal., 15g fat (6g sat. fat), 77mg chol., 1245mg sod., 35g carb. (4g sugars, 2g fiber), 22g pro.

SLOW-COOKER SWISS STEAK

Everyone raves over this rich and tender dish. I make it at least once every two weeks during the winter. I modified my mom's Swiss steak recipe to cook it hands-free in the slow cooker.
—Kathie Morris, Redmond, OR

Prep: 15 min. • **Cook:** 8 hours
Makes: 6 servings

- ¾ cup all-purpose flour
- 1 tsp. pepper
- ¼ tsp. salt
- 2 to 2½ lbs. boneless beef top round steak
- 1 to 2 Tbsp. butter
- 1 can (10¾ oz.) condensed cream of mushroom soup, undiluted
- 1⅓ cups water
- 1 cup sliced celery, optional
- ½ cup chopped onion
- 1 to 3 tsp. beef bouillon granules
- ½ tsp. minced garlic

1. In a shallow bowl, combine the flour, pepper and salt. Cut steak into 6 serving-size pieces; dredge in flour mixture.
2. In a large skillet, brown the steak in butter. Transfer to a 3-qt. slow cooker. Combine the remaining ingredients; pour over steak. Cover and cook on low for 8-9 hours or until the meat is tender.

1 SERVING: 313 cal., 9g fat (4g sat. fat), 92mg chol., 666mg sod., 18g carb. (2g sugars, 2g fiber), 37g pro.

SLOW-COOKER CHICKEN & DUMPLINGS

People can't wait to dive into this homey dish. They're often surprised to learn you can make chicken and dumplings in the slow cooker. The homemade classic takes a little bit of time and work but is worth it.
—Daniel Anderson, Kenosha, WI

Prep: 20 min. • **Cook:** 6 hours + standing
Makes: 8 servings

- 6 boneless skinless chicken thighs, chopped
- ½ tsp. salt, divided
- ½ tsp. pepper, divided
- 1 Tbsp. canola oil
- 3 celery ribs, chopped
- 2 medium carrots, peeled and chopped
- 1 large onion, chopped
- 3 garlic cloves, minced
- 2 Tbsp. tomato paste
- ⅓ cup all-purpose flour
- 4 cups chicken broth, divided
- 2 bay leaves
- 1 tsp. dried thyme

DUMPLINGS
- 2 cups all-purpose flour
- 3 tsp. baking powder
- 1 tsp. salt
- ¼ tsp. pepper
- 1 cup whole milk
- 4 Tbsp. melted butter

1. Sprinkle chicken with ¼ tsp. salt and ¼ tsp. pepper. Meanwhile, in a large skillet, heat oil over medium-high heat. Add chicken; cook and stir until no longer pink, 6-8 minutes. Transfer to a 6-qt. slow cooker.
2. In same skillet, cook celery, carrots and onion until tender, 6-8 minutes. Add garlic, tomato paste and remaining salt and pepper; cook 1 minute. Stir in flour; cook 1 minute longer. Whisk in 2 cups chicken broth; cook and stir until thickened. Transfer mixture to slow cooker. Stir in bay leaves, thyme and remaining chicken broth.

TERIYAKI CHICKEN THIGHS

Here's a slow-cooker sensation: Asian-style chicken and rice. Its sweet and tangy flavor goes over big with my family.
—Gigi Miller, Stoughton, WI

- -

Prep: 15 min. • **Cook:** 4 hours
Makes: 8 servings

- -

3	lbs. boneless skinless chicken thighs
¾	cup sugar
¾	cup reduced-sodium soy sauce
⅓	cup cider vinegar
1	garlic clove, minced
¾	tsp. ground ginger
¼	tsp. pepper
4	tsp. cornstarch
4	tsp. cold water
	Hot cooked rice, optional

1. Place chicken in a 4- or 5-qt. slow cooker. In a small bowl, mix sugar, soy sauce, vinegar, garlic, ginger and pepper; pour over chicken. Cook, covered, on low 4-5 hours or until chicken is tender.

2. Remove the chicken to a serving platter; keep warm. Transfer cooking juices to a small saucepan; skim fat. Bring cooking juices to a boil. In a small bowl, mix cornstarch and cold water until smooth; stir into cooking juices. Return to a boil; cook and stir 1-2 minutes or until thickened. Serve with chicken and, if desired, rice.

5 OZ. COOKED CHICKEN WITH ⅓ CUP SAUCE: 342 cal., 12g fat (3g sat. fat), 113mg chol., 958mg sod., 22g carb. (19g sugars, 0 fiber), 33g pro.

TEST KITCHEN TIP
Boneless skinless chicken thighs work well in the slow cooker. The meat shreds easily, yet stays moist due its slightly higher fat content. When making sauce, heat the liquid to boiling before you stir in the cornstarch mixture. Since you stir the liquid only after cornstarch has been added, this gives you hands-free cooking time.

SAUSAGE PASTA STEW

I rely on my slow cooker to prepare this stew that's a lot like chili and packed with turkey sausage, pasta and vegetables. My gang gobbles it up unaware they're eating healthy.
—*Sara Bowen, Upland, CA*

Prep: 20 min. • **Cook:** 7¼ hours
Makes: 8 servings

- 1   lb. turkey Italian sausage links, casings removed
- 4   cups water
- 1   jar (24 oz.) meatless spaghetti sauce
- 1   can (16 oz.) kidney beans, rinsed and drained
- 1   medium yellow summer squash, halved lengthwise and cut into 1-in. pieces
- 2   medium carrots, sliced
- 1   medium sweet red or green pepper, diced
- ⅓   cup chopped onion
- 1½ cups uncooked spiral pasta
- 1   cup frozen peas
- 1   tsp. sugar
- ¼   tsp. salt
- ¼   tsp. pepper

1. In a nonstick skillet, cook sausage over medium heat until no longer pink; drain and place in a 5-qt. slow cooker. Stir in the water, spaghetti sauce, beans, summer squash, carrots, red pepper and onion.

2. Cover and cook on low for 7-9 hours or until vegetables are tender.

3. Stir in the spiral pasta, frozen peas, sugar, salt and pepper. Cover and cook on high for 15-20 minutes or until pasta is tender.

1⅓ CUPS: 276 cal., 6g fat (2g sat. fat), 30mg chol., 1111mg sod., 38g carb. (0 sugars, 6g fiber), 18g pro.

SLOW-COOKER CURRY PORK

I'm a stay-at-home mom, and the slow cooker helps me create dishes like this pork with a curry and cumin rub. I add a splash of coconut milk for a tropical twist.

—Beverly Peychal, Waukesha, WI

Prep: 15 min. • **Cook:** 3½ hours + standing
Makes: 10 servings

- 1½ tsp. salt
- 1½ tsp. hot or regular curry powder
- 1 tsp. ground cumin
- 1 tsp. dried oregano
- ¾ tsp. onion powder
- ¾ tsp. garlic powder
- ½ tsp. pepper
- ¼ tsp. cayenne pepper
- ¼ tsp. paprika
- ¼ tsp. ground chipotle pepper
- 1½ lbs. potatoes, cut into ½-in. pieces
- 4 medium carrots, thinly sliced
- 3 cups cubed peeled butternut squash (about 1 lb.)
- 1 can (14½ oz.) reduced-sodium chicken broth
- 1 boneless pork loin roast (3 to 4 lbs.)

1. In a small bowl, mix seasonings. In a 6-qt. slow cooker, combine vegetables, chicken broth and 2 tsp. seasoning mixture. Rub the remaining seasoning mixture over roast; place over vegetables. Cook, covered, on low 3½-4½ hours or until meat and vegetables are tender (a thermometer inserted in roast should read at least 145°).
2. Remove roast from slow cooker; tent with foil. Let stand 15 minutes before slicing. Serve with vegetables.
4 OZ. COOKED PORK WITH ½ CUP VEGETABLES: 261 cal., 7g fat (2g sat. fat), 68mg chol., 523mg sod., 21g carb. (3g sugars, 4g fiber), 29g pro. **DIABETIC EXCHANGES:** 4 lean meat, 1½ starch.

READER REVIEW

"Great recipe. Loved the spice combination. Doubled the amount of squash and carrots and added Sriracha for additional spice."

COOKIEMIAMI, TASTEOFHOME.COM

SLOW-COOKED MANDARIN CHICKEN

Oranges and olives are elegantly paired in this different and delectable dish. The chicken is marinated, then cooked slowly in a flavorful sauce, so it stays moist.

—Aney Chatterson, Soda Springs, ID

Prep: 30 min. + marinating • **Cook:** 7 hours
Makes: 4 servings

- 1½ cups water
- 1 cup ketchup
- ¼ cup packed brown sugar
- ¼ cup thawed orange juice concentrate
- ¼ cup reduced-sodium soy sauce
- 2 tsp. ground mustard
- 1 tsp. salt
- 1 tsp. garlic powder
- 1 tsp. ground ginger
- 1 tsp. pepper
- 1 broiler/fryer chicken (3 to 3½ lbs.), cut up and skin removed
- 3 Tbsp. cornstarch
- 3 Tbsp. cold water
- 1 can (11 oz.) mandarin oranges, drained
- ¼ cup chopped green pepper
- ½ cup pitted ripe olives, optional
    Hot cooked rice

1. In a large bowl, combine water, ketchup, brown sugar, orange juice concentrate, soy sauce, mustard, salt, garlic powder, ginger and pepper. Pour half into another large bowl or dish; add chicken pieces and turn to coat. Refrigerate for 8 hours or overnight. Cover and refrigerate remaining marinade.
2. Drain and discard marinade from chicken. Place chicken in a 4 or 5-qt. slow cooker; add reserved marinade. Cover and cook on low for 7-8 hours or until chicken juices run clear.
3. Remove meat to a serving platter; keep warm. Skim fat from cooking juices; transfer to a small saucepan. Bring liquid to a boil. Combine cornstarch and water until smooth. Gradually stir into the saucepan. Bring to a boil; cook and stir for 2 minutes or until thickened. Stir in the oranges, green pepper and olives if desired. Serve sauce with chicken and hot rice.
1 SERVING: 396 cal., 9g fat (2g sat. fat), 110mg chol., 1323mg sod., 40g carb. (32g sugars, 1g fiber), 38g pro.

SLOW-COOKER CHICKEN PARMESAN

When the Packers play the Bears, I plan a party and make sure this is on the menu. Using the slow cooker means I can watch the game, too! I serve the chicken on submarine rolls with a bit of the sauce and some chopped lettuce. Or cut the chicken breasts in half and make sliders.
—*Bonnie Hawkins, Elkhorn, WI*

- -

Prep: 25 min. • **Cook:** 4 hours
Makes: 4 servings

½ cup seasoned bread crumbs
½ cup grated Parmesan cheese
½ tsp. Italian seasoning
½ tsp. pepper
¼ tsp. salt
1 large egg, lightly beaten
1 Tbsp. water
4 (6 oz. each) boneless skinless chicken breast halves
1 jar (24 oz.) marinara sauce
4 slices part-skim mozzarella cheese
Hot cooked pasta, optional

1. In a shallow bowl, combine bread crumbs, Parmesan cheese, Italian seasoning, pepper and salt. In another bowl, combine egg and water. Dip chicken in egg mixture, then in crumb mixture to coat both sides (patting to help adhere). Repeat.
2. Transfer chicken to slow cooker. Pour the sauce over chicken and top with cheese. Cook, covered, on low until a thermometer inserted in chicken reads 165°, 4-6 hours. If desired, serve with hot cooked pasta.
1 SERVING: 475 cal., 17g fat (7g sat. fat), 171mg chol., 1689mg sod., 27g carb. (11g sugars, 4g fiber), 50g pro.

PRESSURE-COOKER CHINESE-STYLE RIBS

It's nice to walk in after a hard day's work and have dinner ready in a short amount of time. I hope you agree these ribs are quick, easy and delicious. Enjoy!
—*Paula Marchesi, Lenhartsville, PA*

- -

Prep: 20 min. • **Cook:** 30 min. + releasing
Makes: 6 servings

3 lbs. boneless country-style pork ribs
6 green onions, cut into 1-in. pieces
1 can (8 oz.) sliced water chestnuts, drained
¾ cup hoisin sauce
½ cup water
3 Tbsp. soy sauce
2 Tbsp. sherry or chicken stock
5 garlic cloves, minced
1 Tbsp. minced fresh gingerroot
1 Tbsp. light corn syrup
1 Tbsp. orange marmalade
1 tsp. pumpkin pie spice
½ tsp. crushed red pepper flakes
1 to 2 Tbsp. cornstarch
2 Tbsp. water
Hot cooked rice, optional
Thinly sliced green onions, optional

1. Place the pork, green onions and water chestnuts in a 6-qt electric pressure cooker. Mix hoisin sauce, water, soy sauce, sherry, garlic, gingerroot, corn syrup, marmalade, pie spice and pepper flakes in a bowl. Pour the sauce over pork. Lock lid and close pressure-release valve. Adjust to pressure-cook on high for 25 minutes. Allow pressure to naturally release for 10 minutes and then quick-release any remaining pressure.
2. Remove pork to a serving platter; keep warm. Skim fat from cooking juices. Select saute setting and adjust for medium heat. Bring to a boil. In a small bowl, mix cornstarch and water until smooth. Gradually stir the cornstarch mixture into the pressure cooker. Bring to a boil; cook and stir until thickened, about 2 minutes. Serve ribs with sauce and, if desired, rice and additional green onions.
1 SERVING: 493 cal., 22g fat (8g sat. fat), 132mg chol., 1115mg sod., 28g carb. (15g sugars, 2g fiber), 42g pro.

BUTTERNUT BEEF STEW

I tweaked this recipe I found in a magazine to satisfy my affinity for sweet and spicy. I puree the tomatoes for a thicker consistency without having to add flour.

—*Erin Lembke, Monroe, WA*

Prep: 30 min. • **Cook:** 7 hours
Makes: 4 servings

- 1¼ lbs. beef stew meat, cut into 1-in. cubes
- 1 Tbsp. canola oil
- 1½ cups cubed peeled butternut squash
- 1 cup chopped cabbage
- ½ cup coarsely chopped sweet red pepper
- 1 celery rib with leaves, chopped
- 1 can (10 oz.) diced tomatoes and green chiles
- ¼ cup packed brown sugar
- 1 can (14½ oz.) beef broth
- 1 Tbsp. adobo sauce
- 1 tsp. dried oregano
- ¼ tsp. salt
- ⅛ tsp. pepper

1. In a large skillet, brown meat in oil on all sides; drain. Transfer to a 3-qt. slow cooker. Stir in the squash, cabbage, red pepper and celery.

2. In a blender, combine diced tomatoes and brown sugar. Cover and process until blended. Pour over vegetables. Combine the broth, adobo sauce, oregano, salt and pepper; add to slow cooker.

3. Cover and cook on low until meat and vegetables are tender, 7-8 hours.

1½ CUPS: 377 cal., 15g fat (4g sat. fat), 88mg chol., 1047mg sod., 31g carb. (17g sugars, 4g fiber), 30g pro.

TEX-MEX CHICKEN WITH BLACK BEANS & RICE

I came up with this recipe for my sister, who appreciates the convenience of tossing canned goods into one big pot. It's a yummy go-to dish for even the busiest day.
—*Elizabeth Dumont, Madison, MS*

Prep: 20 min. • **Cook:** 5 hours
Makes: 6 servings

- 6 chicken leg quarters, skin removed
- 1 envelope taco seasoning, divided
- 1 can (14½ oz.) Mexican diced tomatoes, undrained
- 1 can (10¾ oz.) condensed cream of chicken soup, undiluted
- 1 large onion, chopped
- 1 can (4 oz.) chopped green chiles
- 1 cup uncooked instant rice
- 1 cup canned black beans, rinsed and drained
- 1 cup sour cream
- 1 cup shredded cheddar cheese
- 1½ cups crushed tortilla chips
  Minced fresh cilantro

1. Sprinkle chicken leg quarters with 1 Tbsp. taco seasoning; transfer to a 5- or 6-qt. slow cooker. In a large bowl, combine tomatoes, soup, onion, green chiles and remaining taco seasoning; pour over chicken. Cover and cook on low for 5-7 hours or until chicken is 165° and tender.

2. Prepare rice according to the package directions. Stir in beans; heat through.

3. Remove chicken from cooking juices; stir sour cream into cooking juices. Serve chicken with rice mixture and sauce. Sprinkle servings with cheese, tortilla chips and cilantro.

1 SERVING: 590 cal., 26g fat (12g sat. fat), 139mg chol., 1461mg sod., 46g carb. (5g sugars, 4g fiber), 38g pro.

HERBED TURKEY BREASTS

Tender, moist turkey breast is enhanced with a flavorful citrus and herb marinade in this comforting entree.
—*Laurie Mace, Los Osos, CA*

- -

Prep: 25 min. + marinating • **Cook:** 3½ hours
Makes: 12 servings

1	can (14½ oz.) chicken broth
½	cup lemon juice
¼	cup packed brown sugar
¼	cup fresh sage
¼	cup fresh thyme leaves
¼	cup lime juice
¼	cup cider vinegar
¼	cup olive oil
1	envelope onion soup mix
2	Tbsp. Dijon mustard
1	Tbsp. minced fresh marjoram
1½	tsp. paprika
1	tsp. garlic powder
1	tsp. pepper
½	tsp. salt
2	boneless skinless turkey breast halves (2 lbs. each)

1. In a blender, process first 15 ingredients until blended. Pour marinade into a large bowl; add the turkey. Turn to coat; cover and refrigerate for 8 hours or overnight.
2. Transfer turkey and marinade to a 5-qt. slow cooker. Cover and cook on high until a thermometer reads 165°, 3½-4½ hours.
5 OZ. COOKED TURKEY: 219 cal., 5g fat (1g sat. fat), 87mg chol., 484mg sod., 5g carb. (3g sugars, 0 fiber), 36g pro.

PRESSURE-COOKER BEEF & RICE CABBAGE ROLLS

These cabbage rolls come together in a pinch and always satisfy. We can't get enough!
—*Lynn Bowen, Geraldine, AL*

- -

Prep: 45 min. • **Cook:** 20 min.
Makes: 6 servings

12	cabbage leaves
1	cup cooked brown rice
¼	cup finely chopped onion
1	large egg, lightly beaten
¼	cup fat-free milk
½	tsp. salt
¼	tsp. pepper
1	lb. lean ground beef (90% lean)
½	cup plus 2 Tbsp. water, divided
1	can (8 oz.) tomato sauce
1	Tbsp. brown sugar
1	Tbsp. lemon juice
1	tsp. Worcestershire sauce
2	Tbsp. cornstarch

1. In batches, cook cabbage in boiling water 3-5 minutes or until crisp-tender. Drain; cool slightly. Trim the thick vein from the bottom of each cabbage leaf, making a V-shaped cut.
2. In a large bowl, combine rice, onion, egg, milk, salt and pepper. Add beef; mix lightly but thoroughly. Place about ¼ cup beef mixture on each cabbage leaf. Pull together cut edges of leaf to overlap; fold over filling. Fold in sides and roll up.
3. Place trivet insert and ½ cup water in a 6-qt. electric pressure cooker. Set 6 rolls on trivet, seam side down. In a bowl, mix tomato sauce, brown sugar, lemon juice and Worcestershire sauce; pour half the sauce over cabbage rolls. Top with remaining rolls and sauce.
4. Lock lid and close pressure-release valve. Adjust to pressure-cook on high 15 minutes. Quick-release pressure. A thermometer inserted in beef should read at least 160°.
5. Remove cabbage rolls to a serving platter; keep warm. Remove trivet. In a small bowl, mix cornstarch and remaining 2 Tbsp. water until smooth; stir into pressure cooker. Select the saute setting and adjust for low heat. Simmer, stirring constantly, until sauce is thickened, 1-2 minutes. Serve with rolls.
2 CABBAGE ROLLS: 219 cal., 8g fat (3g sat. fat), 78mg chol., 446mg sod., 19g carb. (5g sugars, 2g fiber), 18g pro. **DIABETIC EXCHANGES:** 2 lean meat, 1 starch.

RED CLAM SAUCE

This recipe tastes as if it's taken a whole day's work. What a classy way to jazz up pasta sauce!
—*JoAnn Brown, Latrobe, PA*

Prep: 25 min. • **Cook:** 3 hours
Makes: 4 servings

- 1 medium onion, chopped
- 1 Tbsp. canola oil
- 2 garlic cloves, minced
- 2 cans (6½ oz. each) chopped clams, undrained
- 1 can (14½ oz.) diced tomatoes, undrained
- 1 can (6 oz.) tomato paste
- ¼ cup minced fresh parsley
- 1 bay leaf
- 1 tsp. sugar
- 1 tsp. dried basil
- ½ tsp. dried thyme
  Additional minced fresh parsley, optional
- 6 oz. linguine, cooked and drained

1. In a small skillet, saute onion in oil until tender. Add garlic; cook 1 minute longer.
2. Transfer to a 1½- or 2-qt. slow cooker. Stir in the clams, tomatoes, tomato paste, parsley, bay leaf, sugar, basil and thyme.
3. Cover and cook on low until the sauce is heated through, 3-4 hours. Discard bay leaf. If desired, sprinkle with additional parsley. Serve with linguine.

1 CUP SAUCE WITH ¾ CUP COOKED LINGUINE: 305 cal., 5g fat (0 sat. fat), 15mg chol., 553mg sod., 53g carb. (14g sugars, 7g fiber), 15g pro.

CIDER-GLAZED HAM

Here is a heartwarming and classic way to serve ham. Apple cider and mustard perfectly accent the ham's rich, smoky flavor.
—*Jennifer Foos-Furer, Marysville, OH*

Prep: 15 min. • **Cook:** 4 hours
Makes: 8 servings

- 1 boneless fully cooked ham (3 lbs.)
- 1¾ cups apple cider or juice
- ¼ cup packed brown sugar
- ¼ cup Dijon mustard
- ¼ cup honey
- 2 Tbsp. cornstarch
- 2 Tbsp. cold water

1. Place ham in a 5-qt. slow cooker. In a small bowl, combine the apple cider, brown sugar, mustard and honey; pour over ham. Cover and cook on low for 4-5 hours or until heated through. Remove ham and keep warm.
2. Pour cooking juices into a small saucepan. Combine cornstarch and water until smooth; stir into cooking juices. Bring to a boil; cook and stir for 2 minutes or until thickened. Serve with ham.

ORANGE-GLAZED HAM: Substitute orange juice for the apple cider.

4 OZ. COOKED HAM: 280 cal., 6g fat (2g sat. fat), 86mg chol., 1954mg sod., 26g carb. (21g sugars, 0 fiber), 31g pro.

Breads, Rolls & Muffins

Here's a delicious mix of sweet and savory breads guaranteed to make your kitchen smell as divine as a bakery. Some require a little elbow grease, while others go from mixing bowl to oven in a jiffy. You're sure to find the perfect companion for any meal—or enjoy them as a snack or sweet treat on their own.

HONEY BAGELS

Who has time to make from-scratch bagels? You do, with this easy recipe! These chewy golden bagels offer a hint of honey and will win over even the pickiest eaters.
—Taste of Home *Test Kitchen*

- -

Prep: 1 hour + standing • **Bake:** 20 min.
Makes: 1 dozen

1	Tbsp. active dry yeast
1¼	cups warm water (110° to 115°)
3	Tbsp. canola oil
3	Tbsp. sugar
3	Tbsp. plus ¼ cup honey, divided
1	tsp. brown sugar
1½	tsp. salt
1	large egg, room temperature
4	to 5 cups bread flour
1	Tbsp. dried minced onion
1	Tbsp. sesame seeds
1	Tbsp. poppy seeds

1. In a large bowl, dissolve yeast in warm water. Add the oil, sugar, 3 Tbsp. honey, brown sugar, salt and egg; mix well. Stir in enough flour to form a soft dough.
2. Turn onto a floured surface; knead until a smooth firm dough forms, 8-10 minutes. Cover and let rest for 10 minutes.
3. Punch dough down. Shape into 12 balls. Push thumb through each center to form a 1½-in. hole. Stretch and shape dough to form an even ring. Place on floured surface. Cover and let rest for 10 minutes; flatten bagels slightly.
4. In a large saucepan or Dutch oven, bring 8 cups water and remaining honey to a boil. Drop bagels, 1 at a time, into boiling water. Cook bagels for 45 seconds; turn and cook for another 45 seconds. Remove bagels with slotted spoon; drain and sprinkle with minced onion, sesame seeds and poppy seeds.
5. Place bagels 2 in. apart on baking sheets lined with parchment. Bake at 425° for 12 minutes. Turn and bake until golden brown, about 5 minutes longer.

1 BAGEL: 265 cal., 5g fat (1g sat. fat), 16mg chol., 303mg sod., 48g carb. (14g sugars, 2g fiber), 7g pro.

SPECIAL CINNAMON ROLLS

My cinnamon rolls studded with raisins and walnuts beat out any sold at the mall. This recipe is perfect for novice bakers because the dough doesn't require any kneading.
—*Brenda Deveau, Cyr, ME*

Prep: 25 min. + rising • **Bake:** 25 min.
Makes: 2 dozen

- 2 pkg. (¼ oz. each) active dry yeast
- ½ cup warm water (110° to 115°)
- 8 cups all-purpose flour
- 1 pkg. (3.4 oz.) instant vanilla pudding mix
- 2 cups warm whole milk (110° to 115°)
- 2 large eggs, room temperature, lightly beaten
- ½ cup sugar
- ½ cup canola oil
- 2 tsp. salt
- ¼ cup butter, melted

FILLING
- 1 cup packed brown sugar
- 2 tsp. ground cinnamon
- 1 cup raisins
- 1 cup chopped walnuts

GLAZE
- 1 cup confectioners' sugar
- 1 to 2 Tbsp. whole milk
- ¼ tsp. vanilla extract

1. In a bowl, dissolve yeast in water. Add next 7 ingredients; mix well (do not knead). Place in a greased bowl; turn once to grease top. Cover and let rise in warm place until doubled, about 1 hour.

2. Punch down. Turn onto a lightly floured surface; divide in half. Roll each half into a 12x8-in. rectangle; brush with butter. Combine filling ingredients; spread over dough. Roll up from long side; seal seam. Slice each filled roll into 12 rolls and place cut side down in 2 greased 13x9-in. baking pans. Cover and let rise until nearly doubled, about 45 minutes.

3. Bake at 350° for 25-30 minutes or until golden brown. Combine glaze ingredients; drizzle over rolls. Cool in pans on wire racks.

1 ROLL: 364 cal., 11g fat (3g sat. fat), 26mg chol., 294mg sod., 60g carb. (26g sugars, 2g fiber), 7g pro.

FETA & CHIVE MUFFINS

This is a spring variation on a savory muffin my husband has made for years. It has a light texture almost like a popover and tastes best still warm right from the oven.
—*Angela Buchanan, Boulder, CO*

Prep: 15 min. • **Bake:** 20 min. • **Makes:** 1 dozen

- 1½ cups all-purpose flour
- 3 tsp. baking powder
- ¼ tsp. salt
- 2 large eggs, room temperature
- 1 cup fat-free milk
- 2 Tbsp. butter, melted
- ½ cup crumbled feta cheese
- 3 Tbsp. minced chives

1. In a large bowl, combine the flour, baking powder and salt. In another bowl, combine the eggs, milk and butter; stir into the dry ingredients just until moistened. Fold in the feta cheese and chives.

2. Fill 12 greased or paper-lined muffin cups two-thirds full. Bake at 400° until a toothpick inserted in the center of a muffin comes out clean, 18-22 minutes. Cool for 5 minutes before removing from pan to a wire rack. Serve warm. Refrigerate leftovers.

1 MUFFIN: 105 cal., 4g fat (2g sat. fat), 43mg chol., 235mg sod., 13g carb. (1g sugars, 1g fiber), 4g pro. **DIABETIC EXCHANGES:** 1 starch, ½ fat.

DID YOU KNOW?
Chives are available as fresh or freeze-dried hollow stems. They have a delicate onion flavor with a mild hint of garlic.

BLACK RASPBERRY BUBBLE RING

I first made this pretty bread years ago for a 4-H project. It helped me win grand champion for my county and took me to the Ohio State Fair. It takes some time to make, but I pull out this recipe any time I want a breakfast or dessert that will really impress.
—Kila Frank, Reedsville, OH

Prep: 35 min. + rising • **Bake:** 25 min.
Makes: 1 loaf (16 wedges)

- 1 pkg. (¼ oz.) active dry yeast
- ¼ cup warm water (110° to 115°)
- 1 cup warm whole milk (110° to 115°)
- ¼ cup plus 2 Tbsp. sugar, divided
- ½ cup butter, melted, divided
- 1 large egg, room temperature
- 1 tsp. salt
- 4 cups all-purpose flour
- 1 jar (10 oz.) seedless black raspberry preserves

SYRUP
- ⅓ cup corn syrup
- 2 Tbsp. butter, melted
- ½ tsp. vanilla extract

1. In a large bowl, dissolve yeast in warm water. Add the milk, ¼ cup sugar, ¼ cup butter, egg, salt and 3½ cups flour. Beat until smooth. Stir in enough remaining flour to form a soft dough.

2. Turn onto a floured surface; knead until smooth and elastic, 6-8 minutes. Place in a greased bowl, turning once to grease top. Cover dough and let rise in a warm place until doubled, about 1¼ hours.

3. Punch dough down. Turn onto a lightly floured surface; divide into 32 pieces. Flatten each into a 3-in. disk. Place about 1 tsp. black raspberry preserves on the center of each piece; bring edges together and seal.

4. Place 16 dough balls in a greased 10-in. fluted tube pan. Brush with half the remaining butter; sprinkle with 1 Tbsp. sugar. Top with remaining balls, butter and sugar. Cover and let rise until doubled, about 35 minutes.

5. Bake at 350° for 25-30 minutes or until golden brown. Combine syrup ingredients; pour over warm bread. Cool for 5 minutes before inverting onto a serving plate.

1 SLICE: 274 cal., 8g fat (5g sat. fat), 34mg chol., 220mg sod., 46g carb. (18g sugars, 1g fiber), 4g pro.

MILK-AND-HONEY WHITE BREAD

Honey adds special flavor to this traditional white bread.
—Kathy McCreary, Goddard, KS

Prep: 15 min. + rising • **Bake:** 30 min.
Makes: 2 loaves (16 slices each)

- 2 pkg. (¼ oz. each) active dry yeast
- 2½ cups warm whole milk (110° to 115°)
- ⅓ cup honey
- ¼ cup butter, melted
- 2 tsp. salt
- 8 to 8½ cups all-purpose flour

1. In a large bowl, dissolve yeast in warm milk. Add honey, butter, salt and 5 cups flour; beat until smooth. Add enough remaining flour to form a soft dough.

2. Turn onto a floured board; knead until smooth and elastic, 6-8 minutes. Place in a greased bowl, turning once to grease top. Cover dough and let rise in a warm place until doubled, about 1 hour.

3. Punch dough down and shape into 2 loaves. Place in greased 9x5-in. loaf pans. Cover and let rise until doubled, about 30 minutes.

4. Bake at 375° for 30-35 minutes or until golden brown. Cover loosely with foil if top browns too quickly. Remove from pans and cool on wire racks.

1 SLICE: 149 cal., 2g fat (1g sat. fat), 6mg chol., 172mg sod., 28g carb. (4g sugars, 1g fiber), 4g pro.

FAVORITE BANANA CHIP MUFFINS

These muffins are one of the first things my husband, U.S. Army Maj. John Duda Jr., gets hungry for when he's home from deployment. I grab the overripe bananas and start my oven!
—*Kimberly Duda, Sanford, NC*

Prep: 20 min. • **Bake:** 20 min. • **Makes:** 1 dozen

1½	**cups all-purpose flour**
⅔	**cup sugar**
1	**tsp. baking soda**
¼	**tsp. ground cinnamon**
⅛	**tsp. salt**
1	**large egg, room temperature**
1⅓	**cups mashed ripe bananas (about 3 medium)**
⅓	**cup butter, melted**
1	**tsp. vanilla extract**
½	**cup semisweet chocolate chips**

1. Preheat oven to 375°. In a large bowl, whisk flour, sugar, baking soda, cinnamon and salt. In another bowl, whisk egg, bananas, melted butter and vanilla until blended. Add to flour mixture; stir just until moistened. Fold in the chocolate chips.

2. Fill 12 greased or paper-lined muffin cups three-fourths full. Bake 17-20 minutes or until a toothpick inserted in center comes out clean. Cool 5 minutes before removing from pan to a wire rack. Serve warm.

1 MUFFIN: 207 cal., 8g fat (5g sat. fat), 31mg chol., 172mg sod., 33g carb. (18g sugars, 2g fiber), 3g pro. **DIABETIC EXCHANGES:** 2 starch, 1½ fat.

APRICOT CRANBERRY BREAD

I was making cranberry bread one day and wanted to try something a little different. I found a jar of apricot jam in the refrigerator and decided to spoon the jam into the center of the bread. It looked lumpy, so I took a knife and cut the jam into the bread. The end result was delicious.
—*Diane Roth, Milwaukee, WI*

Prep: 20 min. • **Bake:** 65 min. + cooling
Makes: 1 loaf

- 2 cups all-purpose flour
- 1 cup sugar
- 1 to 2 tsp. grated orange zest
- 1½ tsp. baking powder
- ½ tsp. baking soda
- ½ tsp. salt
- 1 large egg, room temperature
- ¾ cup water
- ¼ cup vegetable oil
- 1 cup fresh or frozen halved cranberries
- ¼ cup apricot preserves

1. In a large bowl, combine flour, sugar, orange zest, baking powder, baking soda and salt. In a small bowl, beat egg, water and oil; stir into dry ingredients just until moistened. Fold in the cranberries.

2. Pour into a greased and floured 9x5-in. loaf pan. Cut apricots in the preserves into small pieces; spoon preserves over batter. Cut through batter with a knife to swirl. Bake at 350° for 65-70 minutes or until a toothpick inserted in the center of loaf comes out clean. Cool for 10 minutes; remove from pan to a wire rack.

1 SLICE: 155 cal., 4g fat (1g sat. fat), 13mg chol., 157mg sod., 28g carb. (16g sugars, 1g fiber), 2g pro.

CREOLE CORNBREAD

Cornbread is a staple of Cajun and Creole cuisine. This version is a cherished favorite I found in the bottom of my recipe drawer. I hope it becomes one of yours, too.
—Enid Hebert, Lafayette, LA

Prep: 15 min. • **Bake:** 45 min.
Makes: 12 servings

- 2 cups cooked rice
- 1 cup yellow cornmeal
- ½ cup chopped onion
- 1 to 2 Tbsp. seeded chopped jalapeno peppers
- 1 tsp. salt
- ½ tsp. baking soda
- 2 large eggs, room temperature
- 1 cup whole milk
- ¼ cup canola oil
- 1 can (16½ oz.) cream-style corn
- 3 cups shredded cheddar cheese
  Additional cornmeal

1. In a large bowl, combine rice, cornmeal, onion, peppers, salt and baking soda.
2. In another bowl, beat eggs, milk and oil. Add corn; mix well. Stir into rice mixture until blended. Fold in cheddar cheese. Sprinkle a well-greased 10-in. ovenproof skillet with cornmeal. Pour batter into skillet.
3. Bake at 350° until cornbread tests done, 45-50 minutes. Cut into wedges. Serve warm.
NOTE: Wear disposable gloves when cutting hot peppers; the oils can burn skin. Avoid touching your face.
1 PIECE: 272 cal., 14g fat (7g sat. fat), 68mg chol., 551mg sod., 26g carb. (3g sugars, 2g fiber), 10g pro.

BLUEBERRY SCONES

You'll want to stash a few of these homemade morsels in the freezer to serve visitors who drop in unexpectedly. Just pop a frozen scone in the microwave for 20 seconds or so, and you have a warm treat.
—Joan Francis, Spring Lake, NJ

Prep: 20 min. • **Bake:** 15 min.
Makes: 16 scones

- 4 cups all-purpose flour
- 6 Tbsp. sugar
- 4½ tsp. baking powder
- ½ tsp. salt
- ½ cup plus 2 Tbsp. cold butter
- 2 large eggs, room temperature
- ¾ cup plus 2 Tbsp. whole milk, divided
- 1½ cups fresh or frozen blueberries

1. In a bowl, combine the flour, sugar, baking powder and salt; cut in butter until mixture resembles coarse crumbs. In a bowl, whisk eggs and ¾ cup milk; add to dry ingredients just until moistened. Turn dough onto a lightly floured surface; gently knead in blueberries.
2. Divide the dough in half. Pat each portion into an 8-in. circle; cut each into 8 wedges. Place on greased baking sheets. Brush with remaining milk. Bake at 375° for 15-20 minutes or until tops are golden brown. Serve warm.
NOTE: If using frozen blueberries, use without thawing to avoid discoloring the batter.
1 SCONE: 220 cal., 9g fat (5g sat. fat), 48mg chol., 274mg sod., 31g carb. (7g sugars, 1g fiber), 5g pro.

batter evenly over crumb mixture. Top with remaining crumb mixture.

3. Bake at 350° for 50-55 minutes or until a toothpick inserted in the center comes out clean. Cool for 10 minutes before removing sides of pan.

4. Combine confectioners' sugar, extract and enough water to achieve desired consistency; drizzle over coffee cake.

1 PIECE: 351 cal., 14g fat (4g sat. fat), 43mg chol., 260mg sod., 53g carb. (32g sugars, 2g fiber), 5g pro.

SOFT ITALIAN BREADSTICKS

These soft, chewy homemade breadsticks are a cinch to make in the bread machine. They are irresistible when brushed with melted butter and sprinkled with Parmesan cheese and make the perfect accompaniment to soups or Italian entrees. I recommend using the "Dough Only" cycle on your bread machine for best results.
—Christy Eichelberger, Jesup, IA

- -

Prep: 25 min. + rising • **Bake:** 15 min.
Makes: 2 dozen

- 1   cup water (70° to 80°)
- 3   Tbsp. butter, softened
- 1½ tsp. salt
- 3   cups bread flour
- 2   Tbsp. sugar
- 1   tsp. Italian seasoning
- 1   tsp. garlic powder
- 2¼ tsp. active dry yeast

TOPPING
- 1   Tbsp. butter, melted
- 1   Tbsp. grated Parmesan cheese

1. In bread machine pan, place the water, butter, salt, flour, sugar, Italian seasoning, garlic powder and yeast in order suggested by manufacturer. Select the dough setting (check dough after 5 minutes of mixing; add 1-2 Tbsp. water or flour if needed).

2. When cycle is completed, turn dough onto a lightly floured surface; divide in half. Cut each portion into 12 pieces; roll each into a 4-in. to 6-in. rope. Place 2 in. apart on greased baking sheets. Cover and let rise in a warm place until doubled, about 20 minutes.

3. Bake at 350° for 15-18 minutes or until golden brown. Immediately brush with butter; sprinkle with Parmesan cheese. Serve warm.

1 SERVING: 73 cal., 2g fat (1g sat. fat), 5mg chol., 171mg sod., 12g carb. (1g sugars, 0 fiber), 2g pro.

BUTTERCUP SQUASH COFFEE CAKE

My father grows a large squash patch, so each fall, I get an ample amount of his harvest. I make this treat to share with my co-workers. They rave about the moist cake, the crunchy streusel and the applesauce between the layers.
—Mary Jones, Cumberland, ME

- -

Prep: 15 min. • **Bake:** 55 min.
Makes: 12 servings

CRUMB MIXTURE
- ¼ cup packed brown sugar
- ¼ cup sugar
- ¼ cup all-purpose flour
- ¼ cup quick-cooking oats
- ¼ cup chopped nuts
- 1½ tsp. ground cinnamon
- 3   Tbsp. cold butter

CAKE
- ½ cup butter-flavored shortening
- 1   cup sugar
- 2   large eggs, room temperature
- 1   cup mashed cooked buttercup squash
- 1   tsp. vanilla extract
- 2   cups all-purpose flour
- 2   tsp. baking powder
- 1½ tsp. ground cinnamon
- ½ tsp. baking soda
- ½ tsp. salt
- ¼ tsp. ground ginger
- ¼ tsp. ground nutmeg
-     Pinch ground cloves
- ½ cup unsweetened applesauce

GLAZE
- ½ cup confectioners' sugar
- ¼ tsp. vanilla extract
- 1½ tsp. hot water

1. In a small bowl, combine first 6 ingredients. Cut in butter until crumbly and set aside. In a large bowl, cream shortening and sugar until light and fluffy. Beat in 1 egg at a time, beating well after each addition. Beat in the cooked squash and vanilla. Combine dry ingredients; gradually add to creamed mixture and mix well. Spoon half the batter into a greased 9-in. springform pan.

2. Spread applesauce over batter. Sprinkle with half the crumb mixture. Spoon remaining

ORANGE BANANA NUT BREAD

I like this recipe because the orange juice gives the banana bread such a unique flavor. The loaf stays tender even after it's been frozen.
—*Barbara Roethlisberger, Shepherd, MI*

- -

Prep: 15 min. • **Bake:** 50 min. + cooling
Makes: 2 loaves (12 slices each)

- 1½ cups sugar
- 3 Tbsp. canola oil
- 2 large eggs, room temperature
- 3 medium ripe bananas, mashed (about 1¼ cups)
- ¾ cup orange juice
- 3 cups all-purpose flour
- 1½ tsp. baking powder
- 1½ tsp. baking soda
- ½ tsp. salt
- 1 cup chopped walnuts

1. In a bowl, combine the sugar, oil and eggs; mix well. Stir in bananas and orange juice. Combine the dry ingredients; add to banana mixture, beating just until moistened. Stir in walnuts. Pour into 2 greased 8x4-in. loaf pans.

2. Bake at 325° until a toothpick inserted in the center comes out clean, 50-60 minutes. Cool for 10 minutes; remove from pans to a wire rack to cool completely.

FREEZE OPTION: Securely wrap cooled loaves in foil; freeze. To use, thaw at room temperature.

1 SLICE: 176 cal., 6g fat (1g sat. fat), 16mg chol., 164mg sod., 29g carb. (15g sugars, 1g fiber), 3g pro.

SOFT BEER PRETZEL NUGGETS

What goes together better than beer and pretzels? Not much that I can think of. That's why I put them together into one recipe. I'm always looking for new ways to combine fun flavors. I love the way this recipe turned out!
—*Alyssa Wilhite, Whitehouse, TX*

- -

Prep: 1 hour + rising • **Bake:** 10 min./batch
Makes: 8 dozen pretzel nuggets

- 1 bottle (12 oz.) amber beer or nonalcoholic beer
- 1 pkg. (¼ oz.) active dry yeast
- 2 Tbsp. unsalted butter, melted
- 2 Tbsp. sugar
- 1½ tsp. salt
- 4 to 4½ cups all-purpose flour
- 10 cups water
- ⅔ cup baking soda

TOPPING
- 1 large egg yolk
- 1 Tbsp. water
    Coarse salt, optional

1. In a small saucepan, heat beer to 110°-115°; remove from heat. Stir in yeast until dissolved. In a large bowl, combine butter, sugar, salt, yeast mixture and 3 cups flour; beat on medium speed until smooth. Stir in enough remaining flour to form a soft dough (dough will be sticky).

2. Turn dough onto a floured surface; knead until smooth and elastic, 6-8 minutes. Place in a greased bowl, turning once to grease the top. Cover and let rise in a warm place until doubled, about 1 hour.

3. Preheat oven to 425°. Punch dough down. Turn onto a lightly floured surface; divide and shape into 8 balls. Roll each into a 12-in. rope. Cut each rope into 1-in. pieces.

4. In a Dutch oven, bring 10 cups water and baking soda to a boil. Drop nuggets, 12 at a time, into boiling water. Cook for 30 seconds. Remove with a slotted spoon; drain well on paper towels.

5. Place on greased baking sheets. In a small bowl, whisk the egg yolk and 1 Tbsp. water; brush over pretzels. Sprinkle with coarse salt if desired. Bake 10-12 minutes or until golden brown. Remove from pans to a wire rack to cool.

FREEZE OPTION: Freeze cooled pretzel nuggets in airtight containers. To use, thaw at room temperature or, if desired, microwave on high 20-30 seconds or until heated through.

6 PRETZEL NUGGETS: 144 cal., 2g fat (1g sat. fat), 8mg chol., 302mg sod., 26g carb. (2g sugars, 1g fiber), 4g pro.

TEST KITCHEN TIP
Want rolls instead of nuggets? Just divide and shape the dough into 8 balls; roll each into a 14-in. rope. Starting at an end of each rope, loosely wrap dough around itself to form a coil. Boil, top and bake as directed. You can also make classic pretzel shapes with the same dough.

FROZEN BLUEBERRY MUFFINS

These moist muffins are full of blueberries. I keep frozen berries on hand—it's so easy and convenient to fold them right into the muffin batter without having to wait for them to thaw.
—*Ardyce Piehl, Wisconsin Dells, WI*

Prep: 15 min. • **Bake:** 25 min. + cooling
Makes: about 2 dozen

- 4   cups all-purpose flour
- 4   tsp. baking powder
- ½   tsp. salt
- 1   cup butter, softened
- 2   cups sugar
- 4   large eggs, room temperature
- 1   cup 2% milk
- 2   tsp. vanilla extract
- 2   cups frozen unsweetened blueberries

TOPPING
- 2   Tbsp. sugar
- ½   tsp. ground nutmeg

1. In a large bowl, combine the flour, baking powder and salt. In a large bowl, cream butter and sugar. Add eggs, milk and vanilla; mix well. Stir in dry ingredients just until moistened. Fold in frozen blueberries.

2. Fill 24 greased or paper-lined muffin cups two-thirds full. Combine sugar and nutmeg; sprinkle over muffins. Bake at 375° until a toothpick comes out clean, 20-25 minutes. Cool in pan for 10 minutes before removing to a wire rack.

NOTE: If using frozen blueberries, use without thawing to avoid discoloring the batter.

1 MUFFIN: 238 cal., 9g fat (5g sat. fat), 57mg chol., 209mg sod., 36g carb. (19g sugars, 1g fiber), 4g pro.

MAPLE TWIST COFFEE CAKE

Add this recipe to your keeper file if you're a fan of maple. The coffee cake makes a gorgeous addition to any spread, especially a Christmas morning brunch.
—*Deanna Richter, Elmore, MN*

Prep: 45 min. + rising • **Bake:** 20 min.
Makes: 16 servings

- 1   pkg. (¼ oz.) active dry yeast
- ¾   cup warm whole milk (110° to 115°)
- ¼   cup butter, softened
- 3   Tbsp. sugar
- 1   large egg, room temperature

- 1   tsp. maple flavoring
- ½   tsp. salt
- 2¾   to 3 cups all-purpose flour

FILLING
- ½   cup sugar
- ⅓   cup chopped walnuts
- 1   tsp. ground cinnamon
- 1   tsp. maple flavoring
- ¼   cup butter, melted

GLAZE
- 1   cup confectioners' sugar
- 2   Tbsp. butter, melted
- 1   to 2 Tbsp. whole milk
- ½   tsp. maple flavoring

1. In a large bowl, dissolve yeast in warm milk. Add the butter, sugar, egg, maple flavoring, salt and 1½ cups flour. Beat until smooth. Stir in enough remaining flour to form a soft dough.

2. Turn onto a floured surface; knead until smooth and elastic, 6-8 minutes. Place in a greased bowl, turning once to grease top. Cover and let rise in a warm place until doubled, about 1 hour. Meanwhile, in a small

bowl, combine the sugar, walnuts, cinnamon and maple flavoring; set aside.

3. Punch dough down. Turn onto a lightly floured surface; divide into thirds. Roll each portion into a 12-in. circle; place 1 circle on a greased baking sheet or 12-in. baking pan. Spread with a third of the butter; sprinkle with a third of the filling. Repeat layers twice. Pinch edges of dough to seal.

4. Carefully place a glass in center of circle. With scissors, cut from outside edge just to the glass, forming 16 wedges. Remove glass; twist each wedge 5 or 6 times. Pinch ends to seal and tuck under. Cover and let rise until doubled, about 30 minutes.

5. Bake at 375° until golden brown, 18-20 minutes. In a small bowl, combine the glaze ingredients; set aside. Carefully remove the coffee cake from pan by running a metal spatula under it to loosen; transfer to a wire rack. Drizzle with glaze.

1 PIECE: 236 cal., 10g fat (5g sat. fat), 33mg chol., 134mg sod., 34g carb. (17g sugars, 1g fiber), 4g pro.

PUMPKIN PECAN LOAVES

Among all my pumpkin bread recipes, this caramel-glazed creation is the pick of the crop. Often, I'll wrap up a lovely loaf as a homemade gift for teachers and Sunday school leaders.
—*Brenda Jackson, Garden City, KS*

Prep: 15 min. • **Bake:** 1 hour + cooling
Makes: 2 loaves (16 slices each)

- 3⅓ cups all-purpose flour
- 3 cups sugar
- 2 tsp. baking soda
- 1½ tsp. salt
- 1 tsp. ground cinnamon
- 1 tsp. ground nutmeg
- 1 can (15 oz.) pumpkin
- 1 cup vegetable oil
- 4 large eggs, room temperature, lightly beaten
- ⅔ cup water
- ½ cup chopped pecans
  CARAMEL GLAZE
- ¼ cup butter
- ¼ cup sugar
- ¼ cup packed brown sugar
- ¼ cup heavy whipping cream
- ⅔ cup confectioners' sugar
- 1 tsp. vanilla extract

1. In a bowl, combine the first 6 ingredients. In a separate bowl, combine the pumpkin, oil, eggs and water; mix well. Stir into the dry ingredients just until combined; fold in the pecans.
2. Spoon into 2 greased 9x5-in. loaf pans. Bake at 350° for 60-65 minutes or until a toothpick inserted in the center comes out clean. Cool for 10 minutes before removing from pans to wire racks.
3. For glaze, combine butter, sugar, brown sugar and cream in a saucepan. Cook until sugar is dissolved. Cool for 20 minutes. Stir in the confectioners' sugar and vanilla until smooth. Drizzle over cooled loaves.
1 SLICE: 249 cal., 11g fat (3g sat. fat), 29mg chol., 212mg sod., 36g carb. (25g sugars, 1g fiber), 3g pro.

SOUTHERN BUTTERMILK BISCUITS

The recipe for these four-ingredient biscuits has been handed down for many generations.
—*Fran Thompson, Tarboro, NC*

Takes: 30 min. • **Makes:** 8 biscuits

- ½ cup cold butter, cubed
- 2 cups self-rising flour
- ¾ cup buttermilk
  Melted butter

1. In a large bowl, cut butter into flour until mixture resembles coarse crumbs. Stir in buttermilk just until moistened. Turn onto a lightly floured surface; knead 3-4 times. Pat or lightly roll to ¾-in. thickness. Cut with a floured 2½-in. biscuit cutter.
2. Place on a greased baking sheet. Bake at 425° until golden brown, 11-13 minutes. Brush tops with butter. Serve warm.
NOTE: To make a substitute for one cup of self-rising flour, place 1½ tsp. baking powder and ½ tsp. salt in a measuring cup. Add all-purpose flour to measure 1 cup.
1 BISCUIT: 197 cal., 11g fat (7g sat. fat), 28mg chol., 451mg sod., 22g carb., 1g fiber, 4g pro.

READER REVIEW

"So easy, so tasty! Will put this in my file and it will be well used! I love fresh biscuits straight out of the oven!"
RENA 55, TASTEOFHOME.COM

STRAWBERRIES & CREAM BREAD

My husband and I look forward to this quick bread every summer during strawberry-picking season. Since only fresh berries will do, I'd like to try it with other berries that are in season year-round...so we can enjoy it more often.
—*Suzanne Randall, Dexter, ME*

Prep: 15 min. • **Bake:** 65 min. + cooling
Makes: 1 loaf (12 slices)

½	cup butter, softened
¾	cup sugar
2	large eggs, room temperature
½	cup sour cream
1	tsp. vanilla extract
1¾	cups all-purpose flour
½	tsp. baking powder
½	tsp. baking soda
½	tsp. salt
¼	tsp. ground cinnamon
¾	cup chopped fresh strawberries
¾	cup chopped walnuts, toasted, divided

1. Preheat oven to 350°. In a large bowl, cream butter and sugar until light and fluffy. Beat in eggs. Add sour cream and vanilla; mix well.

2. In another bowl, whisk the flour, baking powder, baking soda, salt and cinnamon; gradually stir into creamed mixture just until moistened. Fold in strawberries and ½ cup nuts.

3. Pour into a greased 8x4-in. loaf pan. Sprinkle with remaining nuts. Bake until a toothpick inserted in center comes out clean 65-70 minutes or. Cool in pan for 10 minutes before removing to a wire rack to cool completely.

1 SLICE: 199 cal., 11g fat (5g sat. fat), 47mg chol., 196mg sod., 21g carb. (10g sugars, 1g fiber), 4g pro.

QUICK JALAPENO HUSH PUPPIES

The crunchy exterior of these southern bites is a nice contrast to the moist cornbread on the inside. Jalapeno peppers and hot sauce add a hint of heat.
—Taste of Home *Test Kitchen*

Prep: 15 min. • **Cook:** 5 min./batch
Makes: 2½ dozen

- 1½ cups yellow cornmeal
- ½ cup all-purpose flour
- 1 tsp. baking powder
- 1 tsp. salt
- 2 large eggs, lightly beaten
- ¾ cup 2% milk
- 2 jalapeno peppers, seeded and minced
- ¼ cup finely chopped onion
- 1 tsp. Louisiana-style hot sauce
  Oil for deep-fat frying

1. In a large bowl, combine the cornmeal, flour, baking powder and salt. In another bowl, beat the eggs, milk, jalapenos, onion and hot sauce. Stir into dry ingredients just until combined.

2. In a cast-iron or other heavy skillet, heat oil to 375°. Drop tablespoonfuls of batter, a few at a time, into hot oil. Fry until golden brown on both sides. Drain on paper towels. Serve warm.

NOTE: Wear disposable gloves when cutting hot peppers; the oils can burn skin. Avoid touching your face.

1 HUSH PUPPY: 56 cal., 3g fat (0 sat. fat), 14mg chol., 94mg sod., 7g carb. (0 sugars, 1g fiber), 1g pro.

BOHEMIAN KOLACHES

In Eastern Europe, a kolache is typically shaped into a circle, which is a symbol of good luck, prosperity and eternity. My mother-in-law gave me this recipe.
—*Maxine Hron, Quincy, IL*

- -

Prep: 30 min. + rising • **Bake:** 10 min.
Makes: about 28 rolls

- 2 pkg. (¼ oz. each) active dry yeast
- ½ cup sugar, divided
- 2 cups warm 2% milk (110° to 115°)
- 5¾ to 6½ cups all-purpose flour
- 4 large egg yolks, room temperature
- 1 tsp. salt
- ¼ cup butter, softened
- 2 cups canned prune, poppy seed, cherry or lemon pie filling
- 1 large egg white, beaten

1. In a small bowl, dissolve yeast and 1 Tbsp. sugar in warm milk; let stand 10 minutes. In large bowl, combine 2 cups flour, remaining sugar, egg yolks, salt, butter and yeast/milk mixture. Mix until smooth. Add enough remaining flour to make a stiff dough.

2. Turn out onto a floured surface and knead until smooth and elastic, 6-8 minutes. Add additional flour, if necessary. Place dough in greased bowl, turning once to grease top. Cover; let rise in a warm place until doubled in bulk, about 1 hour.

3. Punch dough down and allow to rise again. Roll out on floured surface to ½-in. thickness. Cut with large glass or 2½-in. cutter. Place on greased baking sheets; let rise until doubled, about 45 minutes.

4. Firmly press indentation in center and fill each roll with a heaping tablespoon of fruit filling. Brush dough with egg white. Bake at 350° for 10-15 minutes or until rolls are light golden brown.

1 SERVING: 164 cal., 3g fat (2g sat. fat), 37mg chol., 116mg sod., 29g carb. (9g sugars, 1g fiber), 4g pro.

QUICK FOCACCIA BREAD

Green olives complement my speedy version of the beloved Italian bread. Try the focaccia with minestrone or Italian wedding soup, or serve it with an antipasto tray for a hearty appetizer everyone will love.
—*Ivy Laffoon, Ceres, CA*

- -

Takes: 30 min. • **Makes:** 8 servings

- 1 loaf (1 lb.) frozen bread dough, thawed
- ½ cup sliced pimiento-stuffed olives
- ½ cup shredded Colby-Monterey Jack cheese
- ½ cup shredded Parmesan cheese
- 1 tsp. Italian seasoning
- 2 Tbsp. olive oil

1. On an ungreased baking sheet, pat dough into a 12x6-in. rectangle. Build up edges slightly. Top with olives, cheeses and Italian seasoning; press gently into dough. Drizzle with oil.

2. Bake at 350° until cheese is melted and golden brown, 15-20 minutes. Let stand for 5 minutes before slicing.

1 SLICE: 249 cal., 11g fat (3g sat. fat), 10mg chol., 623mg sod., 31g carb. (2g sugars, 2g fiber), 9g pro.

GREEN ONION ROLLS

Better double the batch—these savory, elegant rolls will disappear fast.
—*Jane Kroeger, Key Largo, FL*

- -

Prep: 30 min. + rising • **Bake:** 20 min.
Makes: 1 dozen

  1 **Tbsp. butter**
1½ **cups chopped green onions**
 ½ **tsp. pepper**
 ¾ **tsp. garlic salt, optional**
  1 **loaf (1 lb.) frozen bread**
     dough, thawed
 ½ **cup shredded part-skim**
     mozzarella cheese
 ⅓ **cup grated Parmesan cheese**

1. Preheat oven to 375°. In a large skillet, heat butter over medium-high heat; saute green onions until tender. Stir in pepper and, if desired, garlic salt. Remove from heat.
2. On a lightly floured surface, roll dough into a 12x8-in. rectangle. Spread with the onion mixture. Sprinkle with cheeses.
3. Roll up jelly-roll style, starting with a long side; pinch seam to seal. Cut into 12 slices; place in greased muffin cups. Cover with greased plastic wrap; let rise in a warm place until doubled, about 30 minutes. Preheat oven to 375°.
4. Bake until golden brown, 18-20 minutes. Remove from pan to a wire rack. Serve warm.
1 ROLL: 142 cal., 4g fat (1g sat. fat), 7mg chol., 415mg sod., 20g carb. (2g sugars, 2g fiber), 6g pro.

BUTTER & HERB LOAF

This is one of my family's favorite bread recipes. They love it with a warm bowl of soup when there's a chill in the air.
—*Lillian Hatcher, Plainfield, IL*

- -

Prep: 45 min. + rising • **Bake:** 20 min. + cooling
Makes: 2 loaves (16 slices each)

  4 **to 5 cups all-purpose flour**
  1 **pkg. (¼ oz.) active dry yeast**
 ¼ **cup sugar**
  1 **tsp. salt**
1¼ **cups 2% milk**
 ⅓ **cup butter, cubed**
  2 **large eggs, room temperature**
FILLING
 ½ **cup butter, softened**
  1 **garlic clove, minced**
 ½ **tsp. dried minced onion**
 ½ **tsp. dried basil**
 ⅓ **tsp. caraway seeds**
 ¼ **tsp. dried oregano**
 ⅛ **tsp. cayenne pepper**

1. In a large bowl, combine 2 cups flour, yeast, sugar and salt. In a small saucepan, heat milk and butter to 120°-130°. Add to the dry ingredients; beat just until moistened. Add the eggs; beat until smooth. Stir in enough remaining flour to form a soft dough.
2. Turn onto a floured surface; knead until smooth and elastic, 6-8 minutes. Place in a greased bowl, turning once to grease top. Cover dough and let rise in a warm place until doubled, about 1 hour.
3. In a small bowl, combine filling ingredients; set aside. Punch down dough; divide in half. Turn onto a lightly floured surface. Roll each portion into a 15x9-in. rectangle. Spread the filling over each to within ½ in. of edges. Roll up jelly-roll style, starting with a short side; pinch seams to seal and tuck ends under.
4. Place seam side down in 2 greased 9x5-in. loaf pans. Cover and let rise in a warm place until doubled, about 30 minutes.
5. Bake at 350° for 20-25 minutes or until golden brown. Cool for 10 minutes before removing loaves from pans to wire racks to cool completely.
1 SLICE: 109 cal., 5g fat (3g sat. fat), 27mg chol., 116mg sod., 13g carb. (2g sugars, 0 fiber), 3g pro. **DIABETIC EXCHANGES:** 1 starch, 1 fat.

BLUEBERRY KUCHEN

I look forward to warm weather when I can get beautiful, plump blueberries to use in this easy-to-make dessert. I freeze extra berries so I have them available any time I want this treat. It's divine served with a scoop of ice cream.
—Anne Krueger, Richmond, BC

- -

Prep: 10 min. • **Bake:** 40 min.
Makes: 12 servings

- 1½ cups all-purpose flour
- ¾ cup sugar
- 2 tsp. baking powder
- 1½ tsp. grated lemon zest
- ½ tsp. ground nutmeg
- ¼ tsp. salt
- ⅔ cup whole milk
- ¼ cup butter, melted
- 1 large egg, room temperature, beaten
- 1 tsp. vanilla extract
- 2 cups fresh or frozen blueberries

TOPPING
- ¾ cup sugar
- ½ cup all-purpose flour
- ¼ cup butter, melted

1. In a bowl, combine the first 6 ingredients. Add the milk, butter, egg and vanilla. Beat for 2 minutes or until well blended.
2. Pour into a greased 13x9-in. baking dish. Sprinkle with blueberries. In a bowl, combine sugar and flour; add butter. Toss with a fork until crumbly; sprinkle over blueberries. Bake at 350° for 40 minutes or until the kuchen is lightly browned.
1 PIECE: 271 cal., 9g fat (5g sat. fat), 37mg chol., 189mg sod., 45g carb. (28g sugars, 1g fiber), 3g pro.

TEST KITCHEN TIP
Frozen blueberries are convenient to have on hand as they are a nice addition to a variety of baked goods. To freeze fresh blueberries, place berries on a cookie sheet and put them in the freezer until frozen (about 1½ hours). Then place in airtight containers in the freezer. The berries won't stick together, so you can pour out any portion you desire.

LEMONY ZUCCHINI BREAD

Flecks of zucchini give a third dimension to the popular lemon and poppy seed combo in this moist bread. It's great in summer when zucchini is plentiful, but we enjoy it all year long.
—Carol Funk, Richard, SK

- -

Prep: 25 min. • **Bake:** 50 min. + cooling
Makes: 2 loaves (16 slices each)

- 4 cups all-purpose flour
- 1½ cups sugar
- 1 pkg. (3.4 oz.) instant lemon pudding mix
- 1½ tsp. baking soda
- 1 tsp. baking powder
- 1 tsp. salt
- 4 large eggs, room temperature
- 1¼ cups 2% milk
- 1 cup canola oil
- 3 Tbsp. lemon juice
- 1 tsp. lemon extract
- 2 cups shredded zucchini
- ¼ cup poppy seeds
- 2 tsp. grated lemon zest

1. In a large bowl, combine the flour, sugar, pudding mix, baking soda, baking powder and salt. In another bowl, whisk the eggs, milk, oil, lemon juice and extract. Stir into the dry ingredients just until moistened. Fold in the zucchini, poppy seeds and lemon zest.
2. Pour into 2 greased 9x5-in. loaf pans. Bake at 350° for 50-55 minutes or until a toothpick inserted in the center comes out clean. Cool for 10 minutes before removing from pans to wire racks to cool completely.
1 SLICE: 187 cal., 8g fat (1g sat. fat), 28mg chol., 195mg sod., 25g carb. (12g sugars, 1g fiber), 3g pro.

PARMESAN ZUCCHINI BREAD

This loaf has a rustic, textured look that adds to its appeal. The mild Parmesan flavor nicely complements the zucchini, which adds bits of green color to every tender slice.
—Chris Wilson, Sellersville, PA

Prep: 10 min. • **Bake:** 1 hour + cooling
Makes: 1 loaf (16 slices)

- 3 cups all-purpose flour
- 3 Tbsp. grated Parmesan cheese
- 1 tsp. salt
- ½ tsp. baking powder
- ½ tsp. baking soda
- 2 large eggs, room temperature
- 1 cup buttermilk
- ⅓ cup sugar
- ⅓ cup butter, melted
- 1 cup shredded peeled zucchini
- 1 Tbsp. grated onion

1. In a large bowl, combine flour, cheese, salt, baking powder and baking soda. In another bowl, whisk the eggs, buttermilk, sugar and butter. Stir into dry ingredients just until moistened. Fold in zucchini and onion.

2. Pour into a greased and floured 9x5-in. loaf pan. Bake at 350° until a toothpick inserted in the center comes out clean, about 1 hour. Cool for 10 minutes before removing from pan to a wire rack.

1 SLICE: 156 cal., 5g fat (3g sat. fat), 35mg chol., 288mg sod., 23g carb. (5g sugars, 1g fiber), 4g pro.

WHOLE WHEAT DINNER ROLLS

It warms my heart to see everyone at our table reach for one of my hearty whole wheat rolls. Rich with old-fashioned goodness, they bake up to a beautiful golden brown.
—Ruby Williams, Bogalusa, LA

Prep: 30 min. + rising • **Bake:** 15 min.
Makes: 4 dozen

- 2 pkg. (¼ oz. each) active dry yeast
- 2¼ cups warm water (110° to 115°)
- ½ cup plus 1 Tbsp. sugar
- ¼ cup shortening
- 2 tsp. salt
- 2 large eggs, room temperature
- 3 cups whole wheat flour
- 3½ to 4 cups all-purpose flour
- ¼ cup butter, melted

1. In a large bowl, dissolve yeast in warm water. Add the sugar, shortening, salt, eggs and whole wheat flour. Beat until smooth. Stir in enough all-purpose flour to form a soft dough.

2. Turn onto a floured surface; knead until smooth and elastic, 6-8 minutes. Place in a greased bowl, turning once to grease top. Cover and let rise in a warm place until doubled, about 1 hour.

3. Punch dough down. Turn onto a lightly floured surface; divide into 4 pieces. Shape each into 12 balls. Place 1 in. apart on greased baking sheets. Cover and let rise until doubled, about 25 minutes.

4. Bake at 375° for 11-15 minutes or until browned. Remove from pans to wire racks. Brush with melted butter. Serve warm.

1 ROLL: 89 cal., 2g fat (1g sat. fat), 11mg chol., 111mg sod., 15g carb. (3g sugars, 1g fiber), 2g pro.

GINGER PEAR MUFFINS

This wonderful recipe has been in my files for years. The chunks of fresh pear make each bite moist and delicious.
—*Lorraine Caland, Shuniah, ON*

Prep: 25 min. • **Bake:** 20 min.
Makes: 1½ dozen

- ¾ cup packed brown sugar
- ⅓ cup canola oil
- 1 large egg, room temperature
- 1 cup buttermilk
- 2½ cups all-purpose flour
- 1 tsp. baking soda
- 1 tsp. ground ginger
- ½ tsp. salt
- ½ tsp. ground cinnamon
- 2 cups chopped peeled fresh pears

TOPPING
- ⅓ cup packed brown sugar
- ¼ tsp. ground ginger
- 2 tsp. butter, melted

1. Preheat oven to 350°. In a small bowl, beat brown sugar, oil and egg until well blended. Beat in buttermilk. In a small bowl, combine flour, baking soda, ginger, salt and cinnamon; gradually beat into buttermilk mixture until blended. Stir in pears. Fill 18 paper-lined muffin cups two-thirds full.
2. For topping, combine brown sugar and ginger. Stir in butter until crumbly. Sprinkle over batter.
3. Bake 18-22 minutes or until a toothpick inserted in the center comes out clean. Cool 5 minutes before removing from pans to wire racks. Serve warm.
1 MUFFIN: 174 cal., 5g fat (1g sat. fat), 13mg chol., 162mg sod., 30g carb. (16g sugars, 1g fiber), 3g pro. **DIABETIC EXCHANGES:** 2 starch, 1 fat.

BANANA-ZUCCHINI BREAD

My grandmother made this bread for as long as I can remember, and I've been making it ever since I learned how to bake. Children love it for a snack, and it's good to serve at any meal. It's another delicious way to use zucchini, which is so abundant in late summer.
—*Eva Mae Hebert, Lafayette, LA*

Prep: 20 min. • **Bake:** 50 min. + cooling
Makes: 2 loaves

- 4 large eggs, room temperature
- 2 cups sugar
- 1 cup vegetable oil
- 2 medium ripe bananas, mashed (about 1 cup)
- 3 cups all-purpose flour
- 1½ tsp. baking powder
- 1½ tsp. baking soda
- 1½ tsp. ground cinnamon
- 1 tsp. salt
- 1½ cups shredded unpeeled zucchini
- 1 cup chopped pecans

1. In a bowl, beat eggs. Blend in sugar and oil. Add bananas and mix well. Combine the flour, baking powder, baking soda, cinnamon and salt; stir into egg mixture. Stir in zucchini and pecans just until combined.
2. Pour into 2 greased 9x5-in. loaf pans. Bake at 350° until a toothpick comes out clean, 50 minutes. Cool for 10 minutes. Remove from pans to wire racks to cool completely.
1 SLICE: 194 cal., 10g fat (1g sat. fat), 27mg chol., 160mg sod., 24g carb. (14g sugars, 1g fiber), 2g pro.

READER REVIEW
"If I could give this recipe more than 5 stars, I would. I followed the directions except left out the nuts and added a cup of mini chocolate chips instead— perfection!"
ANNE, TASTEOFHOME.COM

LORRAINE CALAND
Shuniah, ON

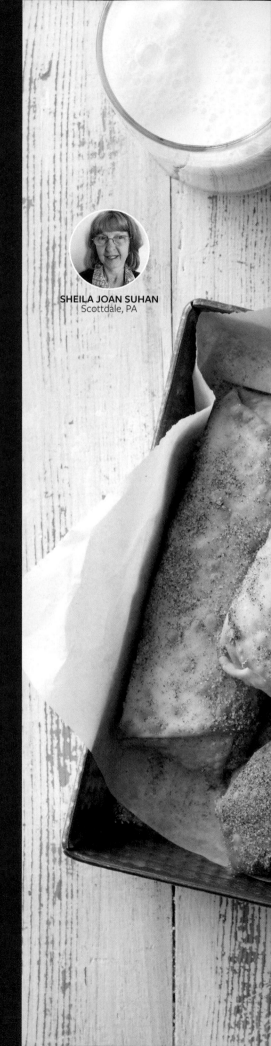

SHEILA JOAN SUHAN
Scottdale, PA

Cakes, Pies & Desserts

From classic cakes and pies to other wow-worthy indulgences, here's a sweet sampling of the dreamiest, yummiest, most irresistible desserts.

AIR-FRYER APPLE PIE EGG ROLLS

This fun riff on handheld apple pies uses egg roll wrappers as vessels for the fruit rather than traditional pie crust. The air-fryer method of cooking results in a crispy, crunchy crust with a tender, juicy filling.
—*Sheila Joan Suhan, Scottdale, PA*

- -

Prep: 25 min. • **Cook:** 15 min./batch
Makes: 8 servings

- 3 cups chopped peeled tart apples
- ½ cup packed light brown sugar
- 2½ tsp. ground cinnamon, divided
- 1 tsp. corn starch
- 8 egg roll wrappers
- ½ cup spreadable cream cheese
   Butter-flavored cooking spray
- 1 Tbsp. sugar
- ⅔ cup hot caramel ice cream topping

1. Preheat air fryer to 400°. In a small bowl, combine apples, brown sugar, 2 tsp. cinnamon and corn starch. With a corner of an egg roll wrapper facing you, spread 1 scant Tbsp. cream cheese to within 1 in. of edges. Place ⅓ cup apple mixture just below center of wrapper. (Cover remaining wrappers with a damp paper towel until ready to use.)
2. Fold bottom corner over filling; moisten remaining wrapper edges with water. Fold side corners toward center over filling. Roll egg roll up tightly, pressing at tip to seal. Repeat.
3. In batches, arrange egg rolls in a single layer in greased air-fryer basket; spritz with cooking spray. Cook until golden brown, 5-6 minutes. Turn; spritz with cooking spray. Cook until golden brown and crisp, 5-6 minutes longer. Combine sugar and remaining ½ tsp. cinnamon; roll hot egg rolls in mixture. Serve with caramel sauce.

1 ROLL: 273 cal., 4g fat (2g sat. fat), 13mg chol., 343mg sod., 56g carb. (35g sugars, 2g fiber), 5g pro.

HOMEMADE VANILLA ICE CREAM

We think this is the best ice cream recipe ever. With only four ingredients, it just might be the easiest, too. No ice cream maker? No problem.
—Taste of Home *Test Kitchen*

Prep: 5 min. • **Process:** 20 min. + freezing
Makes: 1¼ qt.

- 2 cups heavy whipping cream
- 2 cups half-and-half cream
- 1 cup sugar
- 2 tsp. vanilla extract

Combine all ingredients, stirring to dissolve sugar completely. Fill cylinder of ice cream maker no more than two-thirds full; freeze according to manufacturer's directions. (Refrigerate any remaining mixture until ready to freeze.) Serve immediately or store in covered containers in freezer.

NOTE: For raspberry or strawberry ice cream, substitute 2 cups fresh or frozen berries for 1 cup of half-and-half. Puree the berries in a blender or food processor; stir into the other ingredients before freezing.

NOTE: To prepare recipe without an ice cream maker, place a 13x9-in. dish in freezer until cold. Prepare cream mixture as directed; transfer to prepared dish. Freeze until edges of mixture begin to set, 20-30 minutes. Using a hand mixer, beat mixture until smooth. Freeze, covered, until firm, about 3 hours longer, beating again every 30 minutes.

½ CUP: 308 cal., 22g fat (14g sat. fat), 78mg chol., 37mg sod., 23g carb. (23g sugars, 0 fiber), 3g pro.

BUTTERMILK CAKE WITH CARAMEL ICING

This fabulous cake is so tender, it melts in your mouth. It's been a family favorite since the '70s and goes over well at church potlucks.
—Anna Jean Allen, West Liberty, KY

Prep: 35 min. • **Bake:** 45 min. + cooling
Makes: 16 servings

- 1 cup butter, softened
- 2⅓ cups sugar
- 1½ tsp. vanilla extract
- 3 large eggs, room temperature
- 3 cups all-purpose flour
- 1 tsp. baking powder
- ½ tsp. baking soda
- 1 cup buttermilk

ICING
- ¼ cup butter, cubed
- ½ cup packed brown sugar
- ⅓ cup heavy whipping cream
- 1 cup confectioners' sugar

1. Preheat oven to 350°. Grease and flour a 10-in. fluted tube pan.

2. Cream butter and sugar until light and fluffy. Beat in vanilla and 1 egg at a time, beating well after each addition. In another bowl, whisk together flour, baking powder and baking soda; add to the creamed mixture alternately with buttermilk (batter will be thick). Transfer to prepared pan.

3. Bake until a toothpick inserted in center comes out clean, 45-50 minutes. Cool in pan 10 minutes before removing to a wire rack to cool completely.

4. For icing, in a small saucepan, combine the butter, brown sugar and cream; bring mixture to a boil over medium heat, stirring constantly. Remove from the heat; cool for 5-10 minutes. Gradually beat in confectioners' sugar; spoon over cake.

NOTE: To remove cakes easily, use solid shortening to grease plain and fluted tube pans.

1 SLICE: 419 cal., 17g fat (11g sat. fat), 79mg chol., 230mg sod., 63g carb. (44g sugars, 1g fiber), 4g pro.

CHOCOLATE MAYONNAISE CAKE

Mom always made this special chocolate mayo cake for my birthday. It is moist and has a nice light chocolate taste, and the flavorful frosting is the perfect topping.
—*Deborah Amrine, Fort Myers, FL*

Prep: 15 min. • **Bake:** 30 min. + cooling
Makes: 9-12 servings

- 1 cup water
- 1 cup mayonnaise
- 1 tsp. vanilla extract
- 2 cups all-purpose flour
- 1 cup sugar
- 3 Tbsp. baking cocoa
- 2 tsp. baking soda

BROWN SUGAR FROSTING
- ½ cup packed brown sugar
- ¼ cup butter, cubed
- 2 Tbsp. 2% milk
- 1¾ cups confectioners' sugar

1. In a large mixing bowl, combine the water, mayonnaise and vanilla until well blended. In a large bowl, combine the flour, sugar, cocoa and baking soda; gradually beat into mayonnaise mixture until blended.
2. Pour into a greased 9-in. square or 11x7-in. baking pan. Bake at 350° for 30-35 minutes or until a toothpick inserted in the center comes out clean. Cool completely.
3. For frosting, in a small saucepan, cook and stir the brown sugar in butter until bubbly. Remove from the heat; stir in milk. Gradually add confectioners' sugar; beat until smooth. Frost cake.
1 PIECE: 416 cal., 19g fat (4g sat. fat), 17mg chol., 354mg sod., 60g carb. (42g sugars, 1g fiber), 3g pro.

RHUBARB CHEESECAKE SQUARES

Rich and tangy, this cheesecake bar is bound to be a hit with the rhubarb lovers you know—and even those who haven't fallen for the ruby red goodness yet.
—*Sharon Schmidt, Mandan, ND*

Prep: 25 min. • **Bake:** 40 min. + chilling
Makes: 16 servings

- 1¼ cups all-purpose flour
- ½ cup old-fashioned oats
- ½ cup packed brown sugar
- ½ cup cold butter, cubed
- 1 pkg. (8 oz.) cream cheese, softened
- ¾ cup sugar
- ½ tsp. salt
- ¼ tsp. ground cinnamon
- ⅛ tsp. ground nutmeg
- 1 large egg, room temperature, lightly beaten
- ½ tsp. vanilla extract
- 1½ cups diced fresh or frozen rhubarb, thawed

1. Preheat oven to 350°. In a small bowl, mix flour, oats and brown sugar; cut in butter until crumbly. Reserve 1 cup mixture for topping. Press remaining mixture onto bottom of a greased 9-in. square baking pan.
2. For filling, beat cream cheese, sugar, salt and spices until smooth. Add egg and vanilla; beat on low speed just until combined. Fold in rhubarb. Spread over crust. Sprinkle with reserved topping.
3. Bake until golden brown and filling is set, about 40 minutes. Cool on a wire rack 1 hour. Refrigerate dessert, covered, until cold, about 2 hours. Cut into squares.
NOTE: If using frozen rhubarb, measure rhubarb while still frozen, then allow it to thaw completely. Drain in a colander, but do not press liquid out.
1 SQUARE: 216 cal., 11g fat (7g sat. fat), 41mg chol., 171mg sod., 27g carb. (17g sugars, 1g fiber), 3g pro.

YOGURT-RICOTTA CHEESECAKE

I have always liked Italian ricotta cheesecakes. I made a diabetic version and my family couldn't even tell! I serve it with sugar-free strawberry ice cream topping and fresh strawberries.
—*Diane Shipley, Mentor, OH*

Prep: 35 min. • **Bake:** 80 min. + chilling
Makes: 16 servings

- 2 pkg. (8 oz. each) reduced-fat cream cheese
- 2 cups reduced-fat ricotta cheese
  Sugar substitute blend (made with sucralose) equivalent to 1½ cups sugar
- 2 cups (16 oz.) vanilla yogurt
- ½ cup butter, melted
- ¼ cup cornstarch
- 3 Tbsp. all-purpose flour
- 2 Tbsp. lemon juice
- 1 tsp. vanilla extract
- 4 large eggs, room temperature, lightly beaten
  Halved fresh strawberries, optional

1. Preheat oven to 325°. In a large bowl, beat cream cheese, ricotta and sugar blend until smooth. Beat in yogurt, butter, cornstarch, flour, lemon juice and vanilla. Add eggs; beat on low speed just until blended. Pour into a greased 9-in. springform pan. Place pan on a baking sheet.

2. Bake until the center is almost set, 80-85 minutes. Cool on a wire rack 10 minutes. Loosen sides from pan with a knife. Cool 1 hour longer. Refrigerate overnight, covering when completely cooled.

3. Remove rim from pan. If desired, serve cheesecake with strawberries.

NOTE: This recipe was tested with Splenda sugar blend.

1 SLICE: 246 cal., 15g fat (9g sat. fat), 91mg chol., 231mg sod., 19g carb. (16g sugars, 0 fiber), 9g pro.

TEST KITCHEN TIP
It is best to cut a cheesecake right after you remove it from the refrigerator. Dip a clean knife in a glass of hot water and wipe it dry before cutting. Wipe the knife clean after each cut and dip in warm water again. Remove slices to a serving plate with a pie spatula.

APPLE SPICE CAKE WITH BROWN SUGAR FROSTING

I make healthy food choices most of the time, but this apple spice cake is worth the splurge! Every year, I look forward to the opportunity to make my own birthday cake, and I choose this. Add a cup of raisins to the batter before baking if you'd like.
—*Jennifer Owen, Louisville, KY*

- -

Prep: 30 min. • **Bake:** 35 min. + cooling
Makes: 16 servings

- 4 medium Honeycrisp apples, peeled and cut into 1-in. pieces (about 1½ lbs.)
- 2 cups sugar
- ½ cup canola oil
- 2 large eggs, room temperature
- 2 tsp. vanilla extract
- 2 cups all-purpose flour
- 1 Tbsp. pumpkin pie spice
- 2 tsp. baking powder
- 1 tsp. salt
- ½ cup buttermilk
- 1½ cups chopped walnuts, toasted

FROSTING

- 1 pkg. (8 oz.) cream cheese, softened
- ½ cup butter, softened
- 1 cup confectioners' sugar
- 1 cup packed brown sugar
- 1½ tsp. vanilla extract
- 1 tsp. pumpkin pie spice
- 1½ cups chopped walnuts, toasted

1. Preheat oven to 350°. Line the bottoms of 2 greased 9-in. round baking pans with parchment; grease paper.
2. Place apples in a food processor; pulse until finely chopped. In a large bowl, beat sugar, oil, eggs and vanilla until well blended. In another bowl, whisk flour, pie spice, baking powder and salt; gradually beat into sugar mixture alternately with buttermilk. Stir in apples and walnuts.
3. Transfer to prepared pans. Bake until a toothpick inserted in center comes out clean, 35-40 minutes. Cool in pans for 10 minutes before removing to wire racks; remove paper. Cool completely.
4. In a large bowl, beat cream cheese, butter, sugars, vanilla and pie spice until smooth. Spread frosting between layers and over top and sides of cake. Gently press walnuts into frosting on top of cake. Refrigerate leftovers.
1 SLICE: 574 cal., 33g fat (9g sat. fat), 53mg chol., 326mg sod., 67g carb. (51g sugars, 2g fiber), 7g pro.

CONTEST-WINNING RASPBERRY CREAM PIE

This recipe is delicious with either fresh-picked or frozen raspberries. The beauty of that is you can make it all year long. One bite of raspberry pie will instantly turn winter to summer.
—*Julie Price, Nashville, TN*

Prep: 30 min. + chilling • **Makes:** 8 servings

1½ cups crushed vanilla wafers
    (about 45 wafers)
⅓ cup chopped pecans
¼ cup butter, melted
FILLING
1 pkg. (8 oz.) cream cheese, softened
⅔ cup confectioners' sugar
2 Tbsp. orange liqueur
1 tsp. vanilla extract
1 cup heavy whipping cream, whipped
TOPPING
1 cup sugar
3 Tbsp. cornstarch
3 Tbsp. water
2½ cups fresh or frozen
    raspberries, divided

1. Combine the wafer crumbs, pecans and butter. Press onto the bottom and up the sides of a greased 9-in. pie plate.
2. In a large bowl, beat the cream cheese, confectioners' sugar, liqueur and vanilla until light and fluffy. Fold in whipped cream. Spread into crust. Chill until serving.
3. In a small saucepan, combine the sugar and cornstarch; stir in the water and 1½ cups raspberries. Bring to a boil; cook and stir for 2 minutes or until thickened. Transfer to a bowl; refrigerate until chilled.
4. Spread topping over filling. Garnish with remaining berries.
1 PIECE: 507 cal., 28g fat (14g sat. fat), 70mg chol., 196mg sod., 61g carb. (46g sugars, 4g fiber), 4g pro.

BANANA BREAD PUDDING

With its crusty golden top, custardlike inside and smooth vanilla sauce, this bread pudding from my grandmother is a real homespun dessert. I enjoy making it for my grandchildren.
—*Mary Detweiler, Middlefield, OH*

Prep: 10 min. • **Bake:** 40 min.
Makes: 6 servings

4 cups cubed day-old French or
   sourdough bread (1-in. pieces)
¼ cup butter, melted
3 large eggs
2 cups whole milk
½ cup sugar
2 tsp. vanilla extract
½ tsp. ground cinnamon
½ tsp. ground nutmeg
½ tsp. salt
1 cup sliced firm bananas
   (¼-in. pieces)
SAUCE
3 Tbsp. butter
2 Tbsp. sugar
1 Tbsp. cornstarch
¾ cup whole milk
¼ cup light corn syrup
1 tsp. vanilla extract

1. Place the bread cubes in a greased 2-qt. casserole; pour butter over top and toss to coat. In a medium bowl, lightly beat eggs; add milk, sugar, vanilla, cinnamon, nutmeg and salt. Stir in bananas.
2. Pour egg mixture over bread cubes and stir to coat. Bake, uncovered, at 375° for about 40 minutes or until a knife inserted in the center comes out clean.
3. Meanwhile, for sauce, melt butter in a small saucepan. Combine sugar and cornstarch; add to butter. Stir in milk and corn syrup. Cook and stir over medium heat until the mixture comes to a full boil. Boil for 1 minute. Remove from the heat; stir in the vanilla. Serve warm sauce over warm pudding.
1 PIECE: 439 cal., 21g fat (12g sat. fat), 157mg chol., 561mg sod., 56g carb. (38g sugars, 1g fiber), 9g pro.

CHOCOLATE CHIP CHEESECAKE BARS

I received this recipe from a co-worker who made these heavenly bars for a potluck. Since they combine two classic flavors—chocolate chip cookies and cheesecake—in one bite, they were a hit with our three grown children.
—*Jane Nolt, Narvon, PA*

Prep: 20 min. • **Bake:** 45 min.
Makes: 2 dozen

- ¾ cup shortening
- ¾ cup sugar
- ⅓ cup packed brown sugar
- 1 large egg, room temperature
- 1½ tsp. vanilla extract
- 1½ cups all-purpose flour
- 1 tsp. salt
- ¾ tsp. baking soda
- 1½ cups miniature semisweet chocolate chips
- ¾ cup chopped pecans

FILLING

- 2 pkg. (8 oz. each) cream cheese, softened
- ¾ cup sugar
- 2 large eggs, room temperature
- 1 tsp. vanilla extract

1. In a large bowl, cream shortening and sugars until light and fluffy. Beat in egg and vanilla. Combine the flour, salt and baking soda; gradually add to the creamed mixture until blended. Fold in the chocolate chips and pecans.

2. Set aside a third of the dough for topping. Press remaining dough into a greased 13x9-in. baking pan. Bake at 350° for 8 minutes.

3. Meanwhile, in a small bowl, beat cream cheese and sugar until smooth. Beat in eggs and vanilla. Spoon over crust.

4. Drop teaspoonfuls of reserved dough over filling. Bake at 350° for 35-40 minutes or until golden brown. Cool on a wire rack. Cut into bars. Cover and store in the refrigerator.

1 BAR: 176 cal., 11g fat (4g sat. fat), 25mg chol., 117mg sod., 19g carb. (15g sugars, 1g fiber), 2g pro.

APPLE BUTTER PUMPKIN PIE

The addition of apple butter gives this pumpkin pie a slightly fruity flavor. I'm always happy to share tried-and-true recipes like this one.
—*Edna Hoffman, Hebron, IN*

Prep: 25 min. • **Bake:** 50 min. + cooling
Makes: 8 servings

- 3 large eggs, room temperature
- 1 cup canned pumpkin
- 1 cup apple butter
- ¾ cup packed brown sugar
- 1 can (5 oz.) evaporated milk
- ⅓ cup 2% milk
- 1 tsp. vanilla extract
- ½ tsp. salt
- ½ tsp. ground cinnamon
- ⅛ tsp. each ground ginger, cloves and nutmeg
- 1 unbaked pastry shell (9 in.)
  Whipped cream, optional

1. In a large mixing bowl, combine the first 7 ingredients. Whisk in salt and spices until well blended. Pour into pastry shell.

2. Bake at 400° for 50-55 minutes or until a knife inserted in the center comes out clean. Cover edges loosely with foil during the last 20 minutes if necessary. Cool on wire rack. Garnish with whipped cream if desired. Refrigerate leftovers.

NOTE: This recipe was tested with commercially prepared apple butter.

1 PIECE: 328 cal., 10g fat (5g sat. fat), 92mg chol., 304mg sod., 53g carb. (37g sugars, 2g fiber), 5g pro.

4. Place 1 cake layer on a serving plate; spread with half of the filling. Repeat layers. Top with remaining cake layer. Frost top and sides of cake with ganache. In a microwave-safe bowl, combine the chocolate, cream and butter. Microwave at 50% power for 1-2 minutes or until smooth, stirring twice. Cool slightly, stirring occasionally. Drizzle over the cake, allowing some to flow over sides. Refrigerate at least 2 hours before serving.

1 SLICE: 970 cal., 65g fat (30g sat. fat), 88mg chol., 607mg sod., 81g carb. (53g sugars, 3g fiber), 8g pro.

PUMPKIN & WALNUT SQUARES

The buttery crust, crumb topping and creamy pumpkin filling make this dessert popular at potlucks. You should try these squares with a little whipped cream or ice cream—but they taste great plain, too!
—*Ruth Beller, Sun City, CA*

- -

Prep: 25 min. • **Bake:** 50 min. • **Makes:** 2 dozen

1¾	cups all-purpose flour
⅓	cup sugar
⅓	cup packed brown sugar
1	cup cold butter, cubed
1	cup chopped walnuts
2	large eggs, room temperature, lightly beaten
1	can (15 oz.) solid-pack pumpkin
1	can (14 oz.) sweetened condensed milk
1	tsp. ground cinnamon
½	tsp. salt
½	tsp. ground allspice
	Confectioners' sugar, optional

1. Preheat oven to 350°. Mix flour, sugar and brown sugar; cut in butter until crumbly. Stir in walnuts. Reserve 1 cup mixture for topping; press remaining mixture onto bottom and halfway up sides of a 13x9-in. baking dish.
2. In a large bowl, beat eggs, pumpkin, milk, cinnamon, salt and allspice just until smooth. Pour into crust; sprinkle with reserved topping.
3. Bake until golden brown, 50-55 minutes. Cool slightly on a wire rack. Serve warm, or refrigerate and serve cold. If desired, dust with confectioners' sugar. Refrigerate leftovers.

1 SQUARE: 221 cal., 13g fat (6g sat. fat), 41mg chol., 139mg sod., 24g carb. (16g sugars, 1g fiber), 4g pro.

THREE-LAYER CHOCOLATE GANACHE CAKE

This decadent triple-layer beauty is pure chocolate indulgence. The cake layers can be frozen prior to final assembly; in fact, they're easier to work with when frozen.
—*Kathleen Smith, Overland, MO*

- -

Prep: 30 min. • **Bake:** 30 min. + chilling
Makes: 16 servings

4	cups all-purpose flour
2¼	cups sugar
¾	cup baking cocoa
4	tsp. baking soda
2¼	cups mayonnaise
2¼	cups cold brewed coffee
1½	tsp. vanilla extract

FILLING
1	cup sugar
2	Tbsp. cornstarch
1	cup 2% milk
2	tsp. vanilla extract
1	cup butter, softened
¾	cup miniature semisweet chocolate chips

GANACHE
8	oz. semisweet chocolate, chopped
2	cups heavy whipping cream
1	tsp. vanilla extract

GLAZE
8	oz. semisweet chocolate, chopped
¾	cup heavy whipping cream
¼	cup butter, cubed

1. Preheat oven to 350°. Line bottoms of 3 greased 9-in. round baking pans with waxed paper; grease paper. In a large bowl, whisk flour, sugar, cocoa and baking soda. Beat in the mayonnaise, coffee and vanilla. Transfer batter to prepared pans. Bake 30-35 minutes or until a toothpick inserted in center comes out clean. Cool in pans for 10 minutes before removing to wire racks; remove the paper. Cool completely.
2. For the filling, in a small heavy saucepan, mix sugar and cornstarch. Whisk in milk. Cook and stir over medium heat until thickened and bubbly. Reduce heat to low; cook and stir 2 minutes longer. Remove from heat; stir in vanilla. Cool completely. In a large bowl, cream butter. Gradually beat in cooled mixture. Stir in chocolate chips.
3. For the ganache, place chocolate in a large bowl. In a small saucepan, bring cream just to a boil. Pour over the chocolate; let stand for 5 minutes. Stir with a whisk until smooth. Stir in vanilla. Cool to room temperature, stirring occasionally. Refrigerate, covered, until cold. Beat ganache just until soft peaks form, about 15-30 seconds (do not overbeat).

EASY FOUR-LAYER CHOCOLATE DESSERT

I grew up on these nutty, chocolaty layered treats. Now I make them for both my mom and myself, since I know she loves them, too.
—*Kristen Stecklein, Waukesha, WI*

Prep: 20 min. • **Bake:** 15 min. + chilling
Makes: 15 servings

- 1 cup all-purpose flour
- ½ cup cold butter
- 1 cup chopped walnuts, toasted, divided
- 1 pkg. (8 oz.) cream cheese, softened
- 1 cup confectioners' sugar
- 2 cartons (8 oz. each) frozen whipped topping, thawed, divided
- 2½ cups 2% milk
- 2 pkg. (3.9 oz. each) instant chocolate pudding mix
- 1 cup semisweet chocolate chunks
  Chocolate syrup

1. Preheat oven to 350°. Place flour in a small bowl; cut in butter until crumbly. Stir in ½ cup walnuts. Press onto bottom of an ungreased 13x9-in. baking dish. Bake until light golden brown, 12-15 minutes. Cool completely on a wire rack.

2. In a small bowl, beat cream cheese and confectioners' sugar until smooth; fold in 1 carton whipped topping. Spread over crust. In a large bowl, whisk milk and pudding mix for 2 minutes. Gently spread over cream cheese layer. Top with remaining whipped topping. Sprinkle with chocolate chunks and remaining walnuts. Refrigerate until cold.

3. Cut into bars. Just before serving, drizzle with chocolate syrup.

NOTE: To toast nuts, bake in a shallow pan in a 350° oven for 5-10 minutes or cook in a skillet over low heat until lightly browned, stirring occasionally.

1 PIECE: 434 cal., 26g fat (15g sat. fat), 36mg chol., 195mg sod., 46g carb. (27g sugars, 2g fiber), 5g pro.

RHUBARB CRISP

I found this recipe in a box of Quaker Oats about 20 years ago. It's quick and easier to make than pie. It's versatile, too, because you can add strawberries in spring or apples in fall. I pop it into the oven shortly before we sit down to eat so we can enjoy it warm for dessert!
—*C.E. Adams, Charlestown, NH*

Prep: 15 min. • **Bake:** 45 min.
Makes: 8 servings

- ¾ cup sugar
- 3 Tbsp. cornstarch
- 3 cups sliced fresh rhubarb or frozen rhubarb, thawed
- 2 cups sliced peeled apples or sliced strawberries
- 1 cup quick-cooking or old-fashioned oats
- ½ cup packed brown sugar
- ½ cup butter, melted
- ⅓ cup all-purpose flour
- 1 tsp. ground cinnamon
  Vanilla ice cream, optional

1. In a large bowl, combine the sugar and cornstarch. Add the rhubarb and apples or strawberries; toss to coat. Spoon into an 8-in. cast-iron skillet or other ovenproof skillet.

2. In a small bowl, combine the oats, brown sugar, butter, flour and cinnamon until the mixture resembles coarse crumbs. Sprinkle over fruit. Bake at 350° until crisp is bubbly and fruit is tender, about 45 minutes. If desired, serve warm with ice cream.

NOTE: If using frozen rhubarb, measure rhubarb while still frozen, then thaw completely. Drain in a colander, but do not press liquid out.

1 CUP: 320 cal., 12g fat (7g sat. fat), 31mg chol., 124mg sod., 52g carb. (36g sugars, 3g fiber), 3g pro.

NO-BAKE CHOCOLATE CHIP CANNOLI CHEESECAKE

Now you can enjoy the flavor of the classic treat as a cheesecake. I make this in summer because it's light and refreshing. And not having to turn on the oven in hot weather is a bonus.
—*Kristen Heigl, Staten Island, NY*

Prep: 25 min. + chilling • **Makes:** 8 servings

- 1 pkg. (4 oz.) cannoli shells
- ½ cup sugar
- ½ cup graham cracker crumbs
- ⅓ cup butter, melted

FILLING

- 2 pkg. (8 oz. each) cream cheese, softened
- 1 cup confectioners' sugar
- ½ tsp. grated orange zest
- ¼ tsp. ground cinnamon
- ¾ cup part-skim ricotta cheese
- 1 tsp. vanilla extract
- ½ tsp. rum extract
- ½ cup miniature semisweet chocolate chips
  Chopped pistachios, optional

1. Pulse cannoli shells in a food processor until coarse crumbs form. Add sugar, cracker crumbs and melted butter; pulse just until combined. Press onto bottom and sides of a greased 9-in. pie plate. Refrigerate until firm, about 1 hour.

2. Beat the first 4 filling ingredients until blended. Beat in ricotta cheese and extracts. Stir in chocolate chips. Spread into crust.

3. Refrigerate, covered, until set, about 4 hours. If desired, top with pistachios.

1 PIECE: 548 cal., 36g fat (20g sat. fat), 88mg chol., 292mg sod., 51g carb. (38g sugars, 1g fiber), 8g pro.

CRANBERRY APPLE PIE

New England is a prime apple and cranberry growing region. This recipe combines those fruits in a heavenly pie that family and friends request time and again.
—*Betty Winberg, Nashua, NH*

Prep: 15 min. • **Bake:** 1 hour
Makes: 8 servings

- 2 cups sugar
- ¼ cup cornstarch
- ¼ cup orange juice
- ½ tsp. ground cinnamon
- ½ tsp. apple pie spice
- ⅛ tsp. ground nutmeg
- ¼ tsp. lemon juice
- 4 cups sliced peeled tart apples
- 2 cups fresh or frozen cranberries
  Pastry for double-crust pie
- 2 Tbsp. butter

1. In a large bowl, combine the first 7 ingredients. Add apples and cranberries; toss gently. Line a 9-in. pie plate with the bottom pastry. Add filling; dot with butter.

2. Roll remaining pastry to fit top of pie. Cut vents in pastry, using a small apple cutter if desired. Place over filling; seal and flute edges.

3. Bake at 425° for 10 minutes. Reduce heat to 350°; bake 50 minutes longer or until crust is golden brown and filling is bubbly.

1 PIECE: 521 cal., 17g fat (8g sat. fat), 18mg chol., 230mg sod., 92g carb. (60g sugars, 2g fiber), 2g pro.

TEST KITCHEN TIP
When making a 2-crust pie, brush a little water around the edge of the bottom crust before putting on the top crust. This creates a good seal once the 2 are crimped together and prevents any filling from bubbling out between the crusts.

CARAMEL PEANUT FANTASY

Packed with peanuts and gooey with caramel, this do-ahead treat is one sweet dream of a dessert to serve company. With an easy cookie crust and scrumptious candy bar layers, it goes together quickly and will disappear just as fast!
—Taste of Home *Test Kitchen*

Prep: 20 min. • **Bake:** 10 min. + chilling
Makes: 12 servings

- 2 **cups crushed vanilla wafers (about 60 wafers)**
- ⅓ **cup butter, melted**
- 20 **caramels**
- 15 **miniature Snickers candy bars**
- ½ **cup caramel ice cream topping**
- ½ **cup heavy whipping cream, divided**
- 2 **cups salted peanuts, chopped**
- ¾ **cup semisweet chocolate chips**
  Additional chopped salted peanuts, optional

1. In a small bowl, combine wafer crumbs and butter. Press onto the bottom of a greased 9-in. springform pan. Place on a baking sheet. Bake at 350° for 8-10 minutes. Cool crust on a wire rack.

2. In a heavy saucepan, combine the caramels, Snickers candy bars, caramel topping and ¼ cup cream; cook and stir over low heat until smooth and blended. Remove from the heat; stir in peanuts. Spread over crust. Cover and refrigerate for 1 hour.

3. In a microwave, melt chocolate chips and remaining cream; stir until smooth. Spread over caramel layer. If desired, sprinkle with additional peanuts. Cover and refrigerate for 1 hour or until serving.

1 SLICE: 504 cal., 30g fat (11g sat. fat), 32mg chol., 335mg sod., 55g carb. (40g sugars, 4g fiber), 10g pro.

CARROT CAKE

This wonderful recipe dates back to my great-grandmother. You will love the texture the cake gets from pineapple, coconut and, of course, carrots! For lighter appetites or to serve more people, cut it into smaller pieces and place the slices in pretty cupcake liners.
—*Debbie Terenzini-Wilkerson, Lusby, MD*

Prep: 20 min. • **Bake:** 50 min.
Makes: 12 servings

 2 cups all-purpose flour
 2 cups sugar
 2 tsp. ground cinnamon
 1 tsp. baking soda
 ½ tsp. salt
 3 large eggs, room temperature
 1½ cups canola oil
 2 cups finely grated carrots
 1 tsp. vanilla extract
 1 cup well-drained crushed pineapple
 1 cup sweetened shredded coconut
 1 cup chopped nuts

CREAM CHEESE FROSTING
 6 oz. cream cheese, softened
 6 Tbsp. butter, softened
 3 cups confectioners' sugar
 1 tsp. vanilla extract
    Additional chopped nuts

1. In a large bowl, combine the flour, sugar, cinnamon, baking soda and salt. Add the eggs, oil, carrots and vanilla; beat until combined. Stir in pineapple, coconut and nuts.
2. Pour into a greased 13x9-in. baking pan. Bake at 350° for 50-60 minutes or until a toothpick inserted in the center comes out clean. Cool on a wire rack.
3. For frosting, beat cream cheese and butter in a small bowl until fluffy. Add the confectioners' sugar and vanilla; beat until smooth. Frost cake. Sprinkle with additional nuts. Store in the refrigerator.
1 PIECE: 819 cal., 49g fat (12g sat. fat), 76mg chol., 346mg sod., 91g carb. (72g sugars, 3g fiber), 8g pro.

CHOCOLATE CREAM PIE

Our son, John, did lots of 4-H baking as a teenager. His favorite is this old-fashioned creamy chocolate pudding in a flaky crust.
—*Mary Anderson, De Valls Bluff, AR*

Prep: 1¼ hours + chilling • **Makes:** 8 servings

- 1½ **cups sugar**
- ⅓ **cup all-purpose flour**
- 3 **Tbsp. baking cocoa**
- ½ **tsp. salt**
- 1½ **cups water**
- 1 **can (12 oz.) evaporated milk**
- 5 **large egg yolks, lightly beaten**
- ½ **cup butter**
- 1 **tsp. vanilla extract**
- 1 **pastry shell (9 in.), baked**
  Whipped topping and baking cocoa, optional

1. In a large saucepan, combine the first 6 ingredients. Cook and stir over medium-high heat until thickened and bubbly, about 2 minutes. Reduce heat; cook and stir 2 minutes longer. Remove from heat. Whisk 1 cup hot mixture into egg yolks. Return all to pan; bring to a gentle boil, stirring constantly.
2. Remove from the heat; stir in butter and vanilla. Cool slightly. Pour warm filling into crust. Cool for 1 hour. Chill until set. If desired, top with whipped cream and sprinkle with cocoa to serve.
1 PIECE: 488 cal., 25g fat (13g sat. fat), 184mg chol., 413mg sod., 60g carb. (42g sugars, 1g fiber), 7g pro.

🎗 GOLDEN APPLE PIE

Pies are the dessert I like best to prepare. This one's the favorite for family get-togethers, and it has been awarded blue ribbons at a couple of local fairs.
—*Theresa Brazil, Petaluma, CA*

Prep: 30 min. + cooling
Bake: 40 min. + cooling
Makes: 8 servings

- 6 **cups sliced peeled Golden Delicious apples**
- ¾ **cup plus 2 Tbsp. apple juice, divided**
- ¾ **cup sugar**
- 1 **tsp. ground cinnamon**
- ½ **tsp. apple pie spice**
- 2 **Tbsp. cornstarch**
- ¼ **tsp. vanilla extract**

CRUST
- 2½ **cups all-purpose flour**
- 1 **tsp. salt**
- 1 **cup cold butter**
- 6 **to 8 Tbsp. ice water**

1. In a large saucepan, combine the apples, ¾ cup apple juice, sugar, cinnamon and apple pie spice; bring to a boil over medium heat, stirring occasionally. Combine cornstarch and remaining apple juice; add to the saucepan. Return to a boil, stirring constantly. Cook and stir 1 minute more or until thickened. Remove from the heat. Stir in vanilla. Cool to room temperature, stirring occasionally.
2. For crust, combine flour and salt; cut in the butter until mixture is crumbly. Gradually add water, 1 Tbsp. at a time, tossing with a fork until dough can be formed into a ball. Divide in half, making 1 half slightly larger. On a lightly floured surface, roll out larger portion.
3. Line a 9-in. pie plate with bottom pastry; trim even with edge of plate. Add filling. Roll out remaining pastry to fit top of pie; place over filling. Trim, seal and flute edges. Cut slits in top.
4. Bake at 400° for 40-45 minutes or until crust is golden brown and apples are tender. Cool on a wire rack.
1 SLICE: 480 cal., 24g fat (15g sat. fat), 61mg chol., 480mg sod., 65g carb. (30g sugars, 2g fiber), 5g pro.

SURPRISE PUMPKIN CUPCAKES

Cupcakes are a great classroom or workplace treat because they're easily portable. These spiced goodies have a cream cheese surprise.
—Kathleen Dimmich, Easton, PA

Prep: 25 min. • **Bake:** 20 min. + cooling
Makes: 2 dozen

- 1 can (15 oz.) pumpkin
- 2 cups sugar
- 1 cup canola oil
- 4 large eggs, room temperature
- 2 cups all-purpose flour
- 2 tsp. baking powder
- 2 tsp. ground cinnamon
- 1 tsp. baking soda
- ½ tsp. salt

FILLING

- 1 pkg. (8 oz.) cream cheese, softened
- ⅓ cup sugar
- 1 large egg, room temperature
  Confectioners' sugar, optional

1. In a large bowl, beat the pumpkin, sugar, oil and eggs until well blended. In small bowl, combine the flour, baking powder, cinnamon, baking soda and salt; gradually beat into the pumpkin mixture until blended.
2. For filling, in another small bowl, beat cream cheese and sugar until smooth. Add egg; beat on low just until combined.
3. Fill paper-lined muffin cups one-third full. Drop filling by tablespoonfuls into center of each cupcake. Cover with remaining batter.
4. Bake at 350° for 20-25 minutes or until a toothpick inserted in the pumpkin portion comes out clean. Cool for 10 minutes before removing from pans to wire racks to cool completely. Dust with confectioners' sugar if desired. Refrigerate leftovers.

1 CUPCAKE: 250 cal., 14g fat (3g sat. fat), 54mg chol., 179mg sod., 29g carb. (20g sugars, 1g fiber), 3g pro.

BERRY, LEMON & DOUGHNUT HOLE TRIFLE

I was able to whip up this quick, yet impressive, dessert in only a few minutes after my son called and said he was coming home with his college roommates. It's been a family favorite ever since.
—Ellen Riley, Murfreesboro, TN

Takes: 25 min. • **Makes:** 10 servings

- 2 cups cold 2% milk
- 1 pkg. (3.4 oz.) instant lemon pudding mix
- 1 carton (8 oz.) frozen whipped topping, thawed and divided
- 16 to 32 plain doughnut holes
- 3 cups fresh strawberries, halved
- 2 cups fresh blueberries

1. Whisk milk and pudding mix for 2 minutes. Let stand for 2 minutes or until soft-set. Fold in 2½ cups whipped topping; set aside.
2. Place half the doughnut holes in a 3-qt. trifle bowl; spread half the pudding mixture over the top. Top pudding with half the strawberries and blueberries. Repeat layers. Top with remaining whipped topping. Chill until serving.

1 CUP: 250 cal., 11g fat (7g sat. fat), 6mg chol., 250mg sod., 33g carb. (24g sugars, 2g fiber), 3g pro.

JELLY DONUT CAKE

(RECIPE 1)

Cake or donuts? Now you don't have to choose between the two. Impress your family with this easy jelly-filled donut cake. Try your best to center the jelly in the middle of the half-filled Bundt pan so that it will not seep out of the edges of the cake.

—Colleen Delawder, Herndon, VA

- -

Prep: 25 min. + chilling
Bake: 45 min. + cooling
Makes: 12 servings

- 1 cup sugar
- 2 tsp. ground cinnamon
- ½ tsp. salt
- ¼ tsp. ground nutmeg
- ¾ cup unsalted butter, melted
- 2 large eggs, room temperature
- 1 cup 2% milk
- 2 Tbsp. sour cream
- 1 Tbsp. vanilla extract
- 2⅔ cups all-purpose flour
- 2½ tsp. baking powder
- ¾ cup raspberry, strawberry or apple jelly

FROSTING
- 1 pkg. (8 oz.) cream cheese, softened
- 1½ cups confectioners' sugar
- 1 tsp. ground cinnamon
- ½ tsp. vanilla extract

1. Preheat oven to 350°. Grease and flour a 10-in. fluted tube pan. Place sugar, cinnamon, salt and nutmeg in a food processor; process for 30 seconds. Transfer to a large bowl.
2. Beat in melted butter, eggs, milk, sour cream and vanilla until well blended. In another bowl, whisk flour and baking powder; gradually beat into sugar mixture.
3. Pour half of the batter into prepared pan. Spoon jelly over batter to within ½ in. of the edges; top with remaining batter. Bake until a toothpick inserted in center comes out clean, 45-50 minutes. Cool in pan 10 minutes before removing to a wire rack to cool completely.
4. In a large bowl, combine all frosting ingredients; beat until smooth. Spread over cake; sprinkle with additional sugar and cinnamon. Refrigerate at least 1 hour before serving.
NOTE: To remove cakes easily, use solid shortening to grease tube pan.
1 SLICE: 475 cal., 20g fat (12g sat. fat), 83mg chol., 283mg sod., 69g carb. (45g sugars, 1g fiber), 6g pro.

**1 FAVORITE
5 WAYS**
Bundt Cake

3

BANANA POUND CAKE

(RECIPE 2)

I adapted a basic pound cake recipe from my great-aunt for this treat. It makes a moist cake that pops out of the pan perfectly.
—*Nancy Zimmerman,
Cape May Court House, NJ*

- -

Prep: 20 min. • **Bake:** 1¼ hours + cooling
Makes: 12 servings

3	tsp. plus 3 cups sugar, divided
1	cup butter, softened
6	large eggs, room temperature
1	cup mashed ripe bananas (about 2 medium)
1½	tsp. vanilla extract
½	tsp. lemon extract
3	cups all-purpose flour
¼	tsp. baking soda
1	cup sour cream

GLAZE

1½	cups confectioners' sugar
½	tsp. vanilla extract
3	to 4 tsp. whole milk

1. Grease a 10-in. fluted tube pan. Sprinkle with 3 tsp. sugar; set aside.
2. In a large bowl, cream butter and remaining 3 cups sugar until light and fluffy. Add 1 egg at a time, beating well after each addition. Stir in bananas and extracts. Combine flour and baking soda; add to the creamed mixture alternately with sour cream, beating just until combined.
3. Pour into prepared pan (pan will be full). Bake at 325° for 75-85 minutes or until a toothpick inserted in the center comes out clean. Cool for 10 minutes before removing from pan to a wire rack to cool completely.
4. In a small bowl, whisk glaze ingredients until smooth; drizzle over cake. Store in the refrigerator. May be frozen for up to 1 month.
1 SLICE: 600 cal., 22g fat (13g sat. fat), 138mg chol., 192mg sod., 96g carb. (69g sugars, 1g fiber), 7g pro.

LEMON LOVER'S POUND CAKE

(RECIPE 3)

Everyone raves about this pretty dessert—it sure doesn't last long in our family. It also freezes beautifully, so make two and pop one into the freezer for another day.
—*Annettia Mounger, Kansas City, MO*

- -

Prep: 20 min. • **Bake:** 55 min. + cooling
Makes: 12 servings

1	cup butter, softened
3	cups sugar
6	large eggs, room temperature
5	Tbsp. lemon juice
1	Tbsp. grated lemon zest
1	tsp. lemon extract
3	cups all-purpose flour
½	tsp. baking soda
¼	tsp. salt
1¼	cups sour cream

ICING

¼	cup sour cream
2	Tbsp. butter, softened
2½	cups confectioners' sugar
3	Tbsp. lemon juice
2	tsp. grated lemon zest

1. In a large bowl, cream butter and sugar until light and fluffy. Add 1 egg at a time, beating well after each addition. Stir in lemon juice, zest and extract. Combine the flour, baking soda and salt; add to the creamed mixture alternately with sour cream. Beat just until combined.
2. Pour into a greased and floured 10-in. fluted tube pan. Bake at 350° for 55-60 minutes or until a toothpick inserted in the center comes out clean. Cool for 10 minutes before removing from the pan to a wire rack to cool completely.
3. For icing, in a small bowl, beat the sour cream and butter until smooth. Gradually add confectioners' sugar. Beat in lemon juice and zest. Drizzle over the cake. If desired, top with additional grated lemon zest. Store in the refrigerator.
1 SLICE: 658 cal., 26g fat (15g sat. fat), 146mg chol., 286mg sod., 101g carb. (76g sugars, 1g fiber), 8g pro.

MARGARITA CAKE

This margarita cake is perfect for a picnic on a warm day. You'll be surprised at how closely it tastes like the real thing.
—*Dawn Lowenstein, Huntingdon Valley, PA*

- -

Prep: 15 min. • **Bake:** 45 min. + cooling
Makes: 16 servings

- 1 pkg. lemon cake mix (regular size)
- 1 pkg. (3.4 oz.) instant lemon pudding mix
- 1 can (10 oz.) frozen nonalcoholic margarita mix, thawed
- 4 large eggs, room temperature
- ½ cup butter, softened
- 2 Tbsp. lime juice
- 3 tsp. grated lime zest
  GLAZE
- 1½ cups confectioners' sugar
- 3 Tbsp. lime juice

1. Preheat oven to 350°. Grease and flour a 10-in. fluted tube pan. In a large bowl, combine cake mix, pudding mix, margarita mix, eggs, butter, lime juice and zest; beat on low speed for 30 seconds. Beat on medium for 2 minutes.
2. Transfer batter to prepared pan. Bake 45-50 minutes or until a toothpick inserted in the center comes out clean. Cool in pan 10 minutes before removing to a wire rack to cool completely.
3. Meanwhile, combine glaze ingredients. Drizzle over cake.
1 SLICE: 284 cal., 8g fat (5g sat. fat), 62mg chol., 379mg sod., 51g carb. (37g sugars, 1g fiber), 2g pro.

READER REVIEW
"This is hands-down the best Bundt cake I've tasted! The flavor is strong and citrusy and the texture is tender and moist."
NICOLE, TASTEOFHOME.COM

CHERRY CHOCOLATE MARBLE CAKE

Cherries and chocolate are natural partners that make desserts such as this simply scrumptious! The marbled effect is easily achieved by layering the two different batters.
—*Sandra Campbell, Chase Mills, NY*

- -

Prep: 20 min. • **Bake:** 1¼ hours + cooling
Makes: 12 servings

- 1 cup butter, softened
- 2 cups sugar
- 3 large eggs, room temperature
- 6 Tbsp. maraschino cherry juice
- 6 Tbsp. water
- 1 tsp. almond extract
- 3¾ cups all-purpose flour
- 2¼ tsp. baking soda
- ¾ tsp. salt
- 1½ cups sour cream
- ¾ cup chopped maraschino cherries, drained
- ¾ cup chopped walnuts, toasted
- 3 oz. unsweetened chocolate, melted
  Confectioners' sugar, optional

1. In a large bowl, cream butter and sugar until light and fluffy. Add 1 egg at a time, beating well after each addition. Add the cherry juice, water and extract; mix well. Combine the flour, baking soda and salt; add to the creamed mixture alternately with sour cream, beating well after each addition.
2. Divide batter in half. To 1 portion, add cherries and walnuts; mix well. To the second portion, add chocolate; mix well. Spoon half of the cherry mixture into a greased and floured 10-in. fluted tube pan. Cover with half of the chocolate mixture. Repeat layers.
3. Bake at 350° for about 1¼ hours or until a toothpick inserted in the center comes out clean. Cool for 15 minutes; remove from pan to a wire rack to cool completely. Dust with confectioners' sugar if desired.
1 SLICE: 606 cal., 31g fat (16g sat. fat), 94mg chol., 544mg sod., 74g carb. (39g sugars, 3g fiber), 9g pro.

Cookies & Candies

Start here for deliciously fun and blissful bites, all perfect for potlucks, bake sales, special occasions or whenever you're craving a sweet treat. From frosted cookies and chocolate-dipped candies to cream-filled novelties, your cookie jar will be overflowing in no time!

TORCETTI

Our Sicilian grandmother taught my sister and me how to make torcetti. She'd often have us roll out the dough. The melt-in-your-mouth goodness is delightful without being too sweet.
—*Joy Quici, Upland, CA*

- -

Prep: 30 min. + rising
Bake: 15 min./batch + cooling
Makes: 6 dozen

  5   **cups all-purpose flour**
  1   **cup cold butter, cubed**
  1   **cup shortening**
  1   **pkg. (¼ oz.) active dry yeast**
 ½   **cup warm 2% milk (110° to 115°)**
  2   **large eggs, room temperature**
  1   **Tbsp. sugar**
1½   **tsp. vanilla extract**
  2   **cups confectioners' sugar**
       Additional confectioners' sugar

1. Place flour in a large bowl; cut in butter and shortening until mixture resembles coarse crumbs. Set aside. In another large bowl, dissolve yeast in warm milk. Add the eggs, sugar, vanilla and 2 cups of the crumb mixture; beat until well blended. Gradually beat in remaining crumb mixture.

2. Turn onto a floured surface; knead for 3-4 minutes. Place in a greased bowl, turning once to grease top. Cover and let rise in a warm place until doubled, about 1 hour.

3. Punch dough down; divide into 6 portions. Shape each portion into twelve 6-in. ropes about ¼ in. thick; roll in confectioners' sugar. Shape each rope into a loop. Holding both ends of loop, twist together 3 times.

4. Place 2 in. apart on greased baking sheets. Bake at 375° for 12-14 minutes or until golden brown. Roll warm cookies in additional confectioners' sugar. Cool on wire racks.

1 COOKIE: 102 cal., 5g fat (2g sat. fat), 13mg chol., 21mg sod., 12g carb. (5g sugars, 0 fiber), 1g pro. **DIABETIC EXCHANGES:** 1 starch, 1 fat.

PUMPKIN SEED TOFFEE

My kids are allergic to nuts, but they can eat pumpkin seeds. Every fall we save the seeds from our pumpkins to add to various recipes, including this one.
—Suzanne Earl, Spring, TX

Prep: 30 min. + cooling • **Makes:** 2 lbs.

- 1 tsp. plus 2 cups butter, softened, divided
- 2 cups sugar
- ½ cup water
- 2 Tbsp. corn syrup
- 1 tsp. pumpkin pie spice
- ¼ tsp. salt
- 1 cup roasted pumpkin seeds or pepitas

1. Grease a 15x10x1-in. pan with 1 tsp. butter; set aside. In a heavy saucepan, melt the remaining butter. Stir in the sugar, water, corn syrup, pie spice and salt. Cook, stirring continuously, over medium heat until a candy thermometer reads 300° (hard-crack stage).
2. Remove from the heat; stir in pumpkin seeds. Immediately pour into prepared pan. Let stand at room temperature until cool, about 1 hour. Break or cut into bite-sized pieces. Store in an airtight container at room temperature.

1 OZ.: 176 cal., 14g fat (8g sat. fat), 31mg chol., 122mg sod., 14g carb. (13g sugars, 0 fiber), 1g pro.

HIDDEN MINT MORSELS

Is it a cookie or a candy? No matter which answer folks choose, they find these minty morsels yummy. The recipe makes so much that you can whip up dozens of gifts at once.
—Adina Skilbred, Prairie du Sac, WI

Prep: 30 min. + chilling
Bake: 10 min./batch + chilling
Makes: about 10 dozen

- ⅓ cup shortening
- ⅓ cup butter, softened
- ¾ cup sugar
- 1 large egg, room temperature
- 1 Tbsp. 2% milk
- 1 tsp. vanilla extract
- 1¾ cups all-purpose flour
- ⅓ cup baking cocoa
- 1½ tsp. baking powder
- ¼ tsp. salt
- ⅛ tsp. ground cinnamon

PEPPERMINT LAYER
- 4 cups confectioners' sugar
- 6 Tbsp. light corn syrup
- 6 Tbsp. butter, melted
- 2 to 3 tsp. peppermint extract

CHOCOLATE COATING
- 2 pkg. (11½ oz. each) milk chocolate chips
- ¼ cup shortening

1. In a large bowl, cream the shortening, butter and sugar until light and fluffy. Beat in the egg, milk and vanilla. Combine the flour, cocoa, baking powder, salt and cinnamon; gradually add to the creamed mixture. Cover tightly and refrigerate for 8 hours or overnight.
2. On a lightly floured surface, roll dough to ⅛-in. thickness. Cut with a lightly floured 1½-in. round cookie cutter; place cutouts on ungreased baking sheets.
3. Bake at 375° until set, 6-8 minutes. Cool for 2 minutes before removing to wire racks to cool completely.
4. In a large bowl, combine all the peppermint layer ingredients. Knead for 1 minute or until smooth. Shape into 120 balls, ½ in. each. Place a ball on each cookie and flatten to cover the cookie. Place on waxed paper-lined baking sheets; refrigerate for 30 minutes.
5. In a microwave, melt chocolate chips and shortening; stir until smooth. Spread about 1 teaspoonful over each cookie. Chill until firm.

2 MORSELS: 127 cal., 6g fat (3g sat. fat), 11mg chol., 50mg sod., 18g carb. (14g sugars, 0 fiber), 1g pro.

SOUR CREAM DROPS

My mother is an excellent baker, and this is her recipe. These morsels are wonderful for bake sales and school lunches.
—*Tracy Betzler, Reston, VA*

Prep: 20 min. + chilling
Bake: 10 min./batch + cooling
Makes: 2½ dozen

- ¼ cup shortening
- ¾ cup sugar
- 1 large egg, room temperature
- ½ cup sour cream
- ½ tsp. vanilla extract
- 1⅓ cups all-purpose flour
- ¼ tsp. baking powder
- ¼ tsp. baking soda
- ¼ tsp. salt

FROSTING

- 2 Tbsp. butter
- ½ cup confectioners' sugar
- ¼ tsp. vanilla extract
- 3 to 4 tsp. hot water

1. In a large bowl, cream shortening and sugar until light and fluffy. Beat in the egg, sour cream and vanilla. Combine the flour, baking powder, baking soda and salt; add to the creamed mixture and mix well. Chill for at least 1 hour.

2. Drop by tablespoonfuls 2 in. apart onto greased baking sheets. Bake at 425° until lightly browned, 7-8 minutes. Remove to wire racks to cool.

3. For frosting, melt butter in a saucepan until golden brown; stir in confectioners' sugar, vanilla and enough water to achieve a spreading consistency. Frost cooled cookies.

1 COOKIE: 80 cal., 3g fat (1g sat. fat), 9mg chol., 44mg sod., 11g carb. (7g sugars, 0 fiber), 1g pro.

SNICKERS COOKIES

There's a sweet surprise inside these cookies. My mother received the recipe from a fellow teacher at her school. It's a fantastic way to dress up refrigerated cookie dough.
—*Kari Pease, Conconully, WA*

Takes: 30 min. • **Makes:** 2 dozen

- 1 tube refrigerated chocolate chip cookie dough
- 24 miniature Snickers candy bars

Preheat oven to 350°. Cut the dough into ¼-in.-thick slices. Place a candy bar on each slice and wrap dough around it. Place 2 in. apart on ungreased baking sheets. Bake until lightly browned, 8-10 minutes. Remove to wire racks to cool.

1 COOKIE: 123 cal., 5g fat (2g sat. fat), 6mg chol., 59mg sod., 17g carb. (4g sugars, 0 fiber), 2g pro.

> **TEST KITCHEN TIP**
> When using a single baking sheet, put it on the middle rack in your oven. If you are using more than 1 baking sheet, rotate the pans halfway through the baking time. Swap the location of the pans in the oven and rotate each 180 degrees for an even double-batch bake.

LAURA STRICKLIN
Jackson, MS

ORANGE SLICE COOKIES

Soft orange candy slices add a refreshing burst to these crispy vanilla chip cookies. Use kitchen shears to quickly cut the orange candy in small pieces. Occasionally rinse the blades with cold water to reduce sticking.
—*Britt Strain, Idaho Falls, ID*

Prep: 20 min. • **Bake:** 10 min./batch
Makes: about 10 dozen

1	cup orange candy slices
1½	cups sugar, divided
1	cup butter, softened
1	cup shortening
1½	cups packed brown sugar
2	large eggs, room temperature
2	tsp. vanilla extract
4	cups all-purpose flour
2	tsp. baking soda
1	tsp. salt
1	pkg. (10 to 12 oz.) white baking chips
1	cup chopped pecans

1. Cut each orange slice into 8 pieces. Roll in ¼ cup sugar; set aside. In a bowl, cream the butter, shortening, brown sugar and remaining sugar. Add eggs, one at a time, beating well after each addition. Beat in vanilla. Combine the flour, baking soda and salt; gradually add to creamed mixture. Stir in chips, pecans and orange slice pieces.
2. Roll into 1-in. balls. Place 2 in. apart on ungreased baking sheets. Bake at 375° for 10-12 minutes or until golden brown. Remove to wire racks to cool.

1 COOKIE: 92 cal., 5g fat (2g sat. fat), 8mg chol., 58mg sod., 12g carb. (8g sugars, 0 fiber), 1g pro.

RASPBERRY PISTACHIO THUMBPRINTS

Thumbprint cookies are a Christmas classic, and I especially like my updated version with pistachios. The rich buttery bites are not only delicious, but they are also pretty enough to give for gifts—if you manage to share them!
—Laura Stricklin, Jackson, MS

- -

Prep: 25 min. • **Bake:** 15 min./batch + cooling
Makes: about 3 dozen

- 1 cup butter, softened
- ½ cup confectioners' sugar
- 1 tsp. vanilla extract
- 2 cups all-purpose flour
- ¼ tsp. salt
- 1 cup finely chopped pistachios
- ½ cup seedless raspberry jam
  Additional confectioners' sugar, optional

1. Preheat oven to 325°. Cream butter and confectioners' sugar until light and fluffy. Beat in vanilla. In another bowl, whisk flour and salt; gradually beat into creamed mixture. Add the pistachios; mix well.

2. Shape dough into 1-in. balls. Place 1 in. apart on ungreased baking sheets. Press a deep indentation in center of each with your thumb; fill each with ½ tsp. jam.

3. Bake until the bottoms are light brown, 13-16 minutes. Remove from pans to wire racks to cool. If desired, dust with additional confectioners' sugar.

1 COOKIE: 97 cal., 6g fat (3g sat. fat), 12mg chol., 65mg sod., 10g carb. (4g sugars, 0 fiber), 1g pro.

READER REVIEW

"Wow, what a great cookie! Made as directed for Christmas and they were a perfect addition to the other cookies I made. They're sweet little bites, and we loved the combo of pistachios and raspberry jam. Baked them around 13 minutes and they turned out great. Definitely will make again!"

DEBGLASS11, TASTEOFHOME.COM

HONEY WALNUT DELIGHTS

Even after being frozen, these no-fail cookies stay moist and taste freshly baked. They are among my best holiday giveaway treats and are so easy to make. If you prefer, you can use other nut varieties, such as pecans or almonds.
—*Jessica Clemens, Wimbledon, ND*

Prep: 30 min. • **Bake:** 10 min./batch
Makes: about 8 dozen

- 1 **cup butter, softened**
- 2¼ **cups sugar, divided**
- 2 **large eggs, room temperature**
- ½ **cup honey**
- 2 **Tbsp. lemon juice**
- 4 **cups all-purpose flour**
- 2½ **tsp. baking soda**
- 1 **tsp. ground cinnamon**
- ½ **tsp. salt**
- ½ **tsp. ground ginger**
- 1 **cup finely chopped walnuts, toasted**

1. Preheat oven to 350°. In a large bowl, cream butter and 1½ cups sugar until light and fluffy. Beat in eggs, honey and lemon juice. In another bowl, whisk flour, baking soda, cinnamon, salt and ginger; gradually beat into creamed mixture. Stir in walnuts.

2. Shape dough into 1-in. balls; roll in the remaining sugar. Place balls 2 in. apart on ungreased baking sheets. Bake until golden brown, 7-9 minutes. Cool on pans 1 minute. Remove to wire racks to cool completely. Store in an airtight container.

NOTE: To toast nuts, bake in a shallow pan in a 350° oven for 5-10 minutes or cook in a skillet over low heat until lightly browned, stirring occasionally.

1 COOKIE: 66 cal., 3g fat (1g sat. fat), 9mg chol., 60mg sod., 10g carb. (6g sugars, 0 fiber), 1g pro.

BANANA CREAM CHOCOLATE TRUFFLES

This truffle recipe was created from ripe bananas and my imagination, and the outcome blew my family and friends away! I'm not a big fan of bananas, but I could eat these truffles all day long.
—*Michele Lassuy, Orlando, FL*

Prep: 35 min. + freezing
Makes: about 4 dozen

- 1 **pkg. (14.3 oz.) Golden Oreo cookies**
- 1 **pkg. (8 oz.) cream cheese, softened**
- 2 **tsp. banana extract**
- ⅓ **cup mashed ripe banana**
- 1 **lb. milk chocolate candy coating, melted**
  Dried banana chips, coarsely crushed

1. Pulse cookies in a food processor until fine crumbs form. In a bowl, beat cream cheese and extract until blended. Beat in banana. Stir in cookie crumbs. Freeze, covered, until firm enough to shape, about 2 hours.

2. Shape mixture into 1-in. balls. Dip cookie balls in candy coating; place on waxed paper-lined baking sheets. Top immediately with banana chips.

3. Refrigerate until set, about 30 minutes. Store truffles in a covered container in the refrigerator.

1 TRUFFLE: 110 cal., 6g fat (4g sat. fat), 5mg chol., 45mg sod., 13g carb. (9g sugars, 0 fiber), 1g pro.

APRICOT-NUT WHITE FUDGE

We look forward to this luscious apricot-studded fudge every Christmas. It's easy to make and it melts in your mouth. I wrap up small squares of the candy with ribbon and silk holly; it makes great gifts for friends, as well as a nice treat for the family!
—*Betty Claycomb, Alverton, PA*

- -

Prep: 15 min. + chilling • **Makes:** about 2½ lbs.

1   pkg. (8 oz.) cream cheese, softened
4   cups confectioners' sugar
12 oz. white baking chocolate, melted and cooled
1½ tsp. vanilla extract
¾   cup chopped walnuts or pecans
¾   cup chopped dried apricots

1. Line a 9-in. square pan with aluminum foil, letting ends extend over sides by 1 in. Coat with cooking spray; set aside. In a large bowl, beat cream cheese until fluffy. Gradually beat in confectioners' sugar. Gradually add the white chocolate. Beat in the vanilla. Fold in nuts and apricots.

2. Spread into the prepared pan. Cover and refrigerate for 8 hours or overnight. Using foil, lift fudge from pan; cut into 1-in. squares.

1 PIECE: 64 cal., 3g fat (2g sat. fat), 3mg chol., 13mg sod., 10g carb. (9g sugars, 0 fiber), 1g pro.

MINT SANDWICH COOKIES

Canned frosting, peppermint extract and chocolate candy coating quickly turn crackers into these wonderful little no-bake cookies. My children and I like to assemble them for parties and holidays. I hope you and your family enjoy them as much as we do.
—*Melissa Thompson, Anderson, OH*

- -

Prep: 20 min. + standing • **Makes:** 3 dozen

1   can (16 oz.) vanilla frosting
½   tsp. peppermint extract
3   to 5 drops green food coloring, optional
72 butter-flavored crackers
1   lb. dark chocolate candy coating, coarsely chopped

1. In a large bowl, combine the frosting, extract and, if desired, food coloring. Spread filling over half of the crackers; top with remaining crackers.

2. In a microwave, melt chocolate; stir until smooth. Dip cookies in chocolate; allow excess to drip off. Place on waxed paper; let stand until set. Store in an airtight container at room temperature.

1 COOKIE: 155 cal., 8g fat (4g sat. fat), 0 chol., 88mg sod., 21g carb. (16g sugars, 0 fiber), 1g pro.

WHIPPED CREAM KRUMKAKE

Our town of Decorah, in the northeast corner of Iowa, has a rich Norwegian culture. That heritage is evident at holidays and during our annual Nordic Fest, where krumkake is king! This rich, delicious pastry is served at most family dinners and bake sales, and you'll even see demonstrations of krumkake-making in many store windows.
—*Imelda Nesteby, Decorah, IA*

Prep: 20 min. + chilling • **Bake:** 20 min.
Makes: about 3 dozen

- 3 large eggs, room temperature
- 1 cup sugar
- ½ cup sweet butter, melted
- ½ cup heavy whipping cream, whipped
- ½ tsp. nutmeg
- 1½ cups all-purpose flour
  Sweet butter for krumkake plates
  Sweetened whipped cream, optional

1. Beat eggs in a large bowl until very light. Add sugar gradually, beating to blend. Slowly add melted butter, then whipped cream and nutmeg. Mix in flour. (Dough will be the consistency of cookie dough.) Chill the dough thoroughly.

2. Preheat krumkake plates over medium heat for about 10 minutes or until a drop of water dances when dropped onto plates. Brush plates with sweet butter. Place 1 Tbsp. dough in center of lower plate; close iron and press handles together. If excess dough comes out sides, remove with a table knife.

3. Bake for about 30 seconds; flip iron and bake for about 30 seconds on other side. Remove krumkake and immediately roll over a cone-shaped form. Place seam side down on parchment to cool; remove form.

4. Fill cooled cones with sweetened whipped cream if desired. Serve immediately.

1 KRUMKAKE: 81 cal., 4g fat (3g sat. fat), 26mg chol., 7mg sod., 10g carb. (6g sugars, 0 fiber), 1g pro.

5i ❧ CHOCOLATE BILLIONAIRES

A friend gave me this recipe while we were living in Texas. When we moved, I made sure to take it with us. Everyone agrees these candies are the ultimate indulgence.
—*June Humphrey, Strongsville, OH*

Prep: 45 min. + chilling • **Makes:** about 2 lbs.

- 1 pkg. (14 oz.) caramels
- 3 Tbsp. water
- 1½ cups chopped pecans
- 1 cup Rice Krispies
- 3 cups milk chocolate chips
- 1½ tsp. shortening

1. Line 2 baking sheets with waxed paper; grease the paper and set aside. In a large heavy saucepan, combine caramels and water; cook and stir over low heat until smooth. Stir in pecans and cereal until coated. Drop by teaspoonfuls onto prepared pans. Refrigerate for 10 minutes or until firm.

2. Meanwhile, in a microwave, melt the chocolate chips and shortening; stir until smooth. Dip candy into chocolate, coating all sides; allow excess to drip off. Place on prepared pans. Refrigerate until set. Store in an airtight container.

1 OZ.: 172 cal., 10g fat (4g sat. fat), 4mg chol., 51mg sod., 20g carb. (17g sugars, 1g fiber), 2g pro.

TEST KITCHEN TIP
Pecans are dark brown, oval nuts that can be eaten fresh or cooked. They are most often used in sweets or baked goods or sprinkled on salads. Pecans have a higher fat content than other nuts, so they're more prone to going rancid. They'll stay fresh for twice as long in the freezer as they would at room temperature.

CHOCOLATE MARSHMALLOW PEANUT BUTTER SQUARES

I combined a couple of recipes to create these crunchy, chocolaty bars that burst with peanut butter flavor, marshmallows and pretzel pieces. The bars could also pass for fudge!
—*Dawn Lowenstein, Huntingdon Valley, PA*

Prep: 15 min. + chilling • **Cook:** 5 min.
Makes: 5 dozen

- 1 can (14 oz.) sweetened condensed milk
- 1 pkg. (11 oz.) peanut butter and milk chocolate chips
- ½ cup milk chocolate chips
- ½ cup creamy peanut butter
- 1 tsp. vanilla extract
- 1½ cups miniature marshmallows
- 1 cup broken miniature pretzels
- 1 cup Rice Krispies

1. Place first 5 ingredients in a large heavy saucepan; cook and stir over low heat until smooth and blended, about 5 minutes (mixture will be very thick). Remove from heat; stir in remaining ingredients. Spread into a greased 13x9-in. pan.
2. Refrigerate, covered, until firm, about 4 hours. Cut into squares. Store in an airtight container in the refrigerator.
1 SQUARE: 85 cal., 4g fat (2g sat. fat), 3mg chol., 50mg sod., 12g carb. (8g sugars, 0 fiber), 1g pro.

LEMON SNOWFLAKES

You need only four items to whip up these delightful cookies. Confectioners' sugar highlights the cracked tops to give them their snowflake appearance.
—*Linda Barry, Dianna, TX*

Prep: 30 min. • **Bake:** 10 min./batch
Makes: 5½ dozen

- 1 pkg. lemon cake mix (regular size)
- 2¼ cups whipped topping
- 1 large egg, room temperature
  Confectioners' sugar

1. In a large bowl, combine the cake mix, whipped topping and egg until well blended. Batter will be very sticky.
2. Drop by teaspoonfuls into confectioners' sugar; roll lightly to coat. Place on ungreased baking sheets. Bake at 350° for 10-12 minutes or until lightly browned and tops are cracked. Remove to wire racks to cool.
1 COOKIE: 37 cal., 1g fat (1g sat. fat), 3mg chol., 59mg sod., 7g carb. (4g sugars, 0 fiber), 0 pro.

PECAN CARAMEL CANDIES

The perfect combination of salty and sweet, these candies make an ideal treat during the holidays. Get kids involved by having them help you to unwrap the candies and place the pretzels on baking sheets. You'll have several ready to give as gifts in no time!
—*Julie Wemhoff, Angola, IN*

Prep: 30 min. • **Bake:** 5 min. + standing
Makes: 4½ dozen

- 54 pretzels
- 54 Rolo candies (about 11 oz.)
- 54 pecan halves

1. Preheat oven to 250°. Place pretzels 1 in. apart on foil-lined baking sheets. Top each with a Rolo candy.
2. Bake 3-4 minutes or until candies are softened. (Rolos will still retain their shape.) Immediately top with pecans, pressing to spread candy into pretzel. Let stand until set.
1 PIECE: 44 cal., 2g fat (1g sat. fat), 1mg chol., 24mg sod., 6g carb. (4g sugars, 0 fiber), 1g pro.

OAT & COCONUT ICEBOX COOKIES

This recipe was passed down through my family from Grandma Irene and is a favorite of my dad and cousin Dennis. It's a true cookie lover's cookie: crispy on the outside, chewy on the inside and perfectly dunkable.
—*Lori Rowe, Tigerton, WI*

Prep: 20 min. + chilling
Bake: 10 min./batch + cooling
Makes: about 3½ dozen

½ cup butter, softened
½ cup shortening
1 cup sugar
1 cup packed brown sugar
2 large eggs, room temperature
1 tsp. vanilla extract
1½ cups all-purpose flour
1 tsp. baking soda
1 tsp. salt
3 cups old-fashioned oats
½ cup sweetened shredded coconut
½ cup chopped walnuts

1. Cream butter, shortening and sugars until light and fluffy. Beat in the eggs and vanilla. In another bowl, whisk flour, baking soda and salt; gradually beat into creamed mixture. Stir in oats, coconut and walnuts.

2. Divide dough in half. Shape each into a 10-in.-long roll. Wrap in waxed paper; refrigerate overnight.

3. Preheat oven to 375°. Unwrap and cut dough crosswise into ½-in. slices. Place 2 in. apart on ungreased baking sheets. Bake until edges begin to brown, 8-10 minutes. Cool for 2 minutes before removing cookies from pans to wire racks.

1 COOKIE: 142 cal., 7g fat (3g sat. fat), 15mg chol., 117mg sod., 19g carb. (11g sugars, 1g fiber), 2g pro.

PEANUT BUTTER COOKIE CUPS

I'm a busy teacher and pastor's wife. I wouldn't dare show my face at a church dinner or bake sale without these tempting peanut butter treats. They're quick, easy and always a hit.
—*Kristi Tackett, Banner, KY*

Prep: 35 min. • **Bake:** 15 min. • **Makes:** 3 dozen

1 pkg. (17½ oz.) peanut butter cookie mix
36 miniature peanut butter cups, unwrapped

1. Preheat oven to 350°. Prepare cookie mix according to package directions. Roll dough into 1-in. balls. Place balls in greased miniature muffin cups. Press dough evenly onto bottom and up sides of each cup.

2. Bake 11-13 minutes or until set. Immediately place a peanut butter cup in each cup; press down gently. Cool for 10 minutes; carefully remove from pans.

NOTE: You can substitute 2¼ cups of any peanut butter cookie dough for the prepared mix.

1 SERVING: 119 cal., 7g fat (2g sat. fat), 6mg chol., 89mg sod., 13g carb. (3g sugars, 1g fiber), 2g pro.

CREAMY PEANUT BUTTER FUDGE

Christmas wouldn't be the same without this peanut butter fudge. Evaporated milk gives the treat a rich, creamy consistency, and the recipe is always a family favorite.
—*Diana Osborn, Wichita, KS*

- -

Prep: 30 min. + chilling • **Makes:** 81 pieces

- 1 tsp. plus ¼ cup butter, divided
- 1½ cups sugar
- 1 can (5 oz.) evaporated milk
- ¼ tsp. salt
- ⅓ cup butterscotch chips
- ⅓ cup peanut butter chips
- 1 jar (7 oz.) marshmallow creme
- 1 cup chunky peanut butter
- 1 tsp. vanilla extract

1. Line a 9-in. square pan with foil and grease the foil with 1 tsp. butter; set aside.

2. Cube remaining butter and place in a large heavy saucepan. Add the sugar, milk and salt; cook and stir over medium heat until sugar is dissolved. Bring to a rapid boil; boil for 5 minutes or until a candy thermometer reads 230°, stirring constantly.

3. Remove from the heat; stir in chips until melted. Stir in marshmallow creme, peanut butter and vanilla until blended. Pour into prepared pan; refrigerate for 2 hours or until firm.

4. Using foil, lift fudge out of pan. Gently peel off foil; cut fudge into 1-in. squares. Store in an airtight container in the refrigerator.

NOTE: We recommend that you test your candy thermometer before each use by bringing water to a boil; the thermometer should read 212°. Based on your test, adjust your recipe temperature up or down.

1 PIECE: 58 cal., 3g fat (1g sat. fat), 2mg chol., 35mg sod., 8g carb. (6g sugars, 0 fiber), 1g pro.

BERRY-CREAM COOKIE SNAPS

My mother and I came up with these treats by combining two recipes. The snaps are crispy on the outside and light and fluffy on the inside. You can also bake the cookies flat and serve the filling as a dip.
—*Crystal Briddick, Colfax, IL*

Prep: 40 min. + chilling
Bake: 5 min./batch + cooling
Makes: about 2 dozen

- 4 oz. cream cheese, softened
- ¼ cup sugar
- 2 Tbsp. seedless strawberry jam
- ¼ cup heavy whipping cream, whipped
- 1 to 3 drops red food coloring, optional

BATTER
- ½ cup sugar
- ⅓ cup all-purpose flour
- ⅛ tsp. salt
- 2 large egg whites, room temperature
- ¼ tsp. vanilla extract
- ¼ cup butter, melted and cooled
  Chopped fresh strawberries, optional

1. Preheat the oven to 400°. Beat the cream cheese, sugar and jam until blended. Fold in whipped cream and, if desired, food coloring. Refrigerate filling.

2. For batter, whisk sugar, flour and salt; stir in egg whites and vanilla until smooth. Whisk in the butter until blended. Line baking sheets with parchment. Preparing 4 cookies at a time, drop batter by 1½ teaspoonfuls 4 in. apart onto prepared pans. Bake until edges are lightly browned, 5-8 minutes.

3. Loosen each cookie and curl around a wooden spoon handle. Press lightly to seal; hold until set, about 20 seconds. Transfer to waxed paper to cool. Repeat with remaining cookies. If cookies become too cool to shape, return to oven for 1 minute to soften.

4. Just before serving, spoon the filling into cookie shells. Or pipe it by cutting a small hole in the tip of a pastry bag and inserting a star tip, then transferring the filling to bag. After filling shells, dip ends of cookies into chopped strawberries if desired. Refrigerate leftovers.

1 COOKIE: 72 cal., 4g fat (3g sat. fat), 12mg chol., 44mg sod., 8g carb. (7g sugars, 0 fiber), 1g pro.

BASIC COOKIE DOUGH

Skip the store-bought stuff and make cookies from scratch—it's easy! With this basic cookie dough, you can create all sorts of sweet treats. Bake some right away, then pop the extra dough into the freezer to bake later.
—*Gloria McBride, Payson, UT*

- -

Takes: 15 min. • **Makes:** 8 cups

2½ cups butter, softened
 2 cups sugar
 2 large eggs, room temperature
 ¼ cup 2% milk
 2 tsp. vanilla extract
7½ to 8 cups (30 to 32 oz.)
    all-purpose flour
 4 tsp. baking powder
 1 tsp. salt

In a large bowl, cream butter and sugar until light and fluffy, about 5 minutes. Beat in eggs, milk and vanilla. In another bowl, whisk 7½ cups flour, baking powder and salt; gradually beat into creamed mixture, adding additional flour if necessary. Divide dough into four 2-cup portions. Refrigerate, covered, until needed.

4 TSP. DOUGH: 98 cal., 5g fat (3g sat. fat), 17mg chol., 91mg sod., 12g carb. (4g sugars, 0 fiber), 1g pro.

TEST KITCHEN TIP
Most cookie doughs may be refrigerated or frozen, then baked later. When stored in airtight containers, unbaked cookie doughs can be refrigerated for a week or frozen for up to 3 months. Freeze cookie dough by dropping tablespoonfuls onto baking sheets. Cover and freeze until firm. When the dough is frozen, transfer the dough balls into airtight containers. To use frozen cookie dough: Place dough balls 2 in. apart on greased or ungreased baking sheets. Bake as the recipe directs, until the cookies are lightly browned.

1 FAVORITE
5 WAYS
Basic Cookies

1

5i

CRUMB-TOPPED DATE BARS

Basic dough doubles as a shortbread-like crust and a crumbly topping for these sweet date bars.

—*Gloria McBride, Payson, UT*

- -

Prep: 20 min. • **Bake:** 25 min.
Makes: 2 dozen

1	pkg. (8 oz.) chopped dates
½	cup sugar
½	cup water
1	Tbsp. lemon juice
2	cups Basic Cookie Dough

1. In a saucepan, bring the dates, sugar, water and lemon juice to a boil. Reduce heat; simmer, uncovered, for 5 minutes, stirring occasionally. Remove from the heat; cool.

2. Press half of the cookie dough into a greased 9-in. square baking pan. Spread with date mixture. Crumble remaining dough over filling. Bake at 375° for 25-30 minutes or until top is golden brown. Cool on a wire rack. Cut into bars.

1 BAR: 141 cal., 5g fat (3g sat. fat), 17mg chol., 77mg sod., 23g carb. (15g sugars, 1g fiber), 2g pro.

2

3

5i CLASSIC SUGAR COOKIES

Use cookie cutters to cut seasonal shapes from a few cups of this dough. Prepared frosting and colored sugar make it a snap to decorate the cookies according to the season or holiday.
—*Gloria McBride, Payson, UT*

- -

Prep: 10 min. • **Bake:** 20 min.
Makes: about 3 dozen

  2 cups Basic Cookie Dough
      Colored sugar and frosting of your
      choice

On a lightly floured surface, roll out dough to ¼-in. thickness. Using 2½-in. cookie cutters, cut out desired shapes. Place cutouts 2 in. apart on ungreased baking sheets. Leave plain or sprinkle with colored sugar. Bake at 375° for 8-10 minutes or until the edges are golden brown. Remove to wire racks to cool. Frost plain cookies; sprinkle with colored sugar if desired.
1 COOKIE: 65 cal., 3g fat (2g sat. fat), 11mg chol., 51mg sod., 8g carb. (3g sugars, 0 fiber), 1g pro.

CHOCOLATE MALLOW COOKIES

Cocoa, marshmallows and canned frosting transform basic dough into these delightful treats. I top each with a pecan half.
—*Gloria McBride, Payson, UT*

- -

Prep: 20 min. • **Bake:** 20 min.
Makes: 40 cookies

  2 cups Basic Cookie Dough
  ½ cup sugar
  ½ cup baking cocoa
  1 large egg, room temperature
  ¼ cup 2% milk
  ½ cup chopped pecans
 20 large marshmallows, halved
  1 can (16 oz.) chocolate frosting

In a bowl, combine the cookie dough, sugar, cocoa, egg and milk; mix well. Stir in pecans. Drop by tablespoonfuls 2 in. apart onto ungreased baking sheets. Bake at 375° for 8 minutes. Press a marshmallow half onto the top of each cookie. Bake 2 minutes longer or until marshmallow is puffed. Remove to wire racks to cool. Cut a hole in the corner of a pastry or plastic bag; insert a medium star tip. Fill bag with frosting. Pipe a star onto each cookie.
1 COOKIE: 140 cal., 6g fat (3g sat. fat), 15mg chol., 72mg sod., 21g carb. (14g sugars, 1g fiber), 1g pro.

5

—Gloria McBride, Payson, UT

4

CHERRY SURPRISE COOKIES

There's a rich chocolate surprise tucked into each of these cute bites. Candied cherries add a colorful finishing touch.
—Gloria McBride, Payson, UT

- -

Takes: 20 min. • **Makes:** 3 dozen

> 2 **cups Basic Cookie Dough**
> 36 **to 40 chocolate stars or**
> **chocolate kisses**
> 36 **to 40 candied cherry halves**

Drop cookie dough by heaping teaspoonfuls 2 in. apart onto greased baking sheets. Top each with a chocolate star and wrap dough around it. Top each with a candied cherry half. Bake at 375° for 10-12 minutes or until bottoms are lightly browned. Remove to wire racks to cool.

1 COOKIE: 96 cal., 5g fat (3g sat. fat), 12mg chol., 57mg sod., 13g carb. (7g sugars, 0 fiber), 1g pro.

JELLY SANDWICH COOKIES

Sandwiching jelly between two layers of basic cookie dough creates designs that look like stained glass. Your favorite raisin filling is excellent in these cookies, too.
—Gloria McBride, Payson, UT

- -

Prep: 20 min. • **Bake:** 20 min.
Makes: about 2 dozen

> 2 **cups Basic Cookie Dough**
> **Assorted jellies or jams**

1. On a lightly floured surface, roll out dough to ⅛-in. thickness. Cut with a 2½-in. round cookie cutter. Using a 1½-in. cookie cutter of your choice, cut out the center of half of the cookies.
2. Place whole cookies 2 in. apart on greased baking sheets. Spread with 1 tsp. jelly or jam; top with cutout cookies. Pinch edges with a fork to seal. Bake at 375° for 10-12 minutes or until edges are golden brown. Remove to wire racks to cool.
1 COOKIE: 98 cal., 5g fat (3g sat. fat), 17mg chol., 77mg sod., 12g carb. (4g sugars, 0 fiber), 1g pro.

Seasonal Specialties

No matter what the season, you'll find many reasons to celebrate! From summer's fresh bounty to winter's coziest comfort foods and everything in between, these recipes will turn your gatherings into memorable occasions.

SANTA SUGAR COOKIES

Ho-ho-ho! St. Nick can drop in any time when you bake these cute-as-can-be treats formed with a heart-shaped cookie cutter.
—*Jill Boruff, Soap Lake, WA*

- -

Prep: 1 hour + chilling
Bake: 10 min./batch + cooling
Makes: about 4 dozen

1½	cups butter, softened
1½	cups shortening
1½	cups sugar
1½	cups confectioners' sugar
4½	tsp. vanilla extract
3	large eggs, room temperature
6¾	cups all-purpose flour
1½	tsp. baking soda
1½	tsp. cream of tartar
1½	tsp. salt

FROSTING

2	cans (12 oz. each) whipped vanilla frosting
2	Tbsp. butter, softened
2	cups confectioners' sugar
	Brown and red M&M's minis
	Red colored sugar
	Red jimmies

1. Cream first 4 ingredients until light and fluffy. Beat in vanilla and eggs, 1 at a time. Whisk together flour, baking soda, cream of tartar and salt; gradually add to creamed mixture. Divide dough in half; shape into disks. Wrap and refrigerate until firm enough to roll, 1-2 hours.

2. Preheat oven to 375°. On a lightly floured surface, roll each disk to ¼-in. thickness. Cut with a floured 3½-in. heart-shaped cookie cutter. Place 1 in. apart on ungreased baking sheets. Bake until firm, 8-10 minutes (do not overbake). Remove from pans to wire racks; cool completely.

3. For frosting, beat canned frosting, butter and confectioners' sugar until well-blended. Transfer to a pastry bag fitted with a #16 star tip. Placing hearts point side up, use a small amount of frosting to attach brown M&M's for eyes and red M&M's for noses. Use remaining frosting to pipe hats, beards and mustaches. Sprinkle hats with red sugar and add jimmies for mouths.

1 COOKIE: 299 cal., 15g fat (6g sat. fat), 28mg chol., 198mg sod., 38g carb. (24g sugars, 0 fiber), 2g pro.

VALENTINE'S DAY

RUBIES ON ICE

Just like you and your sweetie, ginger and pomegranate are made for each other. The color of this beverage is tantalizing. If you're looking for a nonalcoholic option, you can easily leave out the vodka for a refreshing and festive drink.

—*Tara Deshpande, New York, NY*

Prep: 15 min. + freezing • **Makes:** 4 servings

- 6 Tbsp. pomegranate seeds
- ½ cup vodka
- 4 Tbsp. pomegranate molasses
- 3 Tbsp. sweetened ginger syrup
- 2 Tbsp. lime juice
- 1 cinnamon stick (3 in.)
  Club soda, chilled
  Lime slices, optional
- 1 to 4 tsp. pomegranate seeds, optional

1. Scatter the pomegranate seeds over an ice cube tray, about 1 tsp. per cube; fill with water and freeze.
2. Combine vodka, molasses, ginger syrup, lime juice and the cinnamon stick. Let steep for 15 minutes. Strain; discard cinnamon stick. Place 4 pomegranate ice cubes in each of 4 tall glasses. Pour molasses mixture evenly into glasses; top off with chilled club soda. Stir well. Garnish with additional pomegranate seeds and lime, if desired.
½ CUP: 148 cal., 0 fat (0 sat. fat), 0 chol., 3mg sod., 21g carb. (17g sugars, 0 fiber), 0 pro.

CHOCOLATE-DIPPED STRAWBERRIES

Plump berries from our strawberry patch turned into a special treat when I dipped them in chocolate. I make these right before dinner and put them in the fridge, so they're ready in time for dessert. Dunk the berries in caramel for a fun twist.

—*Valerie Gee, Depew, NY*

Takes: 20 min. • **Makes:** about 9 strawberries

- 1 pint large strawberries
- 4 oz. semisweet chocolate, chopped
- 1 Tbsp. plus ½ tsp. shortening, divided
- 1 oz. white baking chocolate
- 4 drops food coloring, optional

1. Wash strawberries and gently pat with paper towels until completely dry. In a microwave-safe bowl, melt semisweet chocolate and 1 Tbsp. shortening at 50% power; stir until smooth. Dip each strawberry and place on a waxed paper-lined baking sheet. Freeze strawberries for 5 minutes.
2. Meanwhile, microwave white chocolate and remaining shortening at 30% power until melted; stir until smooth. Stir in food coloring if desired. Drizzle over berries. Refrigerate until serving.

1 STRAWBERRY: 57 cal., 4g fat (2g sat. fat), 1mg chol., 4mg sod., 6g carb. (5g sugars, 1g fiber), 1g pro.

TEST KITCHEN TIP
Don't wash strawberries until you're ready to use them. They stay fresh longer if unwashed, with stems on, in a sealed glass jar in the fridge. Strawberries soak up moisture from washing, which can make them spoil in a hurry. It's not a long way from wet berries to moldy berries.

THOMAS FAGLON
Somerset, NJ

BETTER BRUSSELS SPROUTS

This is the only way my kids will eat Brussels sprouts! The recipe is ideal for me because it's fast, easy, healthy and makes a lovely side dish. Quick-cooking Brussels sprout halves are available in the prepackaged salad aisle at the grocery store. They're a timesaver if you can find them, but you can always just buy whole ones and slice them in half.
—Teri Lee Rasey, Cadillac, MI

BETTER BRUSSELS SPROUTS

This is the only way my kids will eat Brussels sprouts! The recipe is ideal for me because it's fast, easy, healthy and makes a lovely side dish. Quick-cooking Brussels sprout halves are available in the prepackaged salad aisle at the grocery store. They're a timesaver if you can find them, but you can always just buy whole ones and slice them in half.
—Teri Lee Rasey, Cadillac, MI

Takes: 20 min. • **Makes:** 6 servings

- 3   Tbsp. coconut oil
- 1   pkg. (16 oz.) fresh halved Brussels sprouts
- ⅓   cup sliced onions
- ½   cup coarsely chopped cashews
- 1   tsp. granulated garlic
     Salt and pepper to taste

In a large heavy skillet or wok, heat coconut oil over medium heat. Add Brussels sprouts; cook and stir for 5 minutes. Add the onion slices; cook 3 minutes longer, stirring every 20-30 seconds. Add cashews and garlic; cook 1 minute longer. Sprinkle with salt and pepper.
⅔ CUP: 161 cal., 13g fat (7g sat. fat), 0 chol., 81mg sod., 11g carb. (1g sugars, 3g fiber), 5g pro.

ORANGE POMEGRANATE SALMON

A colorful salmon dish makes an impressive addition to your table—and this one is as delicious as it is beautiful. No one will guess how easy it is to cook. I like to serve this with roasted baby potatoes and asparagus for a show-stopping meal.
—Thomas Faglon, Somerset, NJ

Prep: 10 min. • **Bake:** 25 min.
Makes: 4 servings

- 1   small red onion, thinly sliced
- 1   skinned salmon fillet (about 2 lbs.)
- ½   tsp. salt
- 1   medium navel orange, thinly sliced
- 1   cup pomegranate seeds
- 2   Tbsp. extra virgin olive oil
- 1   Tbsp. minced fresh dill

1. Preheat oven to 375°. Place a 28x18-in. piece of heavy-duty foil in a 15x10x1-in. baking pan. Place onion slices in a single layer on foil. Top with salmon; sprinkle with salt. Arrange the orange slices over top. Sprinkle with pomegranate seeds and drizzle with oil. Top with a second piece of foil. Bring edges of foil together on all sides and crimp to seal and form a large packet.
2. Bake until fish just begins to flake easily with a fork, 25-30 minutes. Be careful of escaping steam when opening packet. Remove to a serving platter; sprinkle with dill.
4 OZ. COOKED SALMON: 307 cal., 19g fat (3g sat. fat), 76mg chol., 274mg sod., 8g carb. (6g sugars, 1g fiber), 26g pro. **DIABETIC EXCHANGES:** 4 lean meat, 1½ fat, ½ fruit.

ST. PATRICKS'S DAY

3. Add potatoes. Return to a boil. Reduce heat; cover and simmer 1 hour longer or until the potatoes are tender. Combine cornstarch and water until smooth; stir into stew. Bring to a boil; cook and stir for 2 minutes or until thickened. Add peas; heat through. Discard bay leaves.

1 CUP: 301 cal., 13g fat (4g sat. fat), 66mg chol., 441mg sod., 21g carb. (3g sugars, 2g fiber), 23g pro.

GUINNESS FLOAT

That very first sip of a Guinness is what inspired this quick and easy dessert. The rich, creamy foam that gathers on the top of a freshly poured draft made me think of vanilla ice cream. At that point, I knew I had to combine the two in a Guinness float.
—*James Schend, Pleasant Prairie, WI*

Takes: 5 min. • **Makes:** 2 floats

- 1 **cup vanilla ice cream, softened if necessary**
- 2 **cups stout beer**
- 2 **Tbsp. chocolate syrup**

Divide ice cream between 2 glasses. Slowly top with beer; drizzle with chocolate syrup. Serve immediately.

1 SERVING: 286 cal., 7g fat (4g sat. fat), 29mg chol., 68mg sod., 36g carb. (31g sugars, 1g fiber), 4g pro.

IRISH BEEF STEW

Rich and hearty, this stew is my husband's favorite. The beef is incredibly tender. Served with crusty bread, it's an ideal cool-weather meal and perfect for any Irish holiday.
—*Carrie Karleen, St. Nicolas, QC*

Prep: 40 min. • **Cook:** 3¼ hours
Makes: 15 servings (3¾ qt.)

- 8 **bacon strips, diced**
- ⅓ **cup all-purpose flour**
- 1 **tsp. salt**
- ½ **tsp. pepper**
- 3 **lbs. beef stew meat, cut into 1-in. cubes**
- 1 **lb. whole fresh mushrooms, quartered**
- 3 **medium leeks (white portion only), chopped**
- 2 **medium carrots, chopped**
- ¼ **cup chopped celery**
- 1 **Tbsp. canola oil**
- 4 **garlic cloves, minced**
- 1 **Tbsp. tomato paste**
- 4 **cups reduced-sodium beef broth**
- 1 **cup dark stout beer or additional reduced-sodium beef broth**
- 2 **bay leaves**
- 1 **tsp. dried thyme**
- 1 **tsp. dried parsley flakes**
- 1 **tsp. dried rosemary, crushed**
- 2 **lbs. Yukon Gold potatoes, cut into 1-in. cubes**
- 2 **Tbsp. cornstarch**
- 2 **Tbsp. cold water**
- 1 **cup frozen peas**

1. In a stockpot, cook diced bacon over medium heat until crisp. Using a slotted spoon, remove to paper towels. In a large shallow dish, combine flour, salt and pepper. Add beef, a few pieces at a time, and shake to coat. Brown beef in the bacon drippings. Remove and set aside.

2. In the same pan, saute the mushrooms, leeks, carrots and celery in oil until tender. Add garlic; cook 1 minute longer. Stir in tomato paste until blended. Add the broth, beer, bay leaves, thyme, parsley and rosemary. Return beef and bacon to pan. Bring to a boil. Reduce heat; cover and simmer for 2 hours or until beef is tender.

CORNED BEEF PIZZA SWIRLS

Offer these fun little bites that taste like a Reuben for St. Patrick's Day. Even better, don't wait—deli meat and cheese make them doable all year long.
—Colleen Delawder, Herndon, VA

Prep: 30 min. + rising • **Bake:** 35 min.
Makes: 12 servings

- 2 tsp. sugar
- 1 tsp. active dry yeast
- 1 cup warm whole milk (110° to 115°)
- 1 Tbsp. olive oil
- 2 tsp. kosher salt
- 2 tsp. caraway seeds
- 2½ cups all-purpose flour

THOUSAND ISLAND SAUCE
- ½ cup mayonnaise
- 3 Tbsp. finely diced dill pickles
- 2 Tbsp. ketchup
- 1 tsp. brown sugar
- ½ tsp. onion powder
- ¼ tsp. pepper
- 2 dashes Louisiana-style hot sauce
  Dash garlic powder

PIZZA SWIRLS
- ¾ lb. thinly sliced corned beef
- ½ lb. thinly sliced lacy Swiss cheese

1. Add sugar and yeast to warm milk; let stand 15 minutes. Beat yeast mixture, oil, kosher salt and caraway seeds until blended. Beat in flour, ½ cup at a time, just until combined. With oiled hands, place dough in a greased bowl, turning once to grease the top. Cover and let rise in a warm place until doubled, about 2 hours.

2. Meanwhile, mix all ingredients for Thousand Island sauce; refrigerate.

3. Punch down dough. To assemble pizza swirls, turn dough onto a well-floured surface; roll into a 15x10-in. rectangle. Arrange corned beef and cheese slices to within ¾ in. of edges. Roll up jelly-roll style, starting with a long side; pinch seam to seal and tuck ends under. Cut crosswise into 1-in. slices. Place slices, sides touching, on a parchment-lined baking sheet.

4. Preheat oven to 375°. Cover pizza swirls with greased foil; let stand 20 minutes. Bake, covered, 20 minutes; remove foil and bake until golden brown, 15-20 minutes longer. Serve warm with Thousand Island sauce.

1 PIZZA SWIRL: 290 cal., 16g fat (6g sat. fat), 36mg chol., 807mg sod., 23g carb. (3g sugars, 1g fiber), 13g pro.

MINT CHOCOLATE CHEESECAKE

I created this mint chocolate cheesecake for our high school's annual fundraiser. We were told that it brought a hefty price and was one of the first desserts to go! If desired, the cookie pieces may be stirred into the batter instead of being added in a layer. Keep the pieces fairly small; otherwise they have a tendency to rise to the top.
—Sue Gronholz, Beaver Dam, WI

Prep: 20 min. • **Bake:** 1¼ hours + chilling
Makes: 16 servings

- 1 cup Oreo cookie crumbs
- 3 Tbsp. sugar
- 2 Tbsp. butter, melted

FILLING
- 4 pkg. (8 oz. each) cream cheese, softened
- 1 cup sugar
- 1 cup white baking chips, melted and cooled
- 6 Tbsp. creme de menthe
- ¼ cup all-purpose flour
- 2 Tbsp. creme de cacao
- ½ tsp. peppermint extract
- 4 large eggs, room temperature, lightly beaten
- 1 cup coarsely crushed Oreo cookies (about 10 cookies)

GANACHE
- ¾ cup semisweet chocolate chips
- 6 Tbsp. heavy whipping cream

1. Preheat oven to 325°. Place a greased 9-in. springform pan on a double thickness of heavy-duty foil (about 18 in. square). Wrap foil securely around pan. In a small bowl, mix cookie crumbs and sugar; stir in butter. Press onto bottom of prepared pan.

2. In a large bowl, beat cream cheese and sugar until smooth. Beat in cooled chips, creme de menthe, flour, creme de cacao and extract. Add eggs; beat on low speed just until blended. Pour half the batter over the crust; sprinkle with crushed Oreos. Carefully spoon remaining batter over top. Place springform pan in a larger baking pan; add 1 in. hot water to larger pan.

3. Bake until center of cheesecake is just set and top appears dull, 75-80 minutes. Remove springform pan from water bath. Cool on a wire rack 10 minutes. Loosen sides from pan with a knife; remove foil. Cool 1 hour longer. Refrigerate overnight, covering cheesecake when completely cooled.

4. Remove rim from pan. Place chocolate chips in a small bowl. In a small saucepan, bring whipping cream just to a boil. Pour over chocolate chips; stir with a whisk until smooth. Spread over cheesecake.

1 SLICE: 518 cal., 33g fat (18g sat. fat), 116mg chol., 296mg sod., 46g carb. (38g sugars, 1g fiber), 7g pro.

EASTER

3. Transfer to prepared pans. Bake until a toothpick inserted in center comes out clean, 24-28 minutes. Cool in pans 10 minutes before removing to wire racks; remove parchment. Cool slightly.

4. For syrup, in a small saucepan, combine sugar and lemon juice. Bring to a boil; cook until liquid is reduced by half. Cool completely.

5. For frosting, beat cream cheese and butter until smooth; beat in confectioners' sugar, lemon juice and salt until blended.

6. Using a long serrated knife, cut each cake horizontally in half. Brush layers with warm syrup; cool completely.

7. Place 1 cake layer on a serving plate; spread with 1 cup frosting. Repeat layers twice. Top with remaining cake layer. Frost top and sides with remaining frosting. If desired, top with lemon slices or edible flowers. Refrigerate leftover cake.

1 SLICE: 841 cal., 48g fat (30g sat. fat), 219mg chol., 656mg sod., 96g carb. (72g sugars, 1g fiber), 8g pro.

SUGAR-GLAZED HAM

This old-fashioned sugar glaze gives your ham a pretty, golden-brown coating just like on the ones Grandma used to make. The mustard and vinegar complement the brown sugar and add tangy flavor. Be prepared to serve seconds!
—*Carol Strong Battle, Heathsville, VA*

Prep: 5 min. • **Bake:** 1¾ hours
Makes: 14 servings

- 1 **fully cooked bone-in ham (5 to 7 lbs.)**
- 1 **cup packed brown sugar**
- 2 **tsp. prepared mustard**
- 1 **to 2 Tbsp. cider vinegar**

1. Preheat oven to 325°. Place ham on a rack in a shallow roasting pan. Using a sharp knife, score surface of ham with ¼-in.-deep cuts in a diamond pattern. Cover and bake until a thermometer reads 130°, 1½-2 hours.

2. Meanwhile, in a small bowl, combine the brown sugar, mustard and enough vinegar to make a thick paste. Remove ham from oven. Spread sugar mixture over ham. Bake ham, uncovered, 15-30 minutes longer or until a thermometer reads 140°.

4 OZ. HAM: 284 cal., 16g fat (6g sat. fat), 57mg chol., 1110mg sod., 15g carb. (15g sugars, 0 fiber), 20g pro.

LEMON LAYER CAKE

This citrusy cake with a luscious cream cheese frosting will garner plenty of raves. The flavor, a duet of sweet and tangy notes, really sings.
—*Summer Goddard, Springfield, VA*

Prep: 35 min. • **Bake:** 25 min. + cooling
Makes: 12 servings

- 1 **cup butter, softened**
- 1½ **cups sugar**
- 2 **large eggs, room temperature**
- 3 **large egg yolks, room temperature**
- 1 **Tbsp. grated lemon zest**
- 2 **Tbsp. lemon juice**
- ¾ **cup sour cream**
- ¼ **cup 2% milk**
- 2½ **cups all-purpose flour**
- 1 **tsp. salt**
- 1 **tsp. baking powder**
- ½ **tsp. baking soda**

SYRUP
- ½ **cup sugar**
- ½ **cup lemon juice**

FROSTING
- 2 **pkg. (8 oz. each) cream cheese, softened**
- 1 **cup butter, softened**
- 4 **cups confectioners' sugar**
- 1½ **tsp. lemon juice**
- ⅛ **tsp. salt**
  Optional: Lemon slices or edible flowers

1. Preheat oven to 350°. Line bottoms of 2 greased 9-in. round baking pans with parchment; grease parchment.

2. Cream butter and sugar until light and fluffy. Add eggs and egg yolks, 1 at a time, beating well after each addition. Beat in lemon zest and juice. In a small bowl, mix sour cream and milk. In another bowl, whisk together flour, salt, baking powder and baking soda; add to creamed mixture alternately with sour cream mixture.

1. In a microwave-safe bowl, stir the sugar, cornstarch and apricot nectar until smooth. Microwave, uncovered, on high until slightly thickened, 4-6 minutes, stirring every 2 minutes. Stir in the vanilla. Refrigerate.
2. In a large bowl, combine the fruit. Drizzle with dressing; gently toss to coat. Cover and refrigerate until serving.

1 CUP: 125 cal., 1g fat (0 sat. fat), 0 chol., 2mg sod., 32g carb. (27g sugars, 3g fiber), 1g pro.

GARLIC PARMESAN ASPARAGUS

Pair any entree with this fresh side dish for a truly succulent meal. With subtle garlic, melted butter and a hint of Parmesan, asparagus never tasted so good.

—Tara Ernspiker, Falling Waters, WV

Takes: 15 min. • **Makes:** 4 servings

- 1 lb. fresh asparagus, trimmed
- 1 garlic clove, minced
- 2 Tbsp. butter, melted
- 1 Tbsp. grated Parmesan cheese

In a large skillet, bring ½ in. water to a boil. Add asparagus and garlic; cook, covered, until asparagus is crisp-tender, 3-5 minutes; drain. Toss asparagus with butter and cheese.

1 SERVING: 71 cal., 6g fat (4g sat. fat), 16mg chol., 74mg sod., 3g carb. (1g sugars, 1g fiber), 2g pro. **DIABETIC EXCHANGES:** 1½ fat, 1 vegetable.

ROASTED TATER ROUNDS WITH GREEN ONIONS & TARRAGON

I am crazy for potatoes, especially when they're roasted and toasted. Toss them with fresh herbs and green onions for a bold finish.

—Ally Phillips, Murrells Inlet, SC

Prep: 25 min. • **Broil:** 10 min.
Makes: 8 servings

- 4 lbs. potatoes (about 8 medium), sliced ¼ in. thick Cooking spray
- 2 tsp. sea salt
- 1 tsp. coarsely ground pepper
- 6 green onions, thinly sliced (about ¾ cup)
- 3 Tbsp. minced fresh parsley
- 2 Tbsp. minced fresh tarragon Olive oil, optional

1. Preheat broiler. Place potatoes in a large microwave-safe bowl; spritz with cooking spray and toss to coat. Microwave, covered, on high 10-12 minutes or until almost tender, stirring halfway through cooking.
2. Spread potatoes into greased 15x10x1-in. baking pans. Spritz with additional cooking spray; sprinkle with salt and pepper.

3. Broil 4-6 in. from heat 10-12 minutes or until golden brown, stirring halfway through cooking. In a small bowl, mix green onions, parsley and tarragon. Sprinkle over potatoes; toss to coat. If desired, drizzle with olive oil.

¾ CUP: 185 cal., 1g fat (0 sat. fat), 0 chol., 497mg sod., 41g carb. (2g sugars, 5g fiber), 5g pro.

FRUIT SALAD WITH APRICOT DRESSING

Whenever I serve this lovely, refreshing salad for picnics, potlucks and holidays, the bowl empties in a hurry!

—Carol Lambert, El Dorado, AR

Takes: 30 min. • **Makes:** 26 servings

- 1 cup sugar
- 1 Tbsp. cornstarch
- 2 cans (5½ oz. each) apricot nectar
- 1 tsp. vanilla extract
- 6 large red apples, coarsely chopped
- 8 medium firm bananas, sliced
- 1 medium fresh pineapple, peeled and cut into chunks (about 5 cups)
- 1 qt. fresh strawberries, quartered
- 2 cups green grapes

CINCO DE MAYO

POTLUCK TACO SALAD

I found this recipe in an old school cookbook, and I've taken it to many potlucks since then. The layers look so pretty in a glass bowl.
—*Sandy Fynaardt, New Sharon, IA*

- -

Takes: 25 min.
Makes: 8 servings (1 cup dressing)

- 1 lb. ground beef
- 1 envelope taco seasoning, divided
- 1 medium head iceberg lettuce, torn
- 1 can (16 oz.) kidney beans, rinsed and drained
- 1 large red onion, chopped
- 4 medium tomatoes, seeded and finely chopped
- 2 cups shredded cheddar cheese
- 4 cups crushed tortilla chips (about 8 oz.)
- 1 bottle (8 oz.) Thousand Island salad dressing
- 2 Tbsp. taco sauce

1. In a large skillet, cook and crumble beef over medium heat until no longer pink, 6-8 minutes; drain. Stir in 3 Tbsp. taco seasoning.
2. In a large bowl, layer beef mixture, lettuce, beans, onion, tomatoes, cheese and crushed chips. In a small bowl, mix salad dressing, taco sauce and remaining taco seasoning; serve with salad.

1½ CUPS SALAD WITH 2 TBSP. DRESSING:
574 cal., 34g fat (11g sat. fat), 66mg chol., 1109mg sod., 44g carb. (9g sugars, 5g fiber), 23g pro.

QUICK WATERMELON SALSA

On hot days, this sweet salsa with watermelon, pineapple and fresh cilantro is sure to satisfy. You can toss it together in a matter of minutes.
—*Betsy Hanson, Tiverton, RI*

- -

Prep: 15 min. + chilling • **Makes:** 3 cups

- 2 cups chopped seedless watermelon
- 1 can (8 oz.) unsweetened crushed pineapple, drained
- ¼ cup chopped sweet onion
- ¼ cup minced fresh cilantro
- 3 Tbsp. orange juice
- ⅛ tsp. hot pepper sauce
  Tortilla chips

In a large mixing bowl, combine the first 6 ingredients. Cover and refrigerate at least 1 hour. Serve with tortilla chips.
¼ CUP: 23 cal., 0 fat (0 sat. fat), 0 chol., 1mg sod., 5g carb. (5g sugars, 0 fiber), 0 pro.
DIABETIC EXCHANGES: ½ fruit.

TEST KITCHEN TIP
Feel free to add other fresh fruits (like cherries or mango) to this watermelon salsa. It'll be bright, colorful, and add a nice sweet-tart flavor. Not a fan of cilantro? Try adding fresh mint instead.

SPANISH RICE

You'll find my Spanish rice is so much better than any boxed variety found in grocery stores. Best of all, it can be prepared in about the same time as those so-called convenience foods using items found in your pantry.
—*Anne Yaeger, Washington, DC*

- -

Takes: 25 min. • **Makes:** 6 servings

- ¼   cup butter, cubed
- 2   cups uncooked instant rice
- 1   can (14½ oz.) diced tomatoes, undrained
- 1   cup boiling water
- 2   beef bouillon cubes
- 1   medium onion, chopped
- 1   garlic clove, minced
- 1   bay leaf
- 1   tsp. sugar
- 1   tsp. salt
- ¼   tsp. pepper

In a saucepan, melt butter over medium heat. Add the rice; cook and stir until lightly browned. Add remaining ingredients; bring to a boil. Reduce heat; cover and simmer until the liquid is absorbed and rice is tender, 10-15 minutes. Remove bay leaf.
¾ CUP: 217 cal., 8g fat (5g sat. fat), 20mg chol., 886mg sod., 33g carb. (4g sugars, 2g fiber), 4g pro.

TURKEY ENCHILADAS VERDES

Planning a fiesta night? These authentic-tasting enchiladas in spicy green sauce will please the whole family. You'll be thankful for such a tasty way to use up turkey leftovers.
—*Kiki Power, Arlington, TX*

- -

Prep: 45 min. • **Bake:** 30 min.
Makes: 16 servings

- 32   corn tortillas (6 in.)
- ⅓   cup plus 1 Tbsp. canola oil, divided
- 1   medium onion, chopped
- 3   cups cubed cooked turkey
- 1   can (14½ oz.) Mexican diced tomatoes, undrained
- 1   Tbsp. chopped pickled jalapeno slices
- 1   envelope taco seasoning
- 1   tsp. ground cumin
- ½   tsp. dried oregano
- ½   tsp. dried basil
- 3   cans (10 oz. each) green enchilada sauce
- 1   can (10¾ oz.) condensed cream of chicken soup, undiluted
- 3   cups shredded Monterey Jack cheese, divided

Optional: Sour cream, chopped tomato, chopped cilantro and additional pickled jalapeno slices

1. In a large skillet, fry tortillas in batches, using ⅓ cup oil, for 5 seconds on each side or until golden. Drain on paper towels.
2. In the same skillet, saute onion in remaining oil until tender. Stir in the turkey, tomatoes, jalapenos, taco seasoning, cumin, oregano and basil; heat through.
3. Combine enchilada sauce and soup. Spread ½ cup mixture into each of two 13x9-in. baking dishes. Place 2 Tbsp. turkey mixture down the center of each tortilla; top with 1 Tbsp. cheese. Roll up and place seam side down in prepared dishes. Pour remaining sauce over the top.
4. Cover and bake at 350° for 25-30 minutes or until heated through. Uncover; sprinkle with remaining cheese. Bake 5 minutes longer or until cheese is melted. Garnish with desired optional toppings.
2 ENCHILADAS: 350 cal., 17g fat (5g sat. fat), 40mg chol., 906mg sod., 33g carb. (3g sugars, 3g fiber), 18g pro.

2. For punch, place thawed strawberries in a blender; cover and puree until smooth. Pour into a large serving or punch bowl. Add the apricot nectar, orange juice concentrate, water, lemon juice and sugar; stir until sugar is dissolved. Just before serving, stir in ginger ale and add ice ring.

1 CUP: 140 cal., 0 fat (0 sat. fat), 0 chol., 7mg sod., 36g carb. (34g sugars, 1g fiber), 1g pro.

HERBY PEA SALAD

We love spring vegetables. One Mother's Day I came up with this flavorful green salad that everyone enjoyed. You could increase the dressing and mix in some cooked small cooked pasta, like acini de pepe, for a pasta salad.
—*Ann Sheehy, Lawrence, MA*

- -

Takes: 30 min. • **Makes:** 8 servings

- 1 Tbsp. olive oil
- 2 medium leeks (white portion only), thinly sliced
- 3 small zucchini, halved and sliced
- ½ lb. fresh asparagus, trimmed and cut into 2-in. pieces
- 3 cups frozen petite peas (about 16 oz.), thawed
- 2 Tbsp. each minced fresh chives and parsley
- 1 to 2 Tbsp. minced fresh tarragon

DRESSING
- 3 Tbsp. olive oil
- 2 Tbsp. rice or white wine vinegar
- ¾ tsp. salt
- ½ tsp. Dijon mustard
- ¼ tsp. pepper

1. In a large skillet, heat oil over medium heat. Add leeks; cook and stir 4-6 minutes or until tender. In a Dutch oven, place steamer basket over 1 in. water. In batches, place the zucchini and asparagus in basket. Bring water to a boil. Reduce heat to maintain a low boil; steam, covered, 4-5 minutes or until crisp-tender. Remove and immediately drop into ice water. Drain and pat dry.

2. In a large bowl, combine the peas, leeks, zucchini mixture and herbs. In a small bowl, whisk dressing ingredients. Pour over salad; toss to coat. Serve immediately.

1 CUP: 140 cal., 0 fat (0 sat. fat), 0 chol., 7mg sod., 36g carb. (34g sugars, 1g fiber), 1g pro.

CELEBRATION PUNCH

This pretty fruit punch has just the right amount of sweetness. The ice ring keeps it cool for hours without diluting the flavor.
—*Marci Carl, Northern Cambria, PA*

- -

Prep: 15 min. + freezing
Makes: 16 servings (about 1 gallon)

ICE RING
- 1¾ cups orange juice
- 1½ cups water
- 1 cup halved fresh strawberries
  Fresh mint sprigs

PUNCH
- 2 pkg. (10 oz. each) frozen sweetened sliced strawberries, thawed
- 4 cans (5½ oz. each) apricot nectar
- ¾ cup orange juice concentrate
- 3 cups cold water
- 1 cup lemon juice
- ¾ cup sugar
- 1 liter ginger ale, chilled

1. For ice ring, in a bowl, combine the orange juice and water. Pour 2 cups into a 4½-cup ring mold. Freeze until solid. Top with fresh strawberries and mint. Slowly pour remaining juice mixture into mold to almost cover strawberries and mint. Freeze until solid.

HOMEMADE SAGE SAUSAGE PATTIES

Oregano, garlic and sage add savory flavor to these quick-to-fix ground pork patties. I've had this Pennsylvania Dutch recipe for years, and it always brings compliments.
—*Diane Hixon, Niceville, FL*

Prep: 10 min. + chilling • **Cook:** 15 min.
Makes: 8 servings

- 1 lb. ground pork
- ¾ cup shredded cheddar cheese
- ¼ cup buttermilk
- 1 Tbsp. finely chopped onion
- 2 tsp. rubbed sage
- ¾ tsp. salt
- ¾ tsp. pepper
- ⅛ tsp. garlic powder
- ⅛ tsp. dried oregano

1. In a bowl, combine all ingredients, mixing lightly, but thoroughly. Shape into eight ½-in.-thick patties. Refrigerate 1 hour.
2. In a large cast-iron or other heavy skillet, cook the patties over medium heat until a thermometer reads 160°, 6-8 minutes on each side.
1 PATTY: 162 cal., 11g fat (5g sat. fat), 49mg chol., 323mg sod., 1g carb. (0 sugars, 0 fiber), 13g pro.

ARTICHOKE & ONION FRITTATA

The combination of fresh flavors make this pretty egg bake a great entree for a special occasion brunch or light luncheon.
—*Joyce Moynihan, Lakeville, MN*

Prep: 15 min. • **Bake:** 35 min.
Makes: 8 servings

- 1 pkg. (8 oz.) frozen artichoke hearts
- 1 Tbsp. butter
- 1 Tbsp. olive oil
- 1 medium onion, chopped
- 1 garlic clove, minced
- ¼ tsp. dried oregano
- ¾ cup shredded Parmesan cheese, divided
- 6 large eggs
- ½ cup 2% milk
- ¼ tsp. salt
- ⅛ tsp. white pepper
- ⅛ tsp. ground nutmeg
- 1 cup shredded Monterey Jack cheese
  Minced chives, optional

1. Cook artichokes according to package directions; drain. Cool slightly; coarsely chop. Preheat oven to 350°.
2. In a large skillet, heat butter and oil over medium-high heat. Add onion; cook and stir until tender. Add garlic; cook 1 minute longer. Stir in oregano and artichokes; remove from the heat.
3. Sprinkle ¼ cup Parmesan cheese in a greased 11x7-in. baking dish. Top with the artichoke mixture.
4. In a large bowl, whisk eggs, milk, salt, pepper and nutmeg. Stir in Monterey Jack cheese and ¼ cup Parmesan cheese. Pour over artichoke mixture.
5. Bake, uncovered, 30 minutes. Sprinkle with remaining Parmesan cheese. Bake 6-8 minutes longer or until a knife inserted in the center comes out clean. If desired, sprinkle with minced chives.
1 PIECE: 192 cal., 13g fat (7g sat. fat), 163mg chol., 373mg sod., 5g carb. (2g sugars, 3g fiber), 13g pro.

SUMMER HARVEST

ANDREA RIVERA
Westbury, NY

1. Cook spaghetti according to package directions; drain.
2. Meanwhile, combine onion, bread crumbs, egg, Parmesan, milk and seasonings. Add beef; mix lightly. With wet hands, shape into 1½-in. balls. Place meatballs on greased grill rack; grill, covered, over medium heat until cooked through, about 10 minutes.
3. For sauce, combine tomatoes, garlic, oil, sugar, salt, oregano and pepper in an 11x7x2-in. disposable foil pan. Grill over medium heat until sauce begins to simmer, about 10 minutes. Stir in basil.
4. Serve meatballs and sauce with spaghetti; top with shredded Parmesan.

1 CUP SPAGHETTI WITH ½ CUP SAUCE AND 3 MEATBALLS: 446 cal., 14g fat (5g sat. fat), 79mg chol., 470mg sod., 55g carb. (7g sugars, 4g fiber), 25g pro.

DILL GARDEN SALAD

This salad shows up on our table several times a week during the summer. I cut up whatever fresh vegetables I have on hand and toss them with this delicious dressing and fresh dill.
—*Bethany Martin, Milton, PA*

- -

Takes: 15 min. • **Makes:** 6 servings

- 3   cups chopped English cucumbers
- 1   large tomato, seeded and cut into ½-in. pieces
- 1   small sweet red pepper, chopped
- 2   Tbsp. chopped sweet onion
- 3   Tbsp. reduced-fat mayonnaise
- 4   tsp. olive oil
- 2   tsp. sugar
- 2   tsp. rice vinegar
- ½   tsp. salt
- ¼   tsp. garlic powder
- ¼   tsp. pepper
- 2½   tsp. snipped fresh dill

In a large bowl, combine cucumbers, tomato, red pepper and onion. In a small bowl, whisk mayonnaise, oil, sugar, vinegar, salt, garlic powder and pepper until blended. Stir in dill. Spoon dressing over salad; toss to coat.

1 CUP: 75 cal., 6g fat (1g sat. fat), 3mg chol., 260mg sod., 6g carb. (4g sugars, 1g fiber), 1g pro. **DIABETIC EXCHANGES:** 1 vegetable, 1 fat.

SUMMERTIME SPAGHETTI WITH GRILLED MEATBALLS

After Hurricane Sandy, we were without power for two weeks. I learned just how much you can cook on a grill, such as these smoky meatballs and tomato sauce.
—*Andrea Rivera, Westbury, NY*

- -

Prep: 25 min. • **Cook:** 10 min.
Makes: 6 servings

- 12   oz. uncooked spaghetti

MEATBALLS
- ½   cup finely chopped onion
- ¼   cup seasoned bread crumbs
- 1   large egg
- 2   Tbsp. grated Parmesan cheese
- 1   Tbsp. 2% milk
- ½   tsp. garlic powder
- ½   tsp. onion powder
- 1   lb. ground beef

TOMATO SAUCE
- 2   lbs. (4 to 5) large tomatoes, chopped
- 3   garlic cloves, minced
- 1   Tbsp. olive oil
- 1   tsp. sugar
- ¾   tsp. salt
- ½   tsp. dried oregano
- ½   tsp. pepper
- 2   Tbsp. minced fresh basil

TOPPING
-      Shredded Parmesan cheese

TASTY MARINATED TOMATOES

My niece introduced me to this colorful recipe some time ago. I make it when I have buffets or large gatherings because it can be prepared hours ahead. This is a wonderful way to use a bumper crop of tomatoes.
—*Myrtle Matthews, Marietta, GA*

- -

Prep: 10 min. + marinating • **Makes:** 8 servings

- 3 large or 5 medium fresh tomatoes, thickly sliced
- ⅓ cup olive oil
- ¼ cup red wine vinegar
- 1 tsp. salt, optional
- ¼ tsp. pepper
- ½ garlic clove, minced
- 2 Tbsp. chopped onion
- 1 Tbsp. minced fresh parsley
- 1 Tbsp. minced fresh basil or 1 tsp. dried basil

Arrange tomatoes in a large shallow dish. Combine remaining ingredients in a jar; cover tightly and shake well. Pour over tomato slices. Cover and refrigerate for several hours.
2 SLICES: 93 cal., 9g fat (1g sat. fat), 0 chol., 4mg sod., 4g carb. (2g sugars, 1g fiber), 1g pro.

ZUCCHINI-CRUSTED PIZZA

It's flavorful, nutritious, versatile, easy to prep ahead and freeze, and fun to make with kids. It also quadruples nicely if you have to serve a crowd. What's not to love?
—*Ruth Hartunian-Alumbaugh, Willimantic, CT*

- -

Prep: 20 min. • **Bake:** 25 min.
Makes: 6 servings

- 2 large eggs, lightly beaten
- 2 cups shredded zucchini (about 1½ medium), squeezed dry
- ½ cup shredded part-skim mozzarella cheese
- ½ cup grated Parmesan cheese
- ¼ cup all-purpose flour
- 1 Tbsp. olive oil
- 1 Tbsp. minced fresh basil
- 1 tsp. minced fresh thyme

TOPPINGS
- 1 jar (12 oz.) roasted sweet red peppers, julienned
- 1 cup shredded part-skim mozzarella cheese
- ½ cup sliced turkey pepperoni

1. Preheat oven to 450°. Mix the first 8 ingredients; transfer to a 12-in. pizza pan coated generously with cooking spray. Spread mixture to an 11-in. circle.
2. Bake until light golden brown, 13-16 minutes. Reduce oven setting to 400°. Add toppings. Bake until cheese is melted, 10-12 minutes longer.
1 SLICE: 219 cal., 12g fat (5g sat. fat), 95mg chol., 680mg sod., 10g carb. (4g sugars, 1g fiber), 14g pro. **DIABETIC EXCHANGES:** 2 medium-fat meat, ½ starch, ½ fat.

FATHER'S DAY

BASIL CORN ON THE COB

Be sure to use your fresh bounty of summer basil for this fantastic corn recipe. Steaming the basil under the husks adds lots of flavor to the ears. Lime makes their sweet taste pop even more.

—Diane Eaton, Campbell, CA

- -

Prep: 25 min. + soaking • **Grill:** 25 min.
Makes: 6 servings

- 6   large ears sweet corn in husks
- 6   Tbsp. butter, softened
- ½   tsp. dried basil
- ¼   tsp. sugar
-      Dash salt
-      Dash garlic salt
- 1   cup fresh basil leaves
-      Lime wedges

1. Carefully peel back corn husks to within 1 in. of bottoms; remove silk. In a small bowl, combine the butter, dried basil, sugar, salt and garlic salt; spread over corn. Place basil leaves over butter mixture. Rewrap corn in husks and secure with kitchen string. Place in a stockpot; cover with cold water. Soak for 20 minutes and drain.
2. Grill corn, covered, over medium heat for 25-30 minutes or until tender, turning often. Serve with lime wedges.
1 SERVING: 225 cal., 13g fat (7g sat. fat), 30mg chol., 145mg sod., 28g carb. (5g sugars, 4g fiber), 5g pro.

GARLIC GRILLED STEAKS

Take steak to new flavor heights by basting your choice of cuts with an amazing garlicky blend that requires only a few minutes to fix. It will be a mouthwatering change of taste at your next outdoor gathering.

—Taste of Home *Test Kitchen*

- -

Takes: 15 min. • **Makes:** 4 servings

- 10   garlic cloves
- 1½   tsp. salt
- ½   tsp. pepper
- 2   Tbsp. olive oil
- 1   Tbsp. lemon juice
- 2   tsp. Worcestershire sauce
- 4   boneless beef strip steaks or ribeye steaks (1 in. thick and 8 oz. each)

1. With a mortar and pestle, crush garlic cloves with salt and pepper. Stir in oil, lemon juice and Worcestershire sauce.
2. Grill steaks, covered, over medium heat 5-7 minutes on each side or until the meat reaches desired doneness (for medium-rare, a thermometer should read 135°; medium, 140°; medium-well, 145°). Brush generously with garlic mixture during the last 4 minutes of cooking.
NOTE: Strip steak may also be labeled as club, New York strip, Kansas City and top loin steak.
1 STEAK: 373 cal., 17g fat (5g sat. fat), 100mg chol., 1013mg sod., 3g carb. (0 sugars, 0 fiber), 48g pro.

GRILLED BANANA BROWNIE SUNDAES

My niece Amanda Jean and I have a lot of fun in the kitchen creating different dishes. One of us will start with a recipe idea and it just grows from there—and so does the mess. In this case, the happy result was our Grilled Banana Brownie Sundae.

—*Carol Farnsworth, Greenwood, IN*

Takes: 15 min. • **Makes:** 8 servings

- 2 medium bananas, unpeeled
- 4 oz. cream cheese, softened
- ¼ cup packed brown sugar
- 3 Tbsp. creamy peanut butter
- 8 prepared brownies (2-in. squares)
- 4 cups vanilla ice cream
- ½ cup hot fudge ice cream topping, warmed
- ½ cup chopped salted peanuts

1. Cut unpeeled bananas crosswise in half, then lengthwise in half. Place quartered bananas on an oiled grill rack, cut side down. Grill, covered, over medium-high heat on each side until lightly browned, 2-3 minutes. Cool slightly.

2. In a small bowl, beat cream cheese, brown sugar and peanut butter until smooth.

3. To serve, remove bananas from peel; place over brownies. Top with the cream cheese mixture, ice cream, hot fudge topping and chopped peanuts.

1 SERVING: 505 cal., 28g fat (11g sat. fat), 62mg chol., 277mg sod., 57g carb. (33g sugars, 3g fiber), 10g pro.

WISCONSIN BUTTER-BASTED BURGERS

It's no secret that Wisconsinites love their dairy—so much that they sometimes top their burgers with a generous pat of butter. My recipe is a lot like the butter burgers you'll find in popular restaurants all over the state.

—*Becky Carver, North Royalton, OH*

Takes: 30 min. • **Makes:** 4 servings

- 1 lb. lean ground beef (90% lean)
- ½ tsp. seasoned salt
- ½ tsp. pepper
- ½ lb. fresh mushrooms
- 2 Tbsp. plus 4 tsp. butter, divided
- 4 hamburger buns, split
  Optional toppings: Tomato slices, lettuce leaves, dill pickle slices, ketchup and mustard

1. Sprinkle ground beef with seasoned salt and pepper. Pulse mushrooms in a food processor until finely chopped. Add to the seasoned beef, mixing lightly but thoroughly. Shape into four ½-in.-thick patties.

2. In a large skillet, heat 2 Tbsp. butter over medium heat. Add burgers; cook 6-8 minutes on each side, basting with butter, until a thermometer reads 160°. Remove from heat; keep warm. Add bun tops to skillet; toast until golden brown.

3. Transfer burgers to bun bottoms. Top each with 1 tsp. butter. Replace bun tops. Serve with toppings.

1 BURGER: 400 cal., 21g fat (10g sat. fat), 96mg chol., 543mg sod., 24g carb. (3g sugars, 1g fiber), 28g pro.

4TH OF JULY PICNIC

3. To serve, spread 1½ cups whipped topping over the gelatin mixture. Toss cut berries with remaining lemon juice; spoon over pie. Sprinkle with toasted coconut and, if desired, additional pistachios. Serve with remaining whipped topping.

FOR HOMEMADE GRAHAM CRACKER CRUST: Toss 2 cups graham cracker crumbs and ⅓ cup sugar with ½ cup melted butter. Press onto the bottom and up sides of an ungreased 9-in. deep-dish pie plate. Bake in a preheated 375° oven until lightly browned, 9-11 minutes. Cool completely on a wire rack before filling.

1 PIECE: 345 cal., 18g fat (9g sat. fat), 0 chol., 217mg sod., 41g carb. (33g sugars, 3g fiber), 4g pro.

FRESH CORN & AVOCADO DIP

I alter my sister's dip recipe by adding finely chopped jalapeno for a little heat. It's a different way of serving corn as a dip that can be made ahead of time and refrigerated until serving.
—*Pat Roberts, Thornton, ON*

Takes: 20 min. • **Makes:** 4 cups

- 2 cups fresh or frozen corn, thawed
- 1 medium ripe avocado, peeled and diced
- 1 small peach, peeled and chopped
- 1 small sweet red pepper, chopped
- 1 small red onion, chopped
- 2 Tbsp. olive oil
- 2 Tbsp. white wine vinegar
- 1 Tbsp. lime juice
- 1½ tsp. ground cumin
- 1 tsp. minced fresh oregano
- 1 garlic clove, crushed
- Salt and pepper to taste
- 1 minced and seeded jalapeno pepper, optional
- Baked tortilla chips

Combine first 11 ingredients; add salt and pepper and, if desired, jalapeno. Serve with tortilla chips.

¼ CUP: 52 cal., 3g fat (0 sat. fat), 0 chol., 4mg sod., 6g carb. (2g sugars, 1g fiber), 1g pro.
DIABETIC EXCHANGES: ½ starch, ½ fat.

BERRY PISTACHIO PIE

My grandmother used to make this pie when I was a small child. A Brooklyn woman gave her the recipe, but my grandmother could never remember the woman's name or the name of the pie, comically dubbing it Lady from Brooklyn's Pie. Feel free to use any flavored gelatin, or try walnuts or pecans instead of pistachios. I use a store-bought graham cracker crust, but you can also use a chocolate graham cracker crust.
—*Judy DeGrottole, New York, NY*

Prep: 25 min. + chilling • **Makes:** 10 servings

- 1 cup boiling water
- 1 pkg. (3 oz.) lemon gelatin
- ¾ cup cold water
- 1 tsp. grated lemon zest
- 2 Tbsp. lemon juice, divided
- 1 carton (12 oz.) whipped topping, divided
- ¾ cup pistachios, chopped
  One 10-in. graham cracker crust (about 9 oz.)
- 1½ cups fresh strawberries, quartered
- 1 cup fresh blueberries
  Sweetened shredded coconut, toasted
  Additional chopped pistachios

1. In a large bowl, add boiling water to gelatin; stir 2 minutes to completely dissolve. Stir in cold water, lemon zest and 1 Tbsp. lemon juice. Refrigerate, covered, until almost firm, 1½-2 hours.
2. Fold 2 cups whipped topping into gelatin. Beat until smooth, 1-2 minutes. Fold in pistachios. Transfer to crust. Refrigerate, covered, at least 4 hours.

4. Remove ribs from oven; discard juices. Brush both sides with barbecue sauce. Grill ribs, covered, on a greased grill rack over low direct heat, turning and brushing occasionally with remaining sauce, until heated through, about 10 minutes. Cut into serving-size pieces; serve with reserved sauce.

1 SERVING: 483 cal., 27g fat (10g sat. fat), 102mg chol., 1107mg sod., 31g carb. (26g sugars, 1g fiber), 30g pro.

ORANGE LEMONADE

This juice is a favorite at our place. I was looking for a way to sweeten lemonade without using more sugar when I came up with the recipe. I'll often double the batch and send a jar next door to my mother-in-law.
—*Wendy Masters, Grand Valley, ON*

Prep: 15 min. + chilling • **Cook:** 5 min. + cooling
Makes: 12 servings (3 qt.)

- 1¾ cups sugar
- 2½ cups water
- 2 Tbsp. grated lemon zest
- 2 Tbsp. grated orange zest
- 1½ cups lemon juice (about 10 lemons)
- 1½ cups orange juice (about 5 oranges)
- 6 cups cold water

1. In a large saucepan, combine sugar and 2½ cups water; cook and stir over medium heat until sugar is dissolved. Cool slightly.
2. Stir in citrus zest and juices. Let stand, covered, 1 hour. Strain syrup; refrigerate, covered, until cold.
3. To serve, fill glasses or pitcher with equal amounts of fruit syrup and water. Add ice and serve.

1 CUP: 136 cal., 0 fat (0 sat. fat), 0 chol., 1mg sod., 35g carb. (33g sugars, 0 fiber), 0 pro.

JIM'S SECRET RECIPE RIBS

For more than 30 years, my brother-in-law Jim kept his famous rib recipe a secret, including from big brother Dennis, my husband. When he finally came around to sharing it, we loved it so much we just had to pass it along. This one's for you, Jim!
—*Vicki Young, Brighton, CO*

Prep: 20 min. + chilling • **Cook:** 3 hours 10 min.
Makes: 8 servings

- 2 racks pork baby back ribs (about 5 lbs.)
- ¼ cup soy sauce
- ¼ cup dried oregano
- 2 Tbsp. onion powder
- 2 tsp. garlic powder
- 1 liter lemon-lime soda
- ½ cup unsweetened pineapple or orange juice, optional

BARBECUE SAUCE
- ½ cup sugar or packed brown sugar
- ½ cup hot water
- 1 cup ketchup
- ¼ cup honey mustard
- ¼ cup barbecue sauce of choice
- 3 Tbsp. lemon juice
- 1½ tsp. white vinegar

1. Brush ribs with soy sauce. Combine the oregano, onion powder and garlic powder; rub over both sides of ribs. Transfer to a large shallow roasting pan; refrigerate, covered, overnight.
2. Preheat oven to 225°. Add lemon-lime soda and, if desired, juice to roasting pan (do not pour over ribs). Bake, covered, until tender, about 3 hours.
3. Meanwhile, for barbecue sauce, dissolve sugar in hot water; combine with remaining ingredients, thinning with additional soda or juice if necessary. Reserve 1 cup for serving.

CAMPFIRE CLASSICS

CAMPFIRE BEAN & HAM SOUP

This is the best beans and ham soup you'll ever taste! Friends rave about this smoky soup that I serve hot off the grill.
—*Tom Greaves, Carrollton, IL*

Prep: 15 min. + standing • **Grill:** 1½ hours
Makes: 12 servings (3 qt.)

- 1   lb. dried navy beans
- 2   small onions
- 8   cups water
- 4   cups cubed fully cooked lean ham (1½ lbs.)
- 2   smoked ham hocks
- 2   cups chopped celery
- 1   cup chopped carrots
- ½   tsp. dried basil
- ½   tsp. pepper

1. Place beans in an ovenproof Dutch oven; add enough water to cover by 2 in. Bring to a boil; boil for 2 minutes. Remove from heat; cover and let stand for 1-4 hours or until beans are softened.
2. Chop 1 onion; slice second onion and separate into rings. Set onions aside. Drain and rinse beans, discarding liquid. Return beans to the pan. Add reserved onions; stir in the remaining ingredients. Cover pan and place on grill rack over indirect medium heat.
3. Cover grill; cook for 1 hour or until beans are almost tender. Uncover Dutch oven; cover grill and cook 30 minutes longer or until beans are tender. Discard ham hocks.
NOTE: For easy cleanup, consider covering the outside of your Dutch oven with heavy-duty foil first.
1 CUP: 197 cal., 3g fat (1g sat. fat), 28mg chol., 612mg sod., 26g carb. (3g sugars, 7g fiber), 19g pro. **DIABETIC EXCHANGES:** 3 lean meat, 1½ starch.

READER REVIEW

"Excellent soup...I did it on the stove and let it simmer. Before I served it, I brought it to a boil and put in the veggies so they didn't get soggy. I would definitely make this again!"

GINABEE, TASTEOFHOME.COM

5i
CAKE & BERRY CAMPFIRE COBBLER

This warm cobbler is one of our favorite ways to end a busy day of fishing, hiking, swimming or rafting. It's yummy with ice cream—and so easy to make!
—*June Dress, Meridian, ID*

Prep: 10 min. • **Grill:** 30 min.
Makes: 12 servings

- 2   cans (21 oz. each) raspberry pie filling
- 1   pkg. yellow cake mix (regular size)
- 1¼ cups water
- ½   cup canola oil
    Vanilla ice cream, optional

1. Prepare grill or campfire for low heat, using 16-20 charcoal briquettes or large wood chips.
2. Line an ovenproof Dutch oven with heavy-duty aluminum foil; add pie filling. In a large bowl, combine the cake mix, water and oil. Spread over pie filling.
3. Cover Dutch oven. When briquettes or wood chips are covered with white ash, place Dutch oven directly on top of 8-10 of them. Using long-handled tongs, place remaining briquettes on pan cover.
4. Cook until filling is bubbly and a toothpick inserted in the topping comes out clean, 30-40 minutes. To check for doneness, use the tongs to carefully lift the cover. If desired, serve with ice cream.
NOTE: This recipe does not use eggs.
1 SERVING: 342 cal., 12g fat (2g sat. fat), 0 chol., 322mg sod., 57g carb. (34g sugars, 2g fiber), 1g pro.

¼ tsp. ground nutmeg
10 cherry Jolly Rancher hard candies, crushed
1 pouch (7 oz.) green decorating icing
½ cup chocolate wafer crumbs
36 pretzel sticks

1. Preheat oven to 350°. In a large bowl, cream butter and sugar until light and fluffy. Beat in eggs and vanilla. In another bowl, whisk flour, baking powder, salt and nutmeg; gradually beat into creamed mixture.

2. Shape level tablespoons of dough into balls; place 2 in. apart on ungreased baking sheets. Flatten slightly with the bottom of a glass. Bake until edges are light brown, 8-10 minutes. Cool on pans 2 minutes before removing to wire racks to cool completely.

3. Meanwhile, spread crushed candies onto a parchment-lined baking sheet. Bake until candy is melted, 5-7 minutes. Cool completely on pan on a wire rack. Break into pieces.

4. Spread icing over cookies; sprinkle with wafer crumbs. Arrange broken candies to make campfire flames. For logs, break pretzel sticks in half. Place 3 halves, broken edge down, in the wet icing. Hold in place until set.

1 COOKIE: 238 cal., 10g fat (6g sat. fat), 36mg chol., 166mg sod., 35g carb. (20g sugars, 1g fiber), 2g pro.

POTATOES PLUS

On our busy farm, meals need to be ready fast. Wrapped in foil packets, these herb-seasoned potatoes and vegetables cook in 30 minutes. They're excellent alongside steak or chicken.
—*Jill Jellett, Leduc, AB*

- -

Prep: 10 min. • **Grill:** 30 min.
Makes: 4 servings

4 medium red potatoes, cubed
1 medium onion, cubed
1 medium sweet red pepper, cubed
½ tsp. seasoned salt
¼ tsp. garlic powder
¼ tsp. each dried basil, dill weed and parsley flakes
¼ cup butter, cubed

1. Combine the vegetables and seasonings; divide among 4 pieces of heavy-duty foil (about 12 in. square). Dot with butter. Fold foil around vegetables and seal tightly.

2. Grill, covered, over medium heat for 15 minutes on each side. Open foil carefully to allow steam to escape.
½ CUP: 206 cal., 12g fat (7g sat. fat), 31mg chol., 315mg sod., 24g carb. (4g sugars, 3g fiber), 3g pro.

CAMPFIRE COOKIES

Once it starts getting chilly in Colorado, it's bonfire weather. What better way to celebrate than with bonfire cookies?
—*Callie Washer, Conifer, CO*

- -

Prep: 45 min. • **Bake:** 10 min./batch + cooling
Makes: 2 dozen

1 cup butter, softened
1½ cups sugar
2 large eggs, room temperature
1 tsp. vanilla extract
3 cups all-purpose flour
1½ tsp. baking powder
¼ tsp. salt

OKTOBERFEST

RED CABBAGE WITH BACON

If you've braised, marinated or served red cabbage raw, try it steamed, then toss with bacon and a tangy sauce. We serve it with pork or chicken.
—*Sherri Melotik, Oak Creek, WI*

- -

Takes: 25 min. • **Makes:** 6 servings

- 1 medium head red cabbage (about 2 lbs.), shredded
- 8 bacon strips, chopped
- 1 small onion, quartered and thinly sliced
- 2 Tbsp. all-purpose flour
- ¼ cup packed brown sugar
- ½ cup water
- ¼ cup cider vinegar
- 1 tsp. salt
- ⅛ tsp. pepper

1. In a large saucepan, place steamer basket over 1 in. water. Place the cabbage in basket. Bring water to a boil. Reduce heat to maintain a simmer; steam, covered, 6-8 minutes or just until tender.

2. Meanwhile, in a large skillet, cook bacon over medium heat until crisp, stirring occasionally. Remove with a slotted spoon; drain on paper towels. Discard drippings, reserving 2 Tbsp. in pan.

3. Add onion to drippings; cook and stir over medium-high heat 4-6 minutes or until tender. Stir in flour and brown sugar until blended. Gradually stir in water and vinegar. Bring to a boil, stirring constantly; cook and stir until thickened, 1-2 minutes. Stir in cabbage, bacon, salt and pepper.

¾ CUP: 188 cal., 9g fat (3g sat. fat), 15mg chol., 635mg sod., 23g carb. (15g sugars, 3g fiber), 6g pro.

SLOW-COOKED REUBEN BRATS

Sauerkraut gives these beer-simmered brats a big flavor boost, but it's the special chili sauce and melted cheese that put them over the top. Top your favorite burger with some of the chili sauce—you won't be sorry.
—*Alana Simmons, Johnstown, PA*

- -

Prep: 30 min. • **Cook:** 7¼ hours
Makes: 10 servings

- 10 uncooked bratwurst links
- 3 bottles (12 oz. each) light beer or nonalcoholic beer
- 1 large sweet onion, sliced
- 1 can (14 oz.) sauerkraut, rinsed and well-drained
- ¾ cup mayonnaise
- ¼ cup chili sauce
- 2 Tbsp. ketchup
- 1 Tbsp. finely chopped onion
- 2 tsp. sweet pickle relish
- 1 garlic clove, minced
- ⅛ tsp. pepper
- 10 hoagie buns, split
- 10 slices Swiss cheese

1. In a large skillet, brown bratwurst links in batches; drain. In a 5-qt. slow cooker, combine the beer, sliced onion and sauerkraut; add bratwurst. Cook, covered, on low 7-9 hours or until sausages are cooked through.

2. Preheat oven to 350°. In a small bowl, mix mayonnaise, chili sauce, ketchup, chopped onion, relish, garlic and pepper until blended. Spread over cut sides of buns; top with cheese, bratwurst and sauerkraut mixture. Place on an ungreased baking sheet. Bake for 8-10 minutes or until cheese is melted.

1 SANDWICH: 733 cal., 50g fat (16g sat. fat), 94mg chol., 1643mg sod., 45g carb. (10g sugars, 2g fiber), 26g pr

edges. Roll up jelly-roll style, starting with a long slide; pinch seam to seal. Place ropes on a parchment-lined baking sheet. Using a sharp knife, make a ½-in.-deep cut lengthwise down the center of each rope, stopping ½ in. from ends. Keeping cut surfaces facing up, braid ropes. Pinch ends to seal; tuck under.

4. Cover with a kitchen towel and let rise in a warm place until almost doubled, about 30 minutes. Preheat oven to 375°. Bake until golden brown, 30-35 minutes. Remove to a wire rack to cool. To make glaze, combine confectioners' sugar and milk for desired consistency; drizzle over warm stollen.

1 SLICE: 270 cal., 10g fat (4g sat. fat), 13mg chol., 73mg sod., 41g carb. (16g sugars, 2g fiber), 5g pro.

POTLUCK GERMAN POTATO SALAD

This is a hit at our church potlucks. One man says he attends just so he can eat my potato salad! It will go over big at your events, too.
—*Kathleen Rabe, Kiel, WI*

- -

Prep: 20 min. • **Cook:** 25 min.
Makes: 12 servings

- 3   **lbs. small Yukon Gold potatoes, unpeeled (about 10)**
- 2   **celery ribs, chopped**
- 1   **small onion, chopped**
- 1   **cup water**
- ½   **cup white vinegar**
- ¾   **cup sugar**
- 1   **Tbsp. cornstarch**
- ¼   **tsp. salt**
- ¼   **tsp. pepper**
- ½   **lb. bacon strips, cooked and crumbled**

1. Place potatoes in a large saucepan; add water to cover. Bring to a boil. Reduce heat; simmer, uncovered, just until tender, 12-15 minutes. Add celery and onion; continue cooking until vegetables are tender, about 5 minutes longer. Drain; set aside.
2. Meanwhile, in a small saucepan, whisk together next 6 ingredients. Bring to a boil; cook until thickened, about 2 minutes.
3. When cool enough to handle, slice the potatoes; return to large saucepan with celery and onions. Add vinegar mixture, tossing to combine. Add bacon. Simmer mixture until heated through, 10-12 minutes. Serve warm.
⅔ CUP: 194 cal., 3g fat (1g sat. fat), 7mg chol., 181mg sod., 39g carb. (15g sugars, 2g fiber), 5g pro.

OMA'S MARZIPAN STOLLEN

My German grandma made this stollen for us when we were young. I love its homey taste and how it reminds me of her and the German food she made. I often freeze this sweet bread once it's shaped into a braid. Then I can pull it out the night before, let it rise on the counter overnight, and bake it in the morning.
—*Abigail Leszczynski, Beaufort, SC*

- -

Prep: 30 min. + rising • **Bake:** 30 min.
Makes: 1 loaf (16 slices)

- 3   **to 3½ cups all-purpose flour**
- ⅓   **cup sugar**
- 1   **pkg. (¼ oz.) active dry yeast**
- 1¼   **cups 2% milk**
- 6   **Tbsp. butter, cubed**
- 2   **tsp. grated lemon zest**
  FILLING
- 1   **can (12½ oz.) almond cake and pastry filling**
- 1   **cup finely ground almonds**
- 1   **Tbsp. 2% milk**
- 1   **tsp. rum extract**
  GLAZE
- ¼   **cup confectioners' sugar**
- ½   **to 1 tsp. 2% milk**

1. In a large bowl, combine 2 cups flour, sugar and yeast. In a small saucepan, heat milk and butter to 120°-130°. Add to dry ingredients and beat just until moistened. Add the lemon zest; beat until smooth. Stir in just enough remaining flour to form a soft dough (dough will be sticky).
2. Turn onto a floured surface; knead until smooth and elastic, 6-8 minutes. Place in a greased bowl, turning once to grease the top. Cover and let rise in a warm place until doubled, about 1 hour.
3. For filling, in a large bowl, beat almond pastry filling, almonds, milk and extract. Punch dough down; turn onto a floured surface. Divide into thirds. Roll each portion into a 15x6-in. rectangle. Spread each portion with a third of the filling to within ¼ in. of

HALLOWEEN

HOT DOG MUMMIES WITH HONEY MUSTARD DIP

These flaky mummy sandwiches are instant party hits! The accompanying mustard dip adds just the right kick.
—Jessie Sarrazin, Livingston, MT

- -

Prep: 25 min. • **Bake:** 10 min.
Makes: 20 appetizers (about 1 cup dip)

- 1 tube (8 oz.) refrigerated crescent rolls
- 20 miniature hot dogs
- 1 large egg
- 2 tsp. water
  Dijon mustard

DIP
- ½ cup mayonnaise
- 3 Tbsp. Dijon mustard
- 3 Tbsp. honey
- 1 Tbsp. cider vinegar
  Dash hot pepper sauce

1. Separate dough into 2 rectangles; seal seams and perforations. Cut each rectangle horizontally into 10 strips. Wrap 1 strip around each hot dog.
2. Place 1 in. apart on an ungreased baking sheet. In a small bowl, whisk egg and water; brush over tops. Bake at 375° until golden brown, 10-15 minutes. Using mustard, add eyes. In a small bowl, combine the dip ingredients; serve with mummies.
1 APPETIZER WITH 2 TSP. DIP: 128 cal., 10g fat (2g sat. fat), 18mg chol., 287mg sod., 8g carb. (4g sugars, 0 fiber), 2g pro.

PUMPKIN MOUSSE IN A PUMPKIN

Rich and creamy, this mousse is a real showstopper when served in a pumpkin shell. The presentation is sure to impress.
—Taste of Home *Test Kitchen*

- -

Prep: 20 min. + cooling
Bake: 25 min. + cooling • **Makes:** 4 servings

- 1 medium pie pumpkin (about 2 lbs.)
- 2 Tbsp. sugar
- ¾ tsp. ground cinnamon, divided
- ⅓ cup vanilla or white chips
- 2 Tbsp. 2% milk
- 3 oz. cream cheese, softened
- ⅓ cup confectioners' sugar
- ⅓ cup canned pumpkin
- 1 tsp. grated orange zest
- 1 cup heavy whipping cream, whipped

1. Cut top off pumpkin; scoop out and discard seeds. In small bowl, combine the sugar and ½ tsp. cinnamon; sprinkle inside pumpkin. Replace pumpkin top. Place on a baking sheet. Bake at 400° until crisp-tender, 25-30 minutes. Cool on a wire rack.
2. Meanwhile, microwave vanilla chips with milk at 70% power; stir until smooth. Cool to room temperature. In a bowl, beat the cream cheese and confectioners' sugar until smooth. Beat in the pumpkin, orange peel, reserved melted chips and remaining cinnamon. Fold in whipped cream. Spoon into pie pumpkin. Refrigerate leftovers.
NOTE: The pumpkin is not fully cooked so that it holds its color and shape. It is used as a serving bowl and is not meant to be eaten.
⅔ CUP: 431 cal., 34g fat (21g sat. fat), 93mg chol., 100mg sod., 30g carb. (28g sugars, 1g fiber), 4g pro.

SUPERNATURAL SPAGHETTI

The idea for a pizza-flavored spaghetti came to me when I saw someone dip a slice of pizza into a pasta dish. It makes a fun and hearty dish for a Halloween or fall-inspired gathering.
—*Robert Smith, Las Vegas, Nevada*

- -

Prep: 20 min. • **Cook:** 30 min.
Makes: 6 servings

½	lb. lean ground beef (90% lean)
½	lb. Italian turkey sausage links, casings removed
½	cup chopped sweet onion
4	cans (8 ounces each) no-salt-added tomato sauce
3	oz. sliced turkey pepperoni
1	Tbsp. sugar
½	tsp. dried parsley flakes
½	tsp. dried basil
9	oz. uncooked whole wheat spaghetti
3	Tbsp. grated Parmesan cheese
12	fresh mozzarella cheese pearls
12	slices pimiento-stuffed olives

1. In a large nonstick skillet, cook the beef, sausage and onion over medium heat until meat is no longer pink, 6-8 minutes, breaking up meat into crumbles; drain.
2. Stir in tomato sauce, pepperoni, sugar, parsley and basil. Bring to a boil. Reduce heat; simmer, uncovered, 20-25 minutes or until thickened. Meanwhile, cook spaghetti according to package directions.
3. Drain spaghetti and toss with the sauce. Sprinkle with Parmesan cheese. Top each serving with 2 cheese pearls and 2 olive slices to resemble eyes.
1⅓ CUPS: 400 cal., 12g fat (4g sat. fat), 65mg chol., 764mg sod., 47g carb. (12g sugars, 13g fiber), 25g pro.

PUMPKIN SNACK MIX

This yummy mix is so munchable, a bowl of it never lasts long. Feel free to use candy corn instead of the candy pumpkins—or a mix of both—if desired.
—*Shirley Engstrom, Genoa, NE*

- -

Prep: 25 min. • **Bake:** 1 hour + cooling
Makes: about 5½ qt.

3	qt. popped popcorn
4	cups Cheerios
4	cups Corn or Rice Chex
2	cups salted peanuts
1	cup packed brown sugar
¾	cup light corn syrup
¼	cup butter, cubed
2	tsp. vanilla extract
½	tsp. baking soda
1	pkg. (16 oz.) candy pumpkins

1. In a large greased roasting pan, combine the popcorn, cereal and peanuts. In a large saucepan, combine the brown sugar, corn syrup and butter; bring to a rolling boil. Boil for 6 minutes, stirring occasionally. Remove from the heat; quickly stir in vanilla and baking soda until mixture is light and foamy.
2. Immediately pour over popcorn mixture; toss to coat. Bake, uncovered, at 250° for 1 hour, stirring every 15 minutes. Let mixture cool completely. Stir in candy pumpkins.
¾ CUP: 216 cal., 8g fat (2g sat. fat), 4mg chol., 223mg sod., 34g carb. (20g sugars, 2g fiber), 4g pro.

TEST KITCHEN TIP
Make this snack mix the day before your party. Store in smaller airtight containers or Halloween-themed snack bags for easier packing or on-the-go snacking.

THANKSGIVING

3. Bring edges of foil over turkey to cover. Roast, covered, 1 hour. Carefully open foil and fold it down. Reduce oven setting to 325°. Roast, uncovered, 1½-2 hours longer or until a thermometer inserted in thickest part of thigh reads 170°-175°. Cover loosely with foil if turkey browns too quickly.

4. Remove turkey from oven; tent with foil. Let stand 20 minutes before carving. Discard fruit mixture from cavity. If desired, skim fat and thicken pan drippings for gravy. Serve with turkey.

6 OZ. COOKED TURKEY: 434 cal., 24g fat (10g sat. fat), 184mg chol., 286mg sod., 3g carb. (2g sugars, 1g fiber), 49g pro.

CORNBREAD STUFFING

When my husband and I were newlyweds and far away from family, we invited friends over for Thanksgiving. I combined several dressing recipes to create this one.
—*Pamela Rickman, Valdosta, GA*

- -

Prep: 20 min. • **Bake:** 55 min.
Makes: 12 servings

- 6 cups crumbled cornbread
- 2 cups white bread cubes, toasted
- 1 cup chopped pecans
- ¼ cup minced fresh parsley
- 1 tsp. dried thyme
- ½ tsp. rubbed sage
- ½ tsp. salt
- ½ tsp. pepper
- 1 lb. bulk pork sausage
- 2 Tbsp. butter
- 2 large tart apples, diced
- 1 cup diced celery
- 1 medium onion, finely chopped
- 1¾ to 2¼ cups chicken broth

1. In a large bowl, combine the bread, pecans and seasonings; set aside. Crumble sausage into a large cast-iron or other ovenproof skillet; cook over medium heat until no longer pink, breaking into crumbles. Remove with slotted spoon; drain on paper towels.
2. Add butter to meat drippings; saute the apples, celery and onion until tender. Add to bread mixture; stir in sausage and enough broth to moisten.
3. Spoon mixture into cast-iron skillet; cover and bake at 350° for 45 minutes. Uncover and bake just until set, about 10 minutes.
1 CUP: 326 cal., 18g fat (4g sat. fat), 19mg chol., 780mg sod., 35g carb. (8g sugars, 5g fiber), 8g pro.

CITRUS HERB TURKEY

When it came to a roasting turkey, my grandma had the magic touch. She would wrap hers in foil and cook it on low heat for 8 hours so it would bake up juicy and tender. This version doesn't take that long to cook, but I think it's just as good.
—*Portia Gorman, Los Angeles, CA*

- -

Prep: 40 min. • **Bake:** 2½ hours + standing
Makes: 12 servings

- 1 pkg. (1 oz.) fresh rosemary, divided
- 1 pkg. (1 oz.) fresh thyme, divided
- ¾ cup softened unsalted butter, divided
- 1 turkey (12 to 14 lbs.)
- 2 tsp. seasoned salt
- ½ tsp. garlic powder
- ½ tsp. pepper
- 1 medium apple, chopped
- 1 medium orange, chopped
- 1 small red onion, chopped
- 1 small sweet orange pepper, chopped

1. Preheat oven to 400°. Line a roasting pan with 3 pieces of heavy-duty foil (pieces should be long enough to cover turkey). Mince half the rosemary and thyme from each package (about ¼ cup total). In a small bowl, beat ½ cup butter and minced herbs until blended. With fingers, carefully loosen skin from turkey breast; rub butter mixture under the skin. Secure skin to underside of breast with toothpicks. Mix seasoned salt, garlic powder and pepper; sprinkle over turkey and inside turkey cavity.
2. Cube remaining butter. In a large bowl, combine butter, apple, orange, onion, orange pepper and remaining herb sprigs; spoon inside cavity. Tuck wings under turkey; tie drumsticks together. Place turkey in prepared pan, breast side up.

LUCY MEYRING
Walden, CO

BAKED CRANBERRY PUDDING

This is an old-fashioned dessert that makes us happy. It's especially good served warm with whipped cream.
—Lucy Meyring, Walden, CO

- -

Prep: 20 min. • **Bake:** 55 min. + cooling
Makes: 10 servings

- 2 large eggs, separated
- 1 cup packed brown sugar
- ½ cup heavy whipping cream
- ¼ cup butter, melted
- 2 tsp. vanilla extract
- 1½ cups all-purpose flour
- 3 Tbsp. grated orange zest
- 1 tsp. baking powder
- 1 tsp. ground cinnamon
- ½ tsp. ground nutmeg
- ½ tsp. cream of tartar, divided
- ⅛ tsp. salt
- 3 cups coarsely chopped cranberries

TOPPING
- 1½ cups sugar
- ½ cup orange juice
- 2½ cups whole cranberries
  Orange zest strips and whipped cream, optional

1. Place egg whites in a large bowl; let stand at room temperature for 30 minutes. Preheat oven to 350°.

2. In a large bowl, beat the brown sugar, cream, melted butter, vanilla and egg yolks until well blended. In another bowl, whisk flour, orange zest, baking powder, cinnamon, nutmeg, ¼ tsp. cream of tartar and salt. Add chopped cranberries; toss to coat. Gradually add to sugar mixture, mixing well. (Batter will be stiff.)

3. Add remaining cream of tartar to egg whites; with clean beaters, beat on medium speed until soft peaks form. Fold into batter. Transfer to a greased 9-in. springform pan. Bake until a toothpick inserted in center comes out clean, 45-50 minutes.

4. Meanwhile, for topping, combine sugar and orange juice in a small saucepan. Bring to a boil, stirring frequently; cook until sugar is dissolved, 2-3 minutes. Add cranberries; return to a boil. Reduce heat and simmer, uncovered, until cranberries pop, stirring occasionally, 6-8 minutes. Remove from heat; cover and keep warm.

5. When the pudding tests done, place springform pan in a 15x10x1-in. baking pan. Spoon cranberry mixture over top. Bake for 10 minutes longer.

6. Cool pudding on a wire rack 10 minutes. Loosen the sides from pan with a knife; remove rim from pan. Cool at least 1 hour before serving.

7. If made ahead, pudding can be warmed in a 350° oven for 10 minutes. If desired, top with orange zest and serve with whipped cream.

1 SLICE: 402 cal., 10g fat (6g sat. fat), 71mg chol., 143mg sod., 75g carb. (57g sugars, 3g fiber), 4g pro.

CHEESY MASHED POTATOES

Everyone who tastes these creamy, cheesy potatoes asks me how to make them. Since this casserole bakes at the same temperature as my chicken bundles, I get it started in the oven and pop in the entree a little later.
—Brad Moritz, Limerick, PA

- -

Prep: 40 min. • **Bake:** 40 min.
Makes: 10 servings

- 6 large potatoes, peeled and quartered
- 1 pkg. (8 oz.) cream cheese, softened
- 1 cup shredded cheddar cheese
- ½ cup sour cream
- ⅓ cup chopped onion
- 1 large egg
- 2 tsp. salt
- ½ tsp. pepper
  Additional shredded cheddar cheese, optional

1. Place potatoes in a large saucepan; cover with water. Cover and bring to a boil. Cook for 20-25 minutes or until very tender; drain well.

2. In a bowl, mash potatoes. Add the cream cheese, cheddar cheese, sour cream, onion, egg, salt and pepper; beat until fluffy. Transfer to a greased 2-qt. baking dish. Cover and bake at 350° until heated through, 40-45 minutes. Sprinkle with additional cheese if desired.

¾ CUP: 328 cal., 14g fat (9g sat. fat), 66mg chol., 633mg sod., 42g carb. (4g sugars, 4g fiber), 10g pro.

HANUKKAH

GARLIC CLOVE CHICKEN

My neighbors made this chicken frequently, and I couldn't get enough of it. If you're a garlic lover, you'll add this one to your keeper file.
—*Denise Hollebeke, Penhold, AB*

- -

Prep: 10 min. • **Bake:** 2¼ hours + standing
Makes: 6 servings

- 1 roasting chicken (5 to 6 lbs.)
- 1 small onion, quartered
- 40 garlic cloves, peeled
- ¼ cup canola oil
- 1½ tsp. salt
- 1 tsp. dried parsley flakes
- ½ tsp. dried celery flakes
- ½ tsp. each dried tarragon, thyme and rosemary, crushed
- ¼ tsp. pepper

1. Place chicken breast side up on a rack in a shallow roasting pan. Stuff onion in chicken; tie drumsticks together. Arrange garlic cloves around chicken. In a small bowl, combine the remaining ingredients. Drizzle over chicken and garlic.
2. Cover and bake at 350° for 1¾ hours. Uncover; bake 30-45 minutes longer or until until a thermometer inserted in thickest part of thigh reads 170°-175°, basting occasionally with pan drippings. (Cover loosely with foil if chicken browns too quickly.) Cover and let stand for 10 minutes before slicing.
7 OZ. COOKED CHICKEN: 556 cal., 36g fat (8g sat. fat), 149mg chol., 738mg sod., 8g carb. (1g sugars, 1g fiber), 49g pro.

CARROT RAISIN COUSCOUS

Golden raisins add a slightly sweet flavor to this bright side dish featuring couscous and carrots. It makes a delicious accompaniment to savory roast chicken or any meat entree.
—*Jordan Sucher, Brooklyn, NY*

- -

Prep: 15 min. • **Cook:** 20 min.
Makes: 10 servings

- ⅓ cup port wine or chicken broth
- ⅓ cup golden raisins
- 1 medium onion, chopped
- 3 Tbsp. olive oil, divided
- 1 pkg. (10 oz.) couscous
- 2 cups chicken broth
- ¼ tsp. salt, divided
- ¼ tsp. pepper, divided
- 4 medium carrots, julienned
- 1 Tbsp. sugar
- 1 tsp. molasses

1. In a small saucepan, heat wine until hot. In a small bowl, soak raisins in wine for 5 minutes. Drain raisins, reserving wine.
2. In a large saucepan, saute onion in 1 Tbsp. oil until tender. Stir in couscous. Cook and stir until lightly browned. Stir in the broth, raisins and half the salt and pepper. Bring to a boil. Cover and remove from the heat. Let stand for 5 minutes; fluff with a fork.
3. In a small skillet, saute carrots in remaining olive oil until crisp-tender. Combine sugar, molasses, wine and the remaining salt and pepper. Stir into carrots; heat through.
4. In a large bowl, combine couscous mixture and carrots; toss to combine.
¾ CUP: 188 cal., 5g fat (1g sat. fat), 1mg chol., 277mg sod., 32g carb. (8g sugars, 2g fiber), 5g pro. **DIABETIC EXCHANGES:** 1½ starch, 1 vegetable, 1 fat.

4. Roll up wedges from the wide end and place point side down 2 in. apart on foil-lined baking sheets. Curve ends to form a crescent shape. Brush with egg; sprinkle with additional sugar.
5. Repeat with remaining dough and filling. Bake at 350° for 18-20 minutes or until golden brown. Remove to wire racks to cool.
1 COOKIE: 103 cal., 6g fat (3g sat. fat), 17mg chol., 80mg sod., 12g carb. (8g sugars, 0 fiber), 1g pro.

LATKES WITH LOX

Lox, a salty smoked salmon, is a year-round delicacy. This recipe, inspired by one from the *Jewish Journal*, uses lox a garnish on traditional fried latkes.
—Taste of Home *Test Kitchen*

Prep: 20 min. • **Cook:** 5 min./batch
Makes: 3 dozen

- 2 cups finely chopped onion
- ¼ cup all-purpose flour
- 6 garlic cloves, minced
- 2 tsp. salt
- 1 tsp. coarsely ground pepper
- 4 large eggs, lightly beaten
- 4 lbs. russet potatoes, peeled and shredded
- ¾ cup canola oil

TOPPINGS
- 4 oz. lox
  Optional: Sour cream and minced fresh chives

1. In a large bowl, combine first 5 ingredients. Stir in eggs until blended. Add potatoes; toss to coat.
2. Heat 2 Tbsp. oil in a large nonstick skillet over medium heat. Drop batter by ¼ cupfuls into oil; press lightly to flatten. Fry in batches until golden brown on both sides, using remaining oil as needed. Drain on paper towels. Serve with lox; top with sour cream and chives if desired.
3 LATKES WITH ⅓ OZ. LOX: 270 cal., 16g fat (2g sat. fat), 73mg chol., 610mg sod., 26g carb. (3g sugars, 2g fiber), 6g pro.

CRANBERRY RUGELACH

These traditional Polish treats will keep for a long time in an airtight container. One year, I sent a batch to my sister, but the box got lost. She received it 12 days later and reported that the cookies were worth the wait!
—Jean Doxon, Omaha, NE

Prep: 25 min. + chilling
Bake: 20 min./batch + cooling
Makes: about 5 dozen

- 1 cup butter, softened
- 1 pkg. (8 oz.) cream cheese, softened
- ½ cup sugar
- 2¾ cups all-purpose flour
- 1 tsp. salt

FILLING
- ¾ cup sugar
- ⅔ cup dried cranberries, finely chopped
- ½ cup finely chopped walnuts, toasted
- ⅓ cup butter, melted
- 2 tsp. ground cinnamon
- 1 tsp. ground allspice
- 1 large egg, lightly beaten
  Additional sugar

1. In a large bowl, cream the softened butter, cream cheese and sugar until light and fluffy. Combine flour and salt; gradually add to the creamed mixture and mix well.
2. Turn dough onto a lightly floured surface; knead 3 minutes or until smooth. Divide into 8 portions. Roll each portion into a ball; flatten into a 4-in. circle. Wrap and refrigerate at least 1 hour.
3. In a small bowl, combine sugar, cranberries, walnuts, melted butter, cinnamon and allspice. On a lightly floured surface, roll 1 portion of dough into an 8-in. circle. Sprinkle surface with 3 Tbsp. filling to within ½ in. of edges. Cut into 8 wedges.

CHRISTMAS DINNER

Place pan on middle oven rack; immediately reduce heat to 350°. Roast 1 hour.

2. Toss potatoes, carrots, onion and fennel with next 5 ingredients. Arrange vegetables in a single layer in a 15x10x1-in. baking pan on lowest rack of the oven. Roast the meat and vegetables, stirring the vegetables midway through baking, until meat reaches desired doneness (a thermometer should read 135° for medium-rare, 140° for medium and 145° for medium-well), about 1½ hours. Cover roast loosely with foil during last 30 minutes to prevent overbrowning. Let stand for 15 minutes before carving.

3. Meanwhile, for glaze, combine balsamic vinegar, Madeira wine and brown sugar in a small saucepan. Bring mixture to a boil over medium-high heat and reduce to ½ cup, about 15 minutes. Let glaze cool to room temperature. Serve roast with vegetables and glaze and, if desired, pink peppercorns and fennel fronds.

1 SERVING: 575 cal., 25g fat (8g sat. fat), 0 chol., 828mg sod., 44g carb. (18g sugars, 5g fiber), 42g pro.

CHRISTMAS VEGETABLE SALAD

My sister gave me this recipe for a colorful, crisp salad, and I've been making it for holiday get-togethers, dinner parties and potlucks ever since. It travels well, holds up beautifully on the buffet and is ideal for making ahead. Serve it in a clear bowl so everyone can see the pretty color combination.

—*Mary Dean, Eau Claire, WI*

- -

Prep: 15 min. + marinating • **Makes:** 6 servings

- ¼ cup canola oil
- 1 Tbsp. plus 1½ tsp. lemon juice
- 1 Tbsp. plus 1½ tsp. white wine vinegar
- 1 tsp. salt
- ½ tsp. sugar
  Coarsely ground pepper
- 2 cups thinly sliced cauliflower
- ½ cup sliced pimiento-stuffed olives
- ⅓ cup chopped green pepper
- ⅓ cup chopped red pepper

In a jar with a tight-fitting lid, combine the first 6 ingredients; shake well. In a salad bowl, combine the cauliflower, olives and peppers; drizzle with dressing and toss to coat. Cover and refrigerate for several hours or overnight.

½ CUP: 120 cal., 12g fat (1g sat. fat), 0 chol., 644mg sod., 4g carb. (2g sugars, 2g fiber), 1g pro.

MUSTARD-CRUSTED PRIME RIB WITH MADEIRA GLAZE

This juicy prime rib is spectacular on its own, but the rich Madeira glaze takes it up a notch to wow at special dinners. What's even better is that it roasts with a bed of tender veggies, so you have the whole meal covered in one pan.

—*Kathryn Conrad, Milwaukee, WI*

- -

Prep: 20 min. • **Bake:** 2½ hours + standing
Makes: 8 servings

- 1 bone-in beef rib roast (about 5 lbs.)
- ½ cup stone-ground mustard
- 6 small garlic cloves, minced
- 1 Tbsp. brown sugar
- ½ tsp. salt
- ½ tsp. coarsely ground pink peppercorns, optional

VEGETABLES

- 2 lbs. medium Yukon Gold potatoes, cut into eighths (about 2-in. chunks)
- 4 medium carrots, halved lengthwise and cut into 2-in. pieces
- 1 medium red onion, cut into eighths (but with root end intact)
- 1 medium fennel bulb, cut into eighths
- 3 Tbsp. olive oil
- 1 Tbsp. balsamic vinegar
- 1 tsp. brown sugar
- ¾ tsp. salt
- ½ tsp. pepper

MADEIRA GLAZE

- 1 cup balsamic vinegar
- ½ cup Madeira wine
- 1 tsp. brown sugar
  Cracked pink peppercorns, optional

1. Let roast stand at room temperature for 1 hour. Preheat oven to 450°. Combine the mustard, garlic, brown sugar, salt and, if desired, peppercorns; brush evenly over top and sides of roast but not over bones (mixture may seem loose but will adhere). Place bone side down on a rack in a shallow roasting pan.

SPICY CRAB SALAD TAPAS

I served these at a party and everyone went wild! These have a crispy flaky outside filled with creamy sweet crab that has a little kick. I used scalloped edge cookie cutters to cut my pastry, but a small biscuit cutter works, too.
—Vanessa Mason, Summerdale, AL

Prep: 35 min. + chilling
Bake: 20 min. + cooling
Makes: about 2 dozen

- 1 can (16 oz.) lump crabmeat, drained
- ¼ cup finely chopped sweet red pepper
- ¼ cup finely chopped sweet yellow pepper
- ¼ cup finely chopped green onions
- 1 jalapeno pepper, seeded and finely chopped
- 1 Tbsp. minced fresh cilantro
- 1 Tbsp. lemon juice
- 2 garlic cloves, minced
- 1 tsp. ground mustard
- ½ cup mayonnaise
- ½ tsp. salt
- ¼ tsp. pepper
- 1 pkg. (17.3 oz.) frozen puff pastry, thawed
- 1 large egg
- 1 Tbsp. water
  Minced fresh parsley and seafood seasoning, optional

1. Preheat oven to 375°. Combine the first 12 ingredients. Refrigerate, covered, at least 1 hour.
2. Meanwhile, on a lightly floured surface, unfold puff pastry. Roll each pastry into a 10-in. square; cut each into twenty-five 2-in. squares. Using a round 1½-in. cookie cutter, cut out the centers of half the puff pastry squares. Whisk egg and water; brush over pastry. Place the cutout squares on top of solid squares; transfer to parchment-lined baking sheets.
3. Bake until golden brown, about 18 minutes. Cool to room temperature. Once cool, spoon 1 heaping tablespoonful crab salad into the center of each cooked pastry. If desired, top with minced parsley and seasoning. Serve immediately.
1 APPETIZER: 145 cal., 9g fat (2g sat. fat), 25mg chol., 240mg sod., 11g carb. (0 sugars, 2g fiber), 5g pro.

HOMEMADE EGGNOG

After just one taste, folks will know this homemade holiday treat came from the kitchen, not the store.
—Pat Waymire, Yellow Springs, OH

Prep: 15 min. • **Cook:** 30 min. + chilling
Makes: 12 servings (about 3 qt.)

- 12 large eggs
- 1½ cups sugar
- ½ tsp. salt
- 8 cups whole milk, divided
- 2 Tbsp. vanilla extract
- 1 tsp. ground nutmeg
- 2 cups heavy whipping cream
  Additional nutmeg, optional

1. In a heavy saucepan, whisk together eggs, sugar and salt. Gradually add 4 cups milk; cook and stir over low heat until a thermometer reads 160°-170°, 30-35 minutes. Do not allow to boil. Immediately transfer to a large bowl.
2. Stir in the vanilla, nutmeg and remaining milk. Place bowl in an ice-water bath, stirring until the milk mixture is cool. (If the mixture separates, process in a blender until smooth.) Refrigerate, covered, until cold, at least 3 hours.
3. To serve, beat cream until soft peaks form. Whisk gently into the cooled milk mixture. Top with additional nutmeg if desired.
NOTE: Eggnog may be stored, covered, in the refrigerator for several days. Whisk before serving.
1 CUP: 411 cal., 25g fat (14g sat. fat), 247mg chol., 251mg sod., 35g carb. (35g sugars, 0 fiber), 13g pro.

CHRISTMAS TREATS

1 COOKIE: 169 cal., 8g fat (5g sat. fat), 28mg chol., 66mg sod., 22g carb. (14g sugars, 0 fiber), 2g pro.

CANDY CANE PUNCH

Peppermint ice cream makes this beverage taste—and look—more like a dessert than a punch! I've mixed the sipper many times for ladies' lunches and buffets. For a fun garnish, hang mini candy canes around the punch bowl or on cups.
—*Neva Schnauber, Fort Collins, CO*

Prep: 10 min. + chilling • **Makes:** 3½ qt.

- 2 jars (12 oz. each) strawberry jelly
- 2 liters lemon-lime soda, divided
- 2 qt. peppermint stick ice cream
  Miniature candy canes, optional

In a large saucepan, melt jelly with 2 cups soda. Chill the jelly mixture and remaining soda. Just before serving, place 6 cups ice cream in a punch bowl. Gently stir in jelly mixture. Add remaining soda. Add remaining ice cream by scoopfuls. Garnish with candy canes if desired.

1 CUP: 270 cal., 8g fat (5g sat. fat), 29mg chol., 73mg sod., 48g carb. (43g sugars, 0 fiber), 2g pro.

NEVER-FAIL CUTOUT COOKIES

I've tried numerous recipes for cutout cookies over the years—this one is foolproof. My daughter and granddaughter make these for holidays and social events. Decorating them is the best part. You can try almond flavoring or another flavoring of choice. This recipe is easily doubled if you're going for a big batch.
—*Irene Palm, Mansfield, OH*

Prep: 45 min. + chilling
Bake: 10 min./batch + cooling
Makes: about 5 dozen

- 2 cups butter, softened
- 1 pkg. (8 oz.) cream cheese, softened
- 2 cups sugar
- 2 large egg yolks, room temperature
- 2 tsp. vanilla extract
- 5 cups all-purpose flour
  FROSTING
- 3½ cups confectioners' sugar
- 3 Tbsp. butter, softened
- 1 Tbsp. shortening
- 1 tsp. vanilla extract
- 4 to 5 Tbsp. 2% milk
  Food coloring of choice, optional
  Assorted sprinkles or candies, optional

1. Beat butter, cream cheese and sugar until light and fluffy. Beat in egg yolks and vanilla. Gradually beat in flour. Divide dough into 4 portions; shape each into a disk. Cover; refrigerate until firm enough to roll, about 30 minutes.
2. Preheat oven to 350°. On a lightly floured surface, roll each portion of dough to ¼-in. thickness. Cut with floured 3-in. holiday cookie cutters. Place 1 in. apart on ungreased baking sheets.
3. Bake cookies until edges are light golden, 12-14 minutes. Cool on pans for 5 minutes. Remove to wire racks to cool completely.
4. For frosting, beat confectioners' sugar, butter, shortening, vanilla and enough milk to reach desired consistency. If desired, tint with food coloring. Spread or pipe over cookies. Decorate as desired.

NO-BAKE CHRISTMAS WREATH TREATS

Cornflakes take the place of traditional rice cereal in these sweet no-bake treats from our Test Kitchen. Dressed up with green and red, they're a pretty addition to cookie platters and dessert buffets.

—Taste of Home *Test Kitchen*

Prep: 20 min. + standing • **Cook:** 5 min.
Makes: 8 servings

- 20 large marshmallows
- 2 Tbsp. butter
- Green food coloring
- 3 cups cornflakes
- Red M&M's minis (about 2 Tbsp.)

1. Place the marshmallows and butter in a microwave-safe bowl; microwave, uncovered, on high until marshmallows are puffed and butter is melted, about 45 seconds. Tint with green food coloring. Stir in cornflakes.
2. On a waxed paper-lined baking sheet, divide mixture into 8 portions. With buttered hands, working quickly, shape each into a 3-in. wreath. Decorate immediately with M&M's, pressing to adhere. Let stand until set.
1 WREATH: 134 cal., 4g fat (2g sat. fat), 9mg chol., 116mg sod., 25g carb. (13g sugars, 0 fiber), 1g pro.

GRANNY'S GINGERBREAD CAKE WITH CARAMEL SAUCE

A buttery caramel sauce complements the rich molasses and autumn spices in this classic dessert. Add a dollop of whipped cream for a finishing touch.

—Joy Sparks, Muskegon, MI

Prep: 25 min. • **Bake:** 35 min.
Makes: 9 servings

- 9 Tbsp. butter, softened
- ⅓ cup sugar
- 1 cup molasses
- 1 large egg, room temperature
- 2¼ cups all-purpose flour
- 1 tsp. baking soda
- 1 tsp. ground ginger
- 1 tsp. ground cinnamon
- ¼ tsp. salt
- ¾ cup water

CARAMEL SAUCE
- 1 cup packed brown sugar
- 1 Tbsp. cornstarch
- 1 cup cold water
- ¼ cup butter, cubed
- 1 tsp. vanilla extract
- Whipped cream, optional

1. In a large bowl, cream the butter and sugar until light and fluffy. Beat in molasses and egg until well blended. In another bowl, whisk together the flour, baking soda, ginger, cinnamon and salt; add to creamed mixture alternately with water.
2. Transfer to a greased 9-in. square baking pan. Bake at 325° for 35-40 minutes or until a toothpick inserted in the center comes out clean. Place on a wire rack.
3. For caramel sauce, in a small saucepan, combine brown sugar and cornstarch. Stir in water until smooth. Bring to a boil; cook and stir for 2 minutes or until thickened. Remove from the heat; stir in butter and vanilla until smooth. Serve with warm cake. Top with whipped cream if desired.
1 PIECE: 497 cal., 17g fat (11g sat. fat), 67mg chol., 353mg sod., 83g carb. (51g sugars, 1g fiber), 4g pro.

4. Bake until top springs back when lightly touched, 12-15 minutes (do not overbake). Cool 5 minutes. Invert onto a tea towel dusted lightly with cocoa. Gently peel off parchment. Roll up cake in the towel jelly-roll style, starting with a short side. Cool cake completely on a wire rack.

5. For filling, in a bowl, dissolve the coffee granules in cream; beat until cream begins to thicken. Add sugar; beat until stiff peaks form. Unroll cake; spread filling over cake to within ½ in. of edges. Roll up again, without towel; trim ends. Transfer to a platter, seam side down. Refrigerate, covered, until cold.

6. For frosting, beat all the ingredients until smooth. Spread frosting over cake. Using a fork, make lines in frosting to resemble tree bark. Refrigerate until serving.

1 SLICE: 341 cal., 15g fat (8g sat. fat), 130mg chol., 136mg sod., 49g carb. (40g sugars, 1g fiber), 4g pro.

PEPPERMINT KISSES

These cookies melt in your mouth. They satisfy a sweet tooth when you don't want something rich and heavy.

—*Lynn Bernstetter, Lake Elmo, MN*

Prep: 20 min. • **Bake:** 1½ hours + cooling
Makes: about 3 dozen

2	large egg whites
⅛	tsp. cream of tartar
⅛	tsp. salt
½	cup sugar
2	regular-size peppermint candy canes (one green, one red), crushed

1. Let egg whites stand at room temperature 30 minutes.

2. Preheat oven to 225;. Add cream of tartar and salt to egg whites; beat on medium speed until foamy. Gradually add sugar, 1 Tbsp. at a time, beating on high after each addition. Continue beating until stiff, glossy peaks form.

3. Transfer egg whites to piping bag. Pipe 1½-in. cookies 2 in. apart onto parchment-lined baking sheets. Sprinkle half with crushed red candy canes, half with green, or with both.

4. Bake meringues until firm but not brown, 1½-2 hours. Remove to wire racks to cool completely. Store in an airtight container.

1 COOKIE: 16 cal., 0 fat (0 sat. fat), 0 chol., 12mg sod., 4g carb. (3g sugars, 0 fiber), 0 pro.

MOCHA YULE LOG

This is guaranteed to delight your holiday guests, especially chocolate lovers, with its yummy cocoa cake, creamy mocha filling and homemade frosting. I garnish it with marzipan holly leaves and berries, but you can also top it with shaved chocolate curls and a light dusting of confectioners' sugar.

—*Jenny Hughson, Mitchell, NE*

Prep: 65 min. + chilling
Bake: 15 min. + cooling • **Makes:** 12 servings

5	large eggs, separated
½	cup cake flour
¼	cup baking cocoa
¼	tsp. salt
1	cup sugar, divided
½	tsp. cream of tartar

FILLING

1½	tsp. instant coffee granules
1	cup heavy whipping cream
½	cup confectioners' sugar

FROSTING

⅓	cup butter, softened
2	cups confectioners' sugar
⅓	cup baking cocoa
1	Tbsp. brewed coffee, cooled
1½	tsp. vanilla extract
2	to 3 Tbsp. 2% milk

1. Place egg whites in a small bowl; let stand at room temperature 30 minutes.

2. Meanwhile, preheat oven to 350°. Line the bottom of a greased 15x10x1-in. pan with parchment; grease parchment. Sift the flour, cocoa and salt together twice. In a large bowl, beat the egg yolks until slightly thickened. Gradually add ½ cup sugar, beating on high speed until thick and lemon-colored. Fold in flour mixture.

3. Add cream of tartar to egg whites; with clean beaters, beat on medium until soft peaks form. Gradually add remaining sugar, 1 Tbsp. at a time, beating on high after each addition until sugar is dissolved. Continue beating until soft glossy peaks form. Fold a fourth of the whites into batter, then fold in remaining whites. Transfer batter to prepared pan, spreading evenly.

4. For glaze, mix confectioners' sugar and rum; spread over cake. Cut into squares.
1 PIECE: 337 cal., 13g fat (1g sat. fat), 28mg chol., 179mg sod., 52g carb. (35g sugars, 3g fiber), 4g pro.

PEANUT BUTTER PENGUINS

Could these be any more adorable? To treat your guests to this chocolaty, peanut buttery goodness, just dip Nutter Butter cookies in candy coating and decorate. They're fun to make...even more fun to eat.
—Taste of Home *Test Kitchen*

Prep: 1 hour + standing
Makes: about 2½ dozen

- 1¼ lbs. dark chocolate candy coating, chopped
- 1 pkg. (16 oz.) Nutter Butter cookies
- 32 bright white candy coating disks
- 64 candy eyes
- 32 orange M&M's minis
- 64 orange milk chocolate M&M's

Microwave candy coating; stir until smooth. Dip a cookie in chocolate; allow excess to drip off. Place on waxed paper. Attach white coating disk for belly and 2 candy eyes. Add an M&M mini for beak and 2 regular M&M's for feet. Repeat. Let stand until set.
1 COOKIE: 156 cal., 8g fat (5g sat. fat), 0 chol., 57mg sod., 21g carb. (16g sugars, 1g fiber), 2g pro.

SPICED RUM & PEAR CAKE

The flavors in this cake make it stand out as a special occasion cake. Packed with raisins, fresh sweet pear chunks, rich spices, crunchy walnuts and rum, it's a fine finale for your holiday spread. If you don't cook with alcohol, try substituting apple juice for the rum—it will be just as delicious!
—*Julie Peterson, Crofton, MD*

Prep: 25 min. • **Bake:** 45 min+ cooling
Makes: 20 servings

- ½ cup spiced rum
- 2 cups sugar
- 3 large eggs, room temperature
- ¾ cup canola oil
- 2 tsp. vanilla extract
- 2½ cups all-purpose flour
- 2 tsp. baking powder
- 2 tsp. ground cinnamon
- 1 tsp. salt
- ½ tsp. ground allspice
- 4 large pears (about 2 lbs.), peeled and cut into ½-in. cubes
- 1 cup chopped walnuts
- 1 cup golden raisins

GLAZE
- 1 cup confectioners' sugar
- 2 Tbsp. rum

1. Preheat oven to 350°. In a small heavy saucepan, heat rum over medium heat. Bring to a boil; cook until liquid is reduced by half, 8-10 minutes. Remove from heat; cool.
2. Beat sugar, eggs, oil, vanilla and cooled rum until slightly thickened, about 5 minutes. Sift together the next 5 ingredients; gradually beat into rum mixture. Stir in pears, walnuts and raisins. Transfer batter to a greased and floured 13x9-in. baking pan.
3. Bake until a toothpick inserted in the center comes out clean, 45-50 minutes. Cool cake in pan on rack.

ALPHABETICAL INDEX

SUBSTITUTIONS & EQUIVALENTS

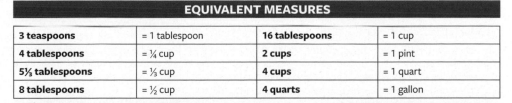

EQUIVALENT MEASURES

3 teaspoons	= 1 tablespoon	**16 tablespoons**	= 1 cup
4 tablespoons	= ¼ cup	**2 cups**	= 1 pint
5⅓ tablespoons	= ⅓ cup	**4 cups**	= 1 quart
8 tablespoons	= ½ cup	**4 quarts**	= 1 gallon

FOOD EQUIVALENTS

Macaroni	1 cup (3½ ounces) uncooked	= 2½ cups cooked
Noodles, Medium	3 cups (4 ounces) uncooked	= 4 cups cooked
Popcorn	⅓-½ cup unpopped	= 8 cups popped
Rice, Long Grain	1 cup uncooked	= 3 cups cooked
Rice, Quick-Cooking	1 cup uncooked	= 2 cups cooked
Spaghetti	8 ounces uncooked	= 4 cups cooked

Bread	1 slice	= ¾ cup soft crumbs, ¼ cup fine dry crumbs
Graham Crackers	7 squares	= ½ cup finely crushed
Buttery Round Crackers	12 crackers	= ½ cup finely crushed
Saltine Crackers	14 crackers	= ½ cup finely crushed

Bananas	1 medium	= ⅓ cup mashed
Lemons	1 medium	= 3 tablespoons juice, 2 teaspoons grated zest
Limes	1 medium	= 2 tablespoons juice, 1½ teaspoons grated zest
Oranges	1 medium	= ¼-⅓ cup juice, 4 teaspoons grated zest

Cabbage	1 head = 5 cups shredded	**Green Pepper**	1 large = 1 cup chopped
Carrots	1 pound = 3 cups shredded	**Mushrooms**	½ pound = 3 cups sliced
Celery	1 rib = ½ cup chopped	**Onions**	1 medium = ½ cup chopped
Corn	1 ear fresh = ⅔ cup kernels	**Potatoes**	3 medium = 2 cups cubed

Almonds	1 pound = 3 cups chopped	**Pecan Halves**	1 pound = 4½ cups chopped
Ground Nuts	3¾ ounces = 1 cup	**Walnuts**	1 pound = 3¾ cups chopped

EASY SUBSTITUTIONS

WHEN YOU NEED...		USE...
Baking Powder	1 teaspoon	½ teaspoon cream of tartar + ¼ teaspoon baking soda
Buttermilk	1 cup	1 tablespoon lemon juice or vinegar + enough milk to measure 1 cup (let stand 5 minutes before using)
Cornstarch	1 tablespoon	2 tablespoons all-purpose flour
Honey	1 cup	1¼ cups sugar + ¼ cup water
Half-and-Half Cream	1 cup	1 tablespoon melted butter + enough whole milk to measure 1 cup
Onion	1 small, chopped (⅓ cup)	1 teaspoon onion powder or 1 tablespoon dried minced onion
Tomato Juice	1 cup	½ cup tomato sauce + ½ cup water
Tomato Sauce	2 cups	¾ cup tomato paste + 1 cup water
Unsweetened Chocolate	1 square (1 ounce)	3 tablespoons baking cocoa + 1 tablespoon shortening or oil
Whole Milk	1 cup	½ cup evaporated milk + ½ cup water

GET COOKING WITH A WELL-STOCKED KITCHEN

In a perfect world, you plan weekly or even monthly menus and have all the ingredients on hand to make each night's dinner. The reality, however, is that you may not get to think about dinner until you walk through the door.

With a reasonably stocked pantry, refrigerator and freezer, you'll still be able to serve a satisfying meal in short order. Consider these tips:

QUICK-COOKING MEATS—such as boneless chicken breasts, chicken thighs, pork tenderloin, pork chops, ground meats, Italian sausage, sirloin and flank steaks, fish fillets and shrimp—should be stocked in the freezer. Wrap individual pieces and portions, so you can remove only the amount you need. For the quickest defrosting, wrap meats for freezing in small, thin packages.

FROZEN VEGETABLES are a real time-saver. Simply pour out the amount needed—no additional preparation is required.

PASTAS, RICE, RICE MIXES AND COUSCOUS are great staples to have in the pantry—and they generally have a long shelf life. Remember that thinner pastas, such as angel hair, cook faster than thicker pastas, and fresh (refrigerated) pasta cooks faster than dried.

DAIRY PRODUCTS like milk, sour cream, cheeses (shredded, cubed or crumbled), eggs, yogurt, butter and margarine are perishable, so check the use-by date on packages and replace as needed.

CONDIMENTS like ketchup, mustard, mayonnaise, salad dressings, salsa, taco sauce, soy sauce, stir-fry sauce, hot sauce, lemon juice and lime juice add flavor to many dishes. Personalize the list to suit your family's tastes.

FRESH FRUIT AND VEGETABLES can make a satisfying pre-dinner snack. Oranges and apples are not as perishable as bananas. Ready-to-use salad greens are perfect for an instant salad.

DRIED HERBS, SPICES, VINEGARS and seasoning mixes add lots of flavor and keep for months.

PASTA SAUCES, OLIVES, BEANS, broths, canned tomatoes, canned vegetables and canned or dried soups are ideal to have on hand for a quick meal—and many of these items are common recipe ingredients.

GET YOUR FAMILY INTO THE HABIT of posting a grocery list. When an item is used up or is almost gone, just add it to the list for your next shopping trip. This way you're less likely to run completely out of an item, and you'll also save time when writing your grocery list.

MAKE THE MOST OF YOUR TIME EVERY NIGHT

With recipes in hand and the kitchen stocked, you're well on the way to a relaxing family meal.
Here are some pointers to help get dinner on the table fast:

PREHEAT THE OVEN OR GRILL before starting on the recipe.

PULL OUT THE REQUIRED INGREDIENTS, mixing tools and cooking tools before beginning any prep work.

USE CONVENIENCE ITEMS whenever possible. Think pre-chopped garlic, onion and peppers, shredded or cubed cheese, seasoning mixes and jarred sauces.

MULTITASK! While the meat is simmering for a main dish, toss a salad together, cook a side dish or start on dessert.

ENCOURAGE HELPERS. Have younger children set the table. Older ones can help with ingredient preparation or can even assemble the recipes themselves.

TAKE CARE OF TWO MEALS IN ONE NIGHT by planning main-dish leftovers or making a double batch of favorite sides.

TRICKS TO TAME HUNGER WHEN IT STRIKES

Are the kids begging for a pre-supper snack? Calm their rumbling tummies with nutritious, not-too-filling noshes.

START WITH A SMALL TOSSED SALAD. Try a ready-to-serve salad mix, and add their favorite salad dressing and a little protein, like cubed cheese or julienned slices of deli meat.

CUT UP AN APPLE and smear a little peanut butter on each slice, or offer other fruits such as seedless grapes, cantaloupe, oranges or bananas. For variety, give kids vanilla yogurt or reduced-fat ranch dressing as a dipper, or combine a little reduced-fat sour cream with a sprinkling of brown sugar. Too busy to cut up the fruit? A fruit snack cup will also do the trick.

DURING THE COLD MONTHS, a small mug of soup with a few oyster crackers on top can really hit the spot.

RAW VEGGIES such as carrots, cucumbers, mushrooms, broccoli and cauliflower are tasty treats, especially when served with a little hummus for dipping. Many of these vegetables can be purchased already cut.

OFFER A SMALL SERVING of cheese and crackers. Look for sliced cheese, and cut the slices into smaller squares to fit the crackers. Choose a cracker that's made from whole wheat, such as an all-natural seven-grain cracker.